Making Music American

Making Music American
1917 and the Transformation of Culture

E. Douglas Bomberger

OXFORD
UNIVERSITY PRESS

OXFORD
UNIVERSITY PRESS

Oxford University Press is a department of the University of Oxford. It furthers
the University's objective of excellence in research, scholarship, and education
by publishing worldwide. Oxford is a registered trade mark of Oxford University
Press in the UK and certain other countries.

Published in the United States of America by Oxford University Press
198 Madison Avenue, New York, NY 10016, United States of America.

Library of Congress Cataloging-in-Publication Data
Names: Bomberger, E. Douglas, 1958– author.
Title: Making music American : 1917 and the transformation of culture /
E. Douglas Bomberger.
Description: New York, NY : Oxford University Press, 2018. |
Includes bibliographical references and index.
Identifiers: LCCN 2018001375| ISBN 9780190872311 (hardcover : alk. paper) |
ISBN 9780190872335 (epub)
Subjects: LCSH: Music—United States—20th century—History and criticism. |
World War, 1914-1918—Music and the war. | Nineteen seventeen, A.D.
Classification: LCC ML200.5 .B66 2018 | DDC 780.973/09041—dc23
LC record available at https://lccn.loc.gov/2018001375

9 8 7 6 5 4 3 2 1

Printed by Sheridan Books, Inc., United States of America

To James and Doris Bomberger

who made my childhood home a place of

cultural, artistic, and intellectual diversity

CONTENTS

ILLUSTRATIONS

PREFACE

By any standard, 1917 was a consequential year for American music. The entry of the United States into World War I in April inspired a flood of musical responses, some predictable and some unforeseen. Patriotic anthems were heard everywhere, but the charged atmosphere made them controversial. The new jazz style provided musical entertainment suited to the mood of a nervous nation. The recording industry made significant innovations that accelerated the pace of musical change. And the European musicians who had dominated classical music in the United States for decades came under suspicion.

The musical events of 1917 unfolded like a novel, and I have chosen to emulate that structure in recounting their history. The eight performers who are the principal characters of this book are representative of musicians active in the United States during this seminal year, and they each exercised a decisive influence on the direction of music in America. Six of the musicians were white, and two were black. Six were men, and two were women. Four were born in the United States, and four were born in Europe. Five were considered classical musicians, and three were known as popular musicians. Three were conductors, two were band members, and three were soloists. None of the eight was primarily a composer. Over the course of this year, their lives intersected and collided in unexpected ways, as the pace of change accelerated and the heat of the war hysteria grew. The narrative method of tracing the year monthly from beginning to end allows for new perspectives on familiar musical events.

The close confluence of events during this year drew me to the project initially and captivated my attention repeatedly during the research phase. Musicians with little in common were thrown together into uneasy alliances. Events that are famous in jazz circles happened simultaneously with events that are infamous in classical music circles. Performers who tried to remain apolitical were forced by circumstances to come down from the fence and take a stand. Politically astute musicians who thought they could control their circumstances through strategic diplomacy saw their good intentions swept away in the flood of national passion.

To understand the musical changes of this seminal year, it is crucial to remember the ways that the musical world of 1917 was different from our own. In an era before the Internet, television, or even radio, live performances were vitally important to music lovers of all types. From the parlor to the vaudeville house to the concert hall, listeners heard live music by performers they could see in person. Recording technology was still relatively primitive, but it played an important role in the events of this year. Print media, particularly daily newspapers, were the primary means of advertising and reviewing musical events.

Despite these differences, the events of 1917 still resonate a century later. Popular and classical music are still heard as symbols of class division in the United States. Musical genres and styles still reflect racial and ethnic divisions. "The Star-Spangled Banner" remains a cultural flashpoint because it symbolizes much more than its melody and lyrics alone. And the print media of 1917 were used for spreading fear, anxiety, and "fake news" as surely as today's electronic media. Music inflames passions because it touches emotions at the core of American culture, and at this crucial juncture in American history, music offers unique insights into the startling changes that shaped the future of our country.

ACKNOWLEDGMENTS

Research for this book was made possible by generous support from Elizabethtown College. Travel support from the college allowed an extended trip to Chicago and New Orleans, along with innumerable short trips to East Coast libraries. A sabbatical leave in fall 2016 gave me the time and freedom for focused writing, while the opportunity to present preliminary findings in campus lectures provided invaluable feedback. The staff of the college's High Library, directed by Sarah Penniman, tracked down obscure resources through interlibrary loan and supported the purchase of secondary literature.

I am indebted to many colleagues for their help and advice, especially Dale Cockrell, Richard Crawford, James Doering, James Haines, David Kenley, Susan Key, Nancy Newman, Brian Newsome, Bruce Boyd Raeburn, and Patrick Warfield. My thinking was sharpened by attendees at conferences of the Society for American Music, the American Musicological Society, the North American Conference on Nineteenth-Century Music, and Rhythm Changes, where preliminary papers were delivered. Robin Rausch and her colleagues in the Library of Congress Music Division were very helpful with their collections and with advice on other divisions in the LOC. I appreciated the help of Karen Bailor and Alison Fulmer of the Boston Symphony Orchestra archives, Maryalice Perrin-Mohr of the New England Conservatory Library, Louise Hilton of the Margaret Herrick Library of the Academy of Motion Picture Arts, and Patrick Lewis of the London (Ontario) Public Library. Bruce Boyd Raeburn, Lynn Abbott, and Alaina Hébert of the Hogan Jazz Archive were unfailingly generous with advice and access to their rich collections.

Suzanne Ryan, Victoria Kouznetsov, and the rest of the Oxford University Press staff have made the publication process pleasant and professional.

Finally, and most importantly, my work would be impossible without the constant support of my wife, Teresa, who deserves a share of the credit for this book.

1917 CHRONOLOGY

9 January   Walter Damrosch leads the New York Symphony Orchestra in an all-Wagner concert in Washington, DC.

27 January   The Original Dixieland Jazz Band (ODJB) makes its New York debut.

1 February   The German navy resumes unrestricted submarine attacks in the Atlantic Ocean. The United States breaks off diplomatic relations two days later.

23 February   Ernestine Schumann-Heink sustains serious injuries in a crash in St. Louis.

26 February   Victor Talking Machine Company records the ODJB in its Manhattan studio.

1 March   Publication of the Zimmermann telegram, in which Germany's foreign minister proposed an alliance with Mexico against the United States.

7–17 March   The Original Creole Band plays at the Winter Garden, just blocks from the ODJB.

19 March   The New York Symphony leaves for a ten-week cross-country tour.

6 April   Congress declares war on Germany.

15 April   Victor releases the ODJB's first record nationally, featuring "Dixie Jass Band One-Step" on the A-side and "Livery Stable Blues" on the B-Side.

2 May   James Reese Europe recruits woodwind players in Puerto Rico for his New York National Guard Band.

5 June   Nearly ten million men register for the first military draft.

22 June   Grand Military Ball and Band Concert introduces Europe's band to the public.

5 August Walter Kingsley's "Whence Comes Jazz?" in the *New York Sun* explains the popularity of the new genre.

18 August Violinist Fritz Kreisler and tenor John McCormack perform for ten thousand at Ocean Grove, New Jersey.

3–6 October Victor records the Boston Symphony Orchestra in its Camden, New Jersey, studio.

12 October A Chicago court ruling on "Livery Stable Blues" declares that jazz and blues are not subject to copyright protection.

12–24 October The Fifteenth New York National Guard regiment endures constant harassment at the training camp in Spartanburg, South Carolina.

30 October When the Boston Symphony Orchestra fails to play "The Star-Spangled Banner" at a concert in Providence, conductor Karl Muck becomes the target of nationwide condemnation.

3 November The Metropolitan Opera eliminates all German operas from its repertoire.

7 November Baltimore police cancel a guest appearance by the Boston Symphony Orchestra after former Maryland governor Edwin Warfield threatens mob violence.

7 November Violinist Fritz Kreisler is denied permission to perform in Pittsburgh.

12 November New Orleans's Storyville is closed under pressure from the military.

26 November Kreisler withdraws from the concert stage.

1 December Victor releases the first records of a full symphony orchestra, recorded by the Boston Symphony Orchestra in October.

4 December Boston Symphony Orchestra cancels concerts in Washington, DC, Baltimore, and Philadelphia because of Justice Department restrictions on enemy aliens.

5 December Walter Damrosch's "official" version of "The Star-Spangled Banner" premieres in New York to widespread criticism.

16 December A benefit concert in Boston features the last performance of Kreisler with Muck.

1 January 1918 Europe's Fifteenth New York National Guard regiment band arrives in France and plays the first of many concerts for French audiences.

Making Music American

CHAPTER 1

ᴄⱱɔ

Prologue

New Year's Eve 1916

New Year's Eve is a day like no other. No matter how bad the previous year has been, revelers drown their disappointments in a celebration and look hopefully to the blank slate of the year ahead. Their optimism and generosity create lucrative opportunities for those who entertain them. The venue where a musician plays on this most festive of days reflects that musician's professional status.

The last day of 1916 was no exception. The world was at war, but the United States was not. For eight musicians, their performances on New Year's Eve 1916 symbolized their places in the musical hierarchy and reminded them where their careers had brought them. For these musicians, 1917 was still a blank slate where unknown opportunities and disappointments waited to be written. The new year would change each of them in ways they could not imagine, and the world of American music would change with them.

Fritz Kreisler (Figure 1.1) played Carnegie Hall in the afternoon. The world's greatest violinist never failed to please his audiences, and this time the hall was packed with out-of-town revelers along with the usual crowd of discriminating Manhattanites. The *New York Times* reviewer found his playing of a Vieuxtemps concerto to be the highlight of the afternoon: "Starting where other fiddlers leave off, as if technical difficulties did not exist for him, Kreisler transformed the star show-piece into a

Figure 1.1 Fritz Kreisler (1875–1962) (Library of Congress).

thing of musical beauty and charm." When the long program came to an
end, the audience refused to let him leave the stage, clamoring for encore after encore. He knew his audience well, and after the concert of serious music, he charmed them with light selections that showed off his
stunning fingerwork. A "Spanish Dance" by Granados brought roars of approval, which he followed with his sentimental "Old Refrain" and then his
breathtaking arrangement of "La Chasse." But what they really wanted to
hear were Kreisler's own compositions, steeped in the atmosphere of his
native Vienna. The Old World charm of these pieces, which never went out
of style, kept the crowds returning year after year. Finally, for the fourth
encore, he played his "Liebesfreud" [Love's Joy], followed by "Schoen
Rosmarin," the quintessential Viennese waltz. No one could match the capricious delicacy of Kreisler's playing, and after these two numbers the
crowd roared louder than ever, stomping their feet and refusing to leave.
Kreisler came out on the stage of America's most famous concert hall one
more time to play his "beg-off"—a "Moment Musical" by Schubert—after
which the house manager turned out the lights in the hall to force them
to leave.

Figure 1.2 Karl Muck (1859–1940) (Courtesy of the Boston Symphony Orchestra Archives).

Two hundred miles to the northeast, **Karl Muck** (Figure 1.2) had the night off. The conductor of the Boston Symphony Orchestra had led two performances of a substantial program of Beethoven, Balakirev, and Schumann in Boston's Symphony Hall on 29 and 30 December; the 31st was a rest day before a tour in the first week of January. The Boston Symphony Orchestra was generally acknowledged as America's greatest, and audiences throughout the country lined up for their performances in other cities. During the first six days of January 1917, the BSO would play in Philadelphia, in Washington, in Baltimore, in New York's Carnegie Hall, in Brooklyn, and again in Carnegie Hall for one final concert. Each program would feature different repertoire, but all of the works would be serious. Music lovers did not come to BSO concerts for light music but for the masterworks of the European repertoire. For Muck, who had earned a PhD in classical philology from the University of Leipzig while also studying music at the Leipzig Conservatory, that meant German music and lots of it. Beethoven was the backbone of his repertoire, but he was also recognized as the world's leading interpreter of Wagner. For the first Carnegie Hall concert on 4 January, he was scheduled to play three Wagner works, along with the imposing Franck Symphony in D minor. Small wonder that he took a day off on New Year's Eve.

The home that Karl and his wife Anita shared at 50 Fenway in Boston was a refuge of comfort for the conductor. Muck was a scholar who studied scores constantly and had little knowledge of the English language, while Anita, in traditional German fashion, took care of the daily concerns of their home so that he could concentrate on his professional duties. When they were preparing to relocate from Berlin to Boston in 1912, Anita had sought the advice of Mrs. George Whitefield Chadwick, the wife of the director of the New England Conservatory and Boston's most famous composer. She was concerned about the apartment they were considering on the most fashionable street in Boston's Back Bay. True, it was in a new building that would allow her to decorate as she chose, but she worried that the dining room was small by German standards and that the location might not admit sufficient natural light during the long winter months. In the end, she took her American friend's advice, and at her new home she was able to create a haven of German *Gemütlichkeit* for her husband.[1] After several years of apartment living, they purchased a "most elegantly furnished four-story private mansion." Its close proximity to Symphony Hall made the conductor's commute even shorter and his wife's home even more luxurious.[2] As Muck prepared for the demanding week of concerts and travel ahead, a night off from performing spent in such familiar and comfortable surroundings was undoubtedly welcome.

Walter Damrosch (Figure 1.3) did not take New Year's Eve off. The members of his New York Symphony Orchestra were well rested after a two-week break, and they treated the matinee audience in Aeolian Hall to a program designed to appeal without overwhelming. Damrosch opened with Dvořák's *New World* Symphony, a perennial favorite with New York audiences. This work, after all, had been written by the Czech composer during his three-year stint as director of the National Conservatory of Music in New York and was said to have been based on African American spirituals, although Dvořák had never specified which ones he used or how. It was enough, though, that the infectious music *sounded* like it could have been based on American folk music. The textures of the symphony were lighter and the rhythms were catchier than the Wagner and Franck that the BSO would play the following week. Damrosch knew that a New Year's Eve concert was not the time to challenge his audience, and he filled out the program with Stravinsky's richly colored *Firebird* suite and the familiar Saint-Saëns Piano Concerto in G minor, played by Olga Samaroff.

Figure 1.3 Walter Damrosch (1862–1950) (Library of Congress).

Damrosch and Samaroff might have been amused, if they bothered to think about it, at the opposite paths they had taken to reach this stage. Damrosch, like Muck, had been born in Germany, but his early years had been very different from those of his illustrious Boston colleague. Damrosch was the son of working musicians: his mother was an opera singer and his father a conductor. When Walter was nine years old, the family moved halfway around the world, from the German city of Breslau to New York, where his father, Leopold, had been hired to conduct a German singing society. Leopold was an entrepreneur who seized the opportunities he found in his adopted home. In 1873, two years after his arrival in America, he founded the New York Oratorio Society, followed by the New York Symphony Society in 1877. When these two groups joined forces for a giant festival in 1881, the nineteen-year-old Walter was enlisted as assistant conductor to prepare some of the choruses. He proved to be so competent that upon his father's untimely death in 1885, the twenty-three-year-old became conductor of both organizations, making him one of New York's most prominent musicians. Walter's New York Symphony was the principal rival of the older New York Philharmonic until their merger in 1928.

Though Walter Damrosch had been born in Germany, his acculturation into American society was the envy of German Americans everywhere. In 1890 he married Margaret Blaine, daughter of one of America's most powerful politicians, James G. Blaine, who served successively as Speaker of the House, senator, and secretary of state. Blaine ran unsuccessfully for president in 1884 but was again appointed secretary of state from 1889 to his death in 1892, a position he held at the time of the Damrosch marriage. Walter enjoyed a long and influential musical career, all the while rubbing shoulders with members of his father-in-law's political circle. Witty and articulate, he retained a hint of a German accent but had a masterful command of English. His powerful friends included Andrew Carnegie, who had constructed the famous concert hall in New York on Walter's recommendation, and Henry Harkness Flagler, whose annual support of $100,000 to the New York Symphony made it possible for Damrosch to hire the best players in the world.

Figure 1.4 Olga Samaroff (1880–1948) (Library of Congress).

Pianist **Olga Samaroff** (Figure 1.4) was born Lucy Mary Agnes Hickenlooper in San Antonio, Texas, and spent her childhood in Galveston. Studying in Paris and Berlin, she developed a formidable piano technique and an impressive repertoire (she became the second pianist in history, after Hans von Bülow, to perform the complete cycle of thirty-two Beethoven sonatas in public). She discovered after her return from Europe that her name and American origin made it difficult to enter the world of classical music at a time when American audiences were enamored of all things European. On the advice of her agent, she changed her name to Olga Samaroff, a name with more sophistication, though no one was fooled by this deception. For her New York debut in 1905, she rented Carnegie Hall and hired Walter Damrosch's New York Symphony to accompany her in two piano concertos by Liszt and Schumann.[3] The successful concert launched her career, and by the time Damrosch played with her on New Year's Eve 1916, she was a world-famous artist in demand throughout the country and playing at *his* request.

Like Muck, **Freddie Keppard** (Figure 1.5) had a rest day. Now considered one of the greatest of the early jazz cornetists, Keppard, a member of the Creole Ragtime Band, played midwestern cities on the WVMA (Western Vaudeville Managers' Association) circuit. The band played "split weeks," usually with Monday through Wednesday in one city and Thursday through Saturday in another. From Thursday through Saturday, 28–30 December, they were the headliners at the Majestic Theater in Bloomington, Illinois. Starting on 1 January they were booked for a succession of three theaters in St. Louis over a ten-day period before moving on to Chicago. As New Year's Eve fell on a Sunday, the band had the day off.

Keppard undoubtedly celebrated in his usual manner. He was known as a heavy drinker who consumed large quantities of gin daily—expensive gin if he had money, cheap gin if he didn't. Band members recounted numerous instances when Keppard's drinking made him late for rehearsals, a shortcoming they grudgingly overlooked because of his prodigious talent. On one occasion he fell asleep by an open train window and awoke to find the left side of his face swollen with frostbite. His legendary response, as related by a jazz writer decades later, stretches plausibility: "But that didn't stop the show. Freddie went on with a poultice and bandaged face. Next day, more drunk than ever, he fell down a flight of stairs, gashing his lower lip deeply. Yet, he played better and louder than ever that night."[4] No such drama is recorded on the last day of 1916, and the band was back at work the next day.

Figure 1.5 Freddie Keppard (1890–1933) (Courtesy of the Hogan Jazz Archive, Tulane University).

Vaudeville was a grueling way to make a living. The short stays in each theater and the need to perform multiple shows each day reflected the desire of the booking agents to provide fast-paced, unpredictable entertainment to their notoriously impatient audiences. A show consisted of five or more different acts, each on stage for about ten minutes. The live acts sometimes alternated with short movies, whose novelty made them a big draw. The entire show was repeated two or more times a day for audiences who paid a dime or a quarter for their seats, and an act's success depended on its ability to grab attention quickly and hold it. The Creole Band was a rare act whose performers were all African Americans. In a white world, however, the easiest way to succeed was to play to stereotypes with a "darky" act. The Creole Band's routine was billed as "Plantation Days," a comedy skit set in the antebellum South. It featured Morgan Prince, a comedian and dancer who played an old slave who could not keep his feet still when the band played ragtime tunes. The comedy routine involved a live chicken and elaborate scenery that travelled with the band. The subject matter and some of the vocal numbers came straight out of the old minstrel show, with its Jim Crow traditions. But the music played by the band was something different from what northern audiences had heard before. Though the band's promoters called it ragtime, its infectious rhythm was unlike any ragtime that vaudeville audiences knew.

In Chicago, **Dominic LaRocca** (Figure 1.6) had a quiet night but not by choice. After years of trouble fueled by alcohol, mobsters, and all-night parties, the Chicago Police Department cracked down hard on cafés in the loop, resulting in "the driest, quietest and most orderly New Year's eve that Chicago has known since Chicago ceased to be a village."[5] New Year's Eve fell on a Sunday that year, resulting in a convenient confluence of two jurisdictions. Since Illinois state law prohibited the sale of alcohol on Sundays and a Chicago city ordinance banned the sale of alcohol after 1 a.m., alcohol was available for only the one hour from midnight to 1 a.m.— making a joke of establishments like the Casino Gardens, where LaRocca and his Original Dixieland Jass Band normally packed 'em in. Revelers who wished to get around the ban rented hotel rooms and stocked them

Figure 1.6 Dominic "Nick" LaRocca (1889–1961) (Courtesy of the Hogan Jazz Archive, Tulane University).

in advance with liquor for their friends. Others went to the theater or to church instead of the cafés. The show *Robinson Crusoe, Jr.*, straight from Broadway and starring Al Jolson supported by "Glittering Galaxies of Gorgeous, Glorious, Gladsome Girlies!" added an extra performance to accommodate those who couldn't bear the thought of a dry cabaret.

LaRocca, like Keppard, had grown up in New Orleans, but his background was notably different. The son of Sicilian immigrants, LaRocca trained to be an electrician, but music was his passion, despite his father's vigorous attempts to discourage it. In the complex social structure of New Orleans, his Sicilian heritage placed him above the African American musicians he heard, but not by much. Most importantly, spending his formative years in the multicultural jambalaya of New Orleans allowed him to hear ragtime, blues, and black gospel music of the African American quarters as well as dance and brass band music in the white quarters. It was his familiarity with these diverse vernacular styles that had made it possible for him to find work as a cabaret musician in Chicago. But his disdain for blacks stayed with him in the North and had a way of surfacing often.[6]

LaRocca also played a style of music that was new to northern audiences, but in Chicago they had a name for it—jass. No one knew for sure how the name came to be applied to music, but it had first appeared in print in the baseball pages of California newspapers around 1912 and in music circles in Chicago in 1915. LaRocca and his band were the hottest purveyors of this new musical style in town, and they created a strong demand for the frenetic dance music after they arrived in March 1916. When Al Jolson first heard the band with a group of theater friends, he was so awestruck that his uneaten plate of food went cold in front of him. He called the New York agent Max Hart to tell him about the group, and Hart set to work trying to book the band for a New York engagement.

Nick LaRocca was ambitious, and Broadway looked like his ticket. An article in the *Chicago Day Book* of 12 December 1916 had raved about the money to be made in New York's entertainment district:

> Men whose business it is to take money from spenders say they never were able to take so much of it before. Ancient Babylon could be set down inside New York's winter pleasure grounds without being noticed; Nebuchadnezzar wouldn't have a reputation outside his own block. Cabarets have sprung up like mushrooms and dance halls thrive as in any new gold camp. "Business is three times as big as the biggest we ever saw before this season," said the manager of the largest cabaret in the city. New York is spending its money and getting what it can for it.[7]

After ten months in Chicago, LaRocca was ready for a new challenge, and he was definitely tired of the Chicago loop, where gangsters were a part of everyday life. After some recent run-ins, he had taken to carrying a revolver in his pocket, and he would be glad to stop looking over his shoulder. Jass was an unknown quantity in New York, and the gig that Hart had arranged was only a two-week trial in a new restaurant on Columbus Circle, but LaRocca was ready to take the risk. He and his band would stay at the Casino Gardens in Chicago until the call came, and then they would be off.

Ernestine Schumann-Heink (Figure 1.7) ended 1916 later than any of the others, as she sang in the New Year on the West Coast. The Austrian contralto owned four estates in the United States, but the one in Grossmont, overlooking the El Cajon Valley in East San Diego, was her favorite. In loyalty to her new home town, she had declined other engagements in order to sing a grand finale concert to close the Panama–California International Exposition at midnight.

San Diego's 1910 population of 37,578 made it the smallest city ever to host an international exposition. It had been open for two years, the first year, 1915, as a national exhibition concurrent with the larger Pan-Pacific Exposition in San Francisco. It was then extended and renamed

Figure 1.7 Ernestine Schumann-Heink (1861–1936) (Library of Congress).

an international exposition in 1916 with the addition of exhibits from European delegations that could not return to their war-torn countries when the San Francisco exposition closed. Schumann-Heink had supported the San Diego exposition generously by purchasing municipal bonds and by giving free concerts on "Schumann-Heink Day," 22 March 1915, and on 23 June 1915. The closing ceremonies for this two-year exposition took place on 31 December 1916. Speeches and a mock military battle by the Twenty-first United States Infantry in the afternoon were followed by a banquet with entertainment by Spanish dancers and by the Hawaiian troupe that had become a nationwide phenomenon during its residency at the exposition. Thanks to the troupe's exposure at the fair, Hawaiian music dominated sheet music, phonograph records, and even the New York cabarets in 1916.

At 11 p.m., the dignitaries gathered at the Plaza de Panama for speeches. After these were dispensed with, buglers played taps for the exposition, followed by Schumann-Heink's angelic rendition of "O Holy Night." Her twenty-minute concert culminated at midnight with "Auld Lang Syne," in which she was joined by the crowd of thousands in Balboa Park. The lights were extinguished, followed by a blaze of fireworks, the unfurling of the flags of the participating nations, and a mammoth sign over the organ reading World Peace—1917. With a son serving in the German navy, Schumann-Heink wished for that outcome as fervently as anyone.

Lt. James Reese Europe (Figure 1.8) was doing what he did best— organizing musicians. Europe had made his reputation as a leader of society orchestras in New York for over a decade. He had organized first the Clef Club, then the Tempo Club, and he had aspirations to eventually create a National Negro Symphony Orchestra, all of which were designed to provide musical opportunities for black musicians. He believed that placing highly skilled black musicians in wealthy white social circles would not only provide employment for the musicians but would break down racial prejudices among their patrons. Starting with his Clef Club in 1910, he created a booking agency to provide entertainment for social functions and to standardize working conditions for black musicians. By 1916, Europe had as many as fifteen musical groups playing social functions at any one time, and he famously made the rounds from one party to the next. There he would give a downbeat to the orchestra, hand the baton to his assistant conductor, and circulate among the patrons, making small talk and building connections that would pay off in the future. Pianist Eubie Blake, recalling Europe as a "master thinker," told an interviewer,

Figure 1.8 James Reese Europe (1881–1919) (National Archives)

"My God, he could see around corners. He could always figure out what was going to happen and be prepared for it. And he knew how to make a plan and *stick* to it."[8]

On New Year's Eve 1916, Europe had his usual cadre of musicians playing parties throughout Manhattan. He was also engaged in hiring musicians for the Royal Poinciana Hotel in West Palm Beach, Florida. He had been instrumental in ending the practice of hiring musicians as cooks or porters in resort hotels and then forcing them to play for free. He insisted that musicians be treated as professionals, and the responsibility of providing music for one of the largest and most glamorous Florida resort hotels reflected his stature. He would leave in a few weeks to spend the winter conducting in Florida.

But Europe's life was about to change dramatically. On 18 September 1916, to the amazement of his friends, he had enlisted in Company K of the Fifteenth Regiment (Colored) of the New York National Guard. On 26 September, his friend Noble Sissle, an experienced vaudeville singer, followed suit. This unit of black soldiers was led by a white commander, Colonel William Hayward, and most of his lieutenants were also white. In response to a serious shortage of black officers, Europe applied for and passed the rigorous physical and mental exams to become an officer; he received a commission as first lieutenant on 11 December 1916. He was about to engage in the most challenging piece of musical organization in his career, for he had been invited by Hayward to take over the leadership of the regimental band. Europe did not particularly like military bands—he had not enlisted for this purpose—and he could not afford to jeopardize his reputation by leading a mediocre band. He agreed to take charge on one condition—that he be given the support necessary to make it the best military band in the country.

Over the course of the twelve months of 1917, these musicians' personal and professional lives all took dramatic and unexpected turns. The plans they had made were undermined and altered by the course of world events. The successes and failures that each of them experienced individually reflected the larger changes taking place in American music during this pivotal year. The old assumptions about music in the United States were upended by social, political, and technological changes, and by New Year's Day of 1918, none of them was the same. Following their stories will allow us to witness firsthand the drastic changes that reshuffled the deck of music in America.

CHAPTER 2

✧

The Old Order

January 1917

During the winter of 1916/17, the richest and most varied concert life in the world was to be found in the northeastern cities of the United States. While Europe's cities suffered financial hardships and the loss of their young men to the war, US audiences enjoyed an embarrassment of riches. From Washington to Boston, each major city had its own orchestra as well as multiple guest concerts by orchestras from Boston, New York, and Philadelphia. Opera productions in these cities were staffed with the best European singers and a host of rising American stars now that the European opera houses were closed or underfunded. The world's most renowned soloists made their homes in America, where they found appreciative audiences and opulent salaries. These artists carried with them the authority of their Old World musical traditions, and here they were able to re-create the concert life of Europe for New World audiences hungry for culture and ready to pay for it. For music lovers in these cities, the opportunities were unprecedented.

No one exemplified the authority of European music more emphatically than Karl Muck. Like all of the Boston Symphony Orchestra conductors since its founding in 1881, he spoke to his players in German. This was partly a matter of practicality; he was none too comfortable with English, and many of his players were either German citizens or recently naturalized

German Americans. But it also reflected the philosophical view that orchestral music was largely a product of German culture.

In January 1917, the BSO's six-day tour took the orchestra for the third time that season to places where it was known and loved. The tour began on New Year's Day in Philadelphia with a program of French and Russian music; it opened with César Franck's dramatic Symphony in D Minor. After intermission, the orchestra played Debussy's sensuous *Prelude to the Afternoon of a Faun*; then Ossip Gabrilowitsch joined the orchestra as soloist in the Rachmaninoff Piano Concerto no. 2, and the program ended with Chabrier's *España* Rhapsody for orchestra. Both the *Inquirer* and the *Public Ledger* noted the large and enthusiastic crowd, which was the case whenever the BSO came to town. Both reviewers also admired the masterful playing of the Russian pianist Gabrilowitsch, who had studied at the St. Petersburg Conservatory and performed for twenty years in Germany before moving to the United States in 1914. The reviewer for the *Public Ledger* expressed surprise that "a concert filled with color, with fragrance, with some of the brightest flowers in the romanticist garden was given last night, and by a conductor usually associated with classic music."[1]

The concert in Washington the following night was as important for who attended as for what the orchestra played. Both the *Post* and the *Times* listed the occupants of reserved boxes, among whom were prominent political leaders and their families. Miss Margaret Wilson, the oldest daughter of President Woodrow Wilson, had served as de facto First Lady after her mother's death in 1914. In her box were William Hitz, a judge of the US District Court for the District of Columbia, and the author La Salle Corbell Pickett, whose account of her husband George Pickett's role in the battle of Gettysburg had helped shape the "Lost Cause" narrative of the Confederacy. Occupying other nearby boxes were German Ambassador Count Johann Heinrich von Bernstorff and Countess von Bernstorff, as well as US Secretary of War Newton D. Baker and his wife. The program contained a Tchaikovsky suite, Weber's *Euryanthe* Overture, and the Schumann Piano Concerto, played by Carl Friedberg, a German pianist who had immigrated to the United States in 1914. According to the *Times*, "Never before in Washington has Dr. Muck shown so much temperament, so much life in his handling of the Boston Symphony Orchestra."[2]

The tour continued in similar fashion. In Baltimore on 3 January, a "huge and enthusiastic" audience heard an "extremely beautiful" concert with a "positively inspired" rendition of the orchestral works.[3] The Brooklyn concert on 5 January featured Beethoven's Eighth Symphony and Weber's *Euryanthe* Overture, both Classical-period works that sparkled under the disciplined precision of Muck's well-drilled orchestra. The concert again featured Gabrilowitsch in the Rachmaninoff Second Concerto and Borodin's *In the Steppes of Central Asia*. The piano soloist earned rave reviews for his passionate rendition of the music of his Russian compatriot.

The two performances in Carnegie Hall on 4 and 6 January were played to the most discriminating audiences and the most demanding critics. Neither concert featured a guest soloist, with the result that "the orchestra is properly made the centre of interest, without the intervention of an artistic personality that may or may not be sympathetic."[4] The first concert opened with the Franck Symphony, which the *Times* critic found to be "profoundly beautiful" but "somewhat long." The audience's applause after the first movement—something that twenty-first-century audiences have been trained not to do—was especially vigorous. Three Wagner overtures were performed after intermission, a programming choice that puzzled all the critics. The audience response was "apathetic," perhaps because that much Wagner at one sitting lacked the variety they expected. After the Romantic-oriented concert on Thursday the 4th, the Saturday matinee on the 6th was mostly Classical: Weber's *Euryanthe* Overture, a Haydn symphony, and Tchaikovsky's First Suite, whose varied timbral combinations emphasize grace, elegance, and wit as opposed to the bombast of the Russian composer's best-known works.

Music criticism in New York was a form of literature, and dozens of reviewers attended these concerts to write often expansive critiques of the repertoire and the performances. Most gave serious consideration to the intentions of the composers and the ability of the performers to bring those intentions to life. Opinions varied widely on the value of individual works, the audience reaction, and even on the success of a performance. There was agreement, though, that the BSO was one of the world's greatest orchestras and that audiences came to their concerts with high expectations. The critic of *Musical America* waxed poetic on this aspect of the organization: "No one is surprised when a beautiful, rich tone is produced from a Stradivarius instrument; in the same manner we come to regard the precision and other musicianly attributes of the Boston Symphony Orchestra as a matter of course. Tradition made it so years ago and what Bostonian is with soul so dead as to apply the higher criticism and inquire if the glorious old tradition lives yet in all of its purity?"[5]

At the head of this legendary orchestra was a man so reserved and distant that he provoked equal parts admiration, curiosity, and exasperation. In the midst of the flights of verbal fancy over the beautiful tone and unequalled discipline of his orchestra were complaints about his repertoire choices. His programming three successive Wagner overtures on Thursday puzzled all who heard the concert, and regarding the Saturday program

Musical America stated bluntly, "Why the orchestra should travel all the way from Boston to do the 'Euryanthe' Overture, a Haydn Symphony and an inconsequential Tschaikowsky suite can be determined only by one intimately acquainted with Dr. Muck's peculiar psychology, which is so baffling to the ordinary run of mortals."[6] The *Musical Courier*, whose editorial tone was often flippant, compared Muck to the heroine of Longfellow's poem "There was a little girl":

> When she was good, she was very good indeed,
> But when she was bad, she was horrid.[7]

After this six-day tour—the orchestra's third visit to these cities since the season began in October 1916—Muck and his orchestra returned to Massachusetts. The orchestra played nineteen concerts in January 1917, only four of them at home in Boston's Symphony Hall. Wherever they went, they were greeted by large and enthusiastic crowds, for a live concert was the only way to hear an orchestra of this caliber. In this era, before radio, television, or the Internet, touring orchestras were essential to American musical life.

Walter Damrosch's New York Symphony was just as active as the BSO during the height of the concert season, performing weekly concerts in New York, touring to nearby cities (Harrisburg, Pennsylvania, among them), and engaging in marathon cross-country tours. The appeal of this orchestra was due in part to the charm of its conductor. Damrosch was known as much for speaking as for conducting. Since the 1880s he had annually given numerous lecture recitals in which he explained the music to be performed by his orchestra. Sometimes he sat alone at a piano, illustrating his points with excerpts from the score, and other times he spoke with the orchestra onstage to demonstrate the themes under discussion. He was also known for his impromptu comments in the middle of concerts, when he would turn to the audience with a friendly smile and begin, "Ladies and gentlemen. . . ." These off-the-cuff remarks were always witty, usually enlightening, and seldom scholarly.

The most popular of his lecture recitals were those devoted to Wagner's operas. He was famous for his detailed analysis of the leitmotifs in these works, which held a special meaning for him. His father, Leopold, had been a friend of Wagner before leaving Europe in 1871, and until his death in 1885, Leopold was one of the composer's most ardent champions in America. Walter continued his father's devotion to this most German of composers through his frequent lecture recitals and regular performances of his works (see Figure 2.1).

On 9 January, the orchestra performed an all-Wagner concert with contralto Julia Claussen in Washington, DC. The concert attracted a distinguished audience of government officials and their families to the Belasco Theater for a program of overtures and arias. The *Washington Post* raved, "If Walter Damrosch never again does anything worthwhile for Washington music lovers, they will always remember him most gratefully for the superb program presented yesterday at the Belasco Theater. To those who know their Wagner the concert was a feast for the heart, and the Symphony Orchestra, of New York, never has played any better."[8] The *Herald* and

Figure 2.1 Photograph of Walter Damrosch conducting ca. 1908 and an autograph from 1927 with an excerpt from Wagner's *Die Meistersinger* inscribed "To Wagner the Prize!" (author's collection).

Times were nearly as effusive, with the reviewer for the latter paper calling Damrosch and Wagner "inseparable" owing to the conductor's ability to bring the composer's mythical world to life.

Though Damrosch, like Muck, toured to the major cities, he led fewer concerts in those cultural centers than his Boston colleague. Instead, he made a specialty of touring to smaller towns not regularly visited by major orchestras. On 12 January, the New York Symphony performed in Zanesville, Ohio, where they earned praise from the audience for featuring a Columbus girl, Helene Pugh, as soloist in the Tchaikovsky Piano Concerto in B-flat Minor. Throughout the month of January, newspapers in Harrisburg stoked excitement for the New York Symphony's performance on 6 February, the only orchestral performance scheduled for the city that season.

Back home in New York, the orchestra often performed in competition with the New York Philharmonic, under the direction of Josef Stransky. As New York was the only city in the country that could support two orchestras of such high caliber, New Yorkers had opportunities afforded no others. The rivalry forced both conductors to update their repertoire constantly with new works, to hire the best soloists available, and to promote their performances relentlessly. Often the concerts of the two orchestras were reviewed in the same column in the city's numerous daily newspapers, and comparisons were inevitable. The critic of the *New York World*, Sylvester Rawling, noted in his review of the 26 January concert that "acute competition is stirring Mr. Damrosch to show depths of power that, hitherto, he has not disclosed to us."[9] This concert included performances of Beethoven's familiar *Leonore* Overture no. 3 and Tchaikovsky's less familiar Symphony no. 2. It also featured Percy Grainger as soloist in the Grieg Piano Concerto. Grainger was an Australian composer and pianist who had studied in Germany and then lived in England for over a decade. Shortly after the war broke out, he immigrated to the United States in September 1914, earning the disapproval of his English friends and critics. His handsome appearance and passionate playing were rapidly making him a favorite of American audiences, and Damrosch capitalized on his popularity and European reputation.

A brief notice in the *New York Times* of 31 January confirmed the conductor's popularity with his players: "Walter Damrosch had a birthday greeting from the Symphony Society at rehearsal yesterday in Aeolian Hall. He arrived to find a dark house, and was suddenly surprised with a blowing of trumpets and beating of drums as the lights were turned on. The orchestra gave the 'dean of American conductors' a bunch of his favorite roses, this year numbering fifty-five."[10] In the prime of his career, he enjoyed artistic admiration, social prestige, and popularity with his players and audiences.

The orchestra that James Reese Europe was putting together for the Royal Poinciana Hotel in Palm Beach was a very different sort of orchestra. His group would be a dance orchestra to entertain vacationers during dinner and to play arrangements of popular music for after-dinner dancing. The orchestra's repertoire and performances were not reviewed by newspaper critics, but its success depended on pleasing the patrons—a much more immediate form of review. In this type of performance, Europe was a past master. During his many years of providing musicians for the rich and powerful throughout the Northeast, he had learned what they wanted to hear and how they expected musicians to behave. Among his most loyal patrons was Philadelphia's Wanamaker family, who had been one of the first to hire Europe to provide music for a party. He subsequently became almost a Wanamaker house musician and provided music for all their social events.

The Royal Poinciana attracted wealthy patrons from the North looking for sun in the winter. The hotel opened in mid-January, and high season lasted through February and March before tapering off in the spring. The patrons were in many cases the same persons who attended symphony orchestra concerts at home, but they did not expect high culture in this setting. Instead, they sought music that would allow them to relax, have a good time, and not think too hard. Europe knew how to select appropriate music for such events, and he also knew how to interact with the clientele. He exuded an air of dignity and self-confidence, but he also avoided undue familiarity. His artistry was evident, but it was not the arrogant artistry of a conductor like Muck.

The other significant difference in this orchestra was that it made money. The size of the orchestra and the salaries of musicians were calculated to turn a profit, and Europe had learned through long experience how to balance the budget in order to pay his musicians fairly and also return a profit for his employers. This was not the primary objective of the Muck and Damrosch orchestras. A full symphony orchestra consisted of just under a hundred musicians, and in order to achieve the level of quality demanded by Boston and New York patrons, these musicians were some of the best in the world. Both Muck and Damrosch went to great lengths to obtain the best available European musicians, which in Damrosch's case had created ongoing battles with the Musicians' Union in New York. World-class woodwind players were especially difficult to find in America, and flutist Georges Barrère of the New York Symphony and oboist Georges Longy of the Boston Symphony—both brought from France at great expense—were unmatched by any orchestra in the world.

Because of the size and quality of their orchestras, Muck and Damrosch could not cover expenses through ticket sales, even with full houses and exclusive prices. In Boston, the founder and chief patron of the orchestra was Henry Lee Higginson. Since its beginnings in 1881, he had exercised constant control over the management of the orchestra. He hired and fired conductors at will (always Europeans, as these were the only acceptable candidates in his view). He demanded that BSO players give their primary loyalty to the orchestra, in exchange for generous salaries and guaranteed employment. He had successfully resisted unionization with the rationale that his conductor could not achieve the requisite standard of quality without being able to rehearse as often and as long as he wished. He gave the conductors absolute artistic control; their mandate was to achieve the highest artistic quality possible. In exchange for these conditions, the millionaire had covered all deficits since the orchestra's founding, thus providing the financial means to develop it into the world's greatest orchestra.[11] In New York, Damrosch enjoyed similar patronage from oil magnate Henry Harkness Flagler, who had covered his orchestra's deficits up to $100,000 since 1914. Both these wealthy men recognized that if American orchestras were to rival the state-supported European orchestras, they would need private funding, since the US government resolutely refused to support the arts in the manner that was customary in Europe.

The Fifteenth Regiment Band faced a similar problem. Army regulations allowed for a twenty-eight-member band, which Jim Europe believed to be inadequate for his aspirations. He told the commander of the regiment, Col. Hayward, that forty-four members was the minimum size he could consider, with sixty members preferable. In order to recruit the extra members, outfit them with uniforms, musical scores, and instruments, and pay bonuses under the table to entice top-flight professional musicians to give up their lucrative careers for army wages, he would need a fund of $10,000. Hayward began raising the money through small donations, but he was not able to approach the sums needed. In despair, he made an appointment with the wealthy industrialist Daniel G. Reid, known as "the Tinplate King." He asked Reid to supply letters of introduction to thirty or forty of his rich friends whom he could ask for $500 each. Reid asked how many donations he hoped to get in all, and when Hayward told him he needed twenty, Reid took his checkbook from his desk and wrote a check for $10,000. "That's a damn sight easier than writing you forty letters of introduction, and it will save you a lot of time too. Here are your twenty victims at $500 each."[12] Europe was stunned when Col. Hayward called to tell him the money had been raised, and his friend Noble Sissle laughingly said, "Well, they called your bluff," earning a barrage of phone books from across the room.[13]

Like Damrosch and Muck, Europe found it impossible to cover the expenses of a large musical ensemble of first-rate musicians without private funds. The wealthy industrialists who supported these organizations—Harkness, Higginson, and Reid—believed that musical ensembles of the highest caliber merited their philanthropy. When Europe departed for Florida in mid-January, Sissle was left with the responsibility of advertising and recruiting for the regimental band, knowing that he had funds to support the quality that Europe had promised to deliver.

Pianist Olga Samaroff was well acquainted with the world of American orchestras, but for a different reason. Shortly after her successful debut with Damrosch's New York Symphony in 1905, she had fallen in love with a church organist and aspiring conductor by the name of Leopold Stokowski. As her fame grew, she helped him achieve his aspirations. She was directly responsible for his conducting debut with the Colonne Orchestra of Paris in 1909, when she recommended him as a last-minute replacement. By the time they married in 1911, he had been appointed conductor of the Cincinnati Symphony Orchestra, and she retired from active performance to take the role of "conductor's wife," hosting teas with society ladies and helping to keep the wheels of his career running smoothly. She was instrumental in securing his appointment as conductor of the Philadelphia Orchestra in 1912, a position he held for three decades as he grew into one of the world's most famous and flamboyant conductors.

Madame Samaroff Stokowski, as she was now known, returned to performing in 1913 and gradually increased the number of her performances to meet the demands of an adoring public. There were few female pianists in the top levels of the classical music world, and her artistry had earned her a solid position as one of the most popular. By the end of January 1917, she had already performed sixty concerts that season. Though she was in demand as a solo recitalist and as a guest with other orchestras, it was her performances with Stokowski's Philadelphia Orchestra that were most anticipated. Between 1914 and 1923 she played over fifty times with the Philadelphians, due as much to the influence of manager Arthur Judson as to her husband.[14]

The last week of January 1917 found them in Pittsburgh, where the Philadelphia Orchestra played an annual series of concerts to great acclaim. For the orchestra's third pair of concerts that season, Stokowski presented an all-French program with his wife as soloist in the Saint-Saëns Piano Concerto no. 2. Advance publicity for the concert featured full-length photos of the tall and strikingly beautiful Samaroff, accompanied by rapturous prose:

> The Philadelphia Orchestra came and conquered, and their Pittsburgh concerts are the chief topic of conversation in music circles. Leopold Stokowski has become a matinee idol in Pittsburgh, as he is in Philadelphia. The next concerts in the series are eagerly awaited, for Olga Samaroff, the brilliant pianist, will appear as soloist with the orchestra. . . . Mme. Samaroff is the wife of Conductor Stokowski, and unusual interest is attached to her appearance under the baton of her distinguished husband. A number of matinee parties have been arranged in honor of Mme. Stokowski, who has many friends in Pittsburgh through her former appearances in that city with the Pittsburgh Orchestra.[15]

Anticipation for the concert was so high that the first of the two concerts, on Monday, 29 January, was moved from the Carnegie Music Hall to the recently built Shriners' Mosque. This much larger auditorium allowed the management to offer six hundred additional seats at "popular prices" (50 cents each) rather than the full price of one dollar. This was the first-ever orchestral performance in the auditorium, and audience members were given a ballot with their program so that they could vote on whether future concerts should also be scheduled there. The program was repeated at a matinee performance in the Nixon Theater on the following Tuesday, 30 January. This change of venue (and presumably a different piano) added extra challenges for the piano soloist.

The *Pittsburgh Press*, the *Post*, and the *Post-Gazette* all gave the concert a rave review, with the first two papers clearly stating that Samaroff was the highlight of the evening. The *Post* critic wrote a detailed description that gives insight into the specific qualities of her playing and also the audience reaction:

> Mme. Samaroff, whose performance of the Saint-Saëns Concerto in G minor, Opus 22, constituted her first appearance before a Pittsburgh audience in a protracted period, carried off the honors of the evening. Her art has much matured since last she was heard here. There is the same beauty of tone, the same clearness and facility of technique, but a new fire. The Saint-Saëns concerto makes no profound demands upon the interpretative artist, but Mme. Samaroff gave to it all the spirit and the brilliance requisite to a noteworthy performance. Her feeling for rhythm was unusual, and her phrasing flawless. She was capably assisted by the orchestra in a remarkably well-knit and finished

performance. A storm of applause followed each of the three movements, and insistent appreciation recalled her half a dozen times at the close of the work.[16]

Following the concert, Stokowski was forced to quell a rumor that had been circulating to the effect that he might not conduct the rest of his orchestra's concerts in Pittsburgh. He clarified that because the orchestra was in such high demand, he had agreed to let his concertmaster direct some of the "less important" concerts to avoid overtaxing himself. He assured his Pittsburgh fans, however, that their concerts were as important to him as those in Philadelphia and that he would not disappoint their expectations. He and his wife both felt the mixed blessing of fame as they struggled to meet the demands of their audience without wearing themselves out.

Among the many European artists who made a home in America, few were as beloved as Ernestine Schumann-Heink. During the prior decade she had built up a loyal following throughout the country and had acquired a sizable fortune in the process. In January 1917 she toured the country, giving concerts and singing with orchestras. She also threw her money and her influence behind an artistic scheme that would take much of her attention during the next six months. Her goal was to re-create in America one of the traditions she missed most about Germany.

The Bayreuth Festival (in German, Bayreuther Festspiele) was the brainchild of Richard Wagner, who believed that his music dramas required a unique theater to stage them properly. After heroic fundraising efforts the theater was completed, and the first festival presented in 1876. It was an artistic triumph for the composer, whose death seven years later did not spell the end of the festival but only made it more revered. His widow, Cosima, took over management of the festival, which took place every year or two until she passed it to her son Siegfried, who ran it from 1906 to 1930. The Bayreuth Festival specialized in the last ten of Wagner's operas, presented in performances that were faithful to the composer's intentions in every way. The artistic orthodoxy they created verged on religious fanaticism.

Since her Bayreuth debut in 1898, Schumann-Heink had performed there often and achieved there some of her greatest artistic successes. She could no longer sing in Bayreuth with the war raging in Europe, but she knew of America's love for Wagner. When the Panama-California International Exposition closed on New Year's Eve 1916, she proposed the idea of an "American Bayreuth" to be held every summer in the Spreckels Organ Pavilion in Balboa Park, San Diego. This festival would stage full performances of Wagner's operas in the outdoor auditorium where she had just sung the final concert of the fair. As a down payment on the scheme, she deposited $10,000 in a San Diego bank and challenged other donors to step forward to support her plan to make San Diego a national center for culture. The initial announcement stated that the first festival would be held in July 1917, just six months away.[17]

Schumann-Heink's nostalgia for the festival she had loved in Germany did not stop her from connecting with American audiences. Touring relentlessly throughout the early months of 1917, she sang with America's most renowned orchestras in its most famous concert halls and also appeared in benefit performances in some unusual venues. Among her favorites were military camps. On 5 January she visited the camp of the Second Battalion of the Twenty-First Regiment in San Diego, where she was elected honorary president of the officers' mess. On Sunday afternoon, 14 January, she serenaded regiments of Ohio troops on border patrol at Camp Pershing, outside El Paso, Texas. She opened her program in a fashion that never failed to please her American audiences: "I am going to sing you boys a song about l-o-v-e. They say the German people can't say 'love,' but always say 'loff.' Now you boys listen closely." She then began with a love song, followed by a sacred song, a Scotch song, a French song, a German song, the popular American song "The Rosary," by Ethelbert Nevin, and ended by leading the troops in "America." She chatted with the Ohio commander in German and accepted flowers and a silver loving cup for her efforts.[18] This informal performance followed a concert in El Paso the night before that was so popular the managers had to set up an extra two hundred seats on the stage after every other seat in the house was sold. The reviewer raved about the fifty-five-year-old singer, "Schumann-Heink, if anything, improves with age, for she never sang better than she did Saturday evening and she fully deserved the great tribute paid her by the splendid audience that poured out to hear her."[19] Though most of her selections were in German, she ended, as usual, with English selections in deference to her audience.

January was also the height of the concert season for Fritz Kreisler. His primary focus that month was the major concert halls of the Northeast, where he was revered above every other violinist. His New York recital on the last day of 1916 had already been his fifth in that city since the concert season began in the fall, and January brought more high-profile performances there, in addition to quick trips to Philadelphia, Pittsburgh, and Rochester and to Burlington, Vermont.

Kreisler did not play as many benefit concerts as Schumann-Heink, but he did participate in an important one on Tuesday, 16 January. On that evening, he and pianist Ignacy Paderewski were soloists with Karl Muck and the Boston Symphony Orchestra in a benefit concert at the Metropolitan Opera House for the Vacation Fund. This organization was dedicated to providing working girls with annual vacation time at full pay by raising funds to reimburse employers and also by encouraging savings accounts by the workers. Thanks to the presence of such high-profile artists on the program, the January concert raised $25,000 for the charity. Kreisler played the Mendelssohn Violin Concerto and a set of solos; Paderewski played the Schumann Piano Concerto and a set of solos. Muck led the orchestra in a performance of Smetana's Overture to *The Bartered Bride* that "has not often been given at a more dizzying pace, with greater finesse, in a more whispered pianissimo in the opening section," followed by Richard Strauss's picturesque *Till Eulenspiegel* and Enescu's *Rumanian Rhapsody*.[20]

For persons who did not have the opportunity to hear Kreisler in person, the burgeoning supply of Victrola records presented an alternative. The recording industry was still in its infancy, and the acoustic recording technology in use at the time could not effectively capture certain instruments or voice types. Both Kreisler and Schumann-Heink were among the most popular recording artists, as the technicians had managed to create pleasing records of their respective performances. The May 1917 complete catalog of Victor Records listed thirty-nine solo records by Kreisler plus fifteen duets with other artists. The same catalog credited Schumann-Heink with forty solo records plus two duets ("sung in German unless noted").[21] Both artists included a mix of classical music and popular favorites, but each recording's length was limited to a little over three minutes. Kreisler's records thus contained none of the concertos or extended solos that were the backbone of his concerts, and Schumann-Heink's records did not include the extended operatic arias for which she was known. Instead both recorded short, light works such as Kreisler's Viennese dance tunes and folk songs. At this point, tenor Enrico Caruso had proven that records had commercial potential, but the field was still very specialized.

During the summer and fall of 1916, the Creole Band had been booked on the Pantages circuit, which took them through western Canada, Montana, and the Pacific Northwest before traversing California from San Francisco to Los Angeles to San Diego. From there they began a gradual move east that would eventually bring them to New York. They began 1917 in St. Louis and reached Chicago by the end of the month by way of dates in Iowa, Indiana, and Illinois.[22] The cartoon in Figure 2.2 illustrates the sort

Figure 2.2 Illustration of vaudeville bill featuring the Creole Band (*Cedar Rapids Evening Gazette*, 12 November 1915, 20).

of mixed bill of vaudeville acts on which they typically performed, in this case a November 1915 bill at the Majestic Theatre in Cedar Rapids, Iowa.

The advance publicity for their performances on the 1916/17 tour promised "wild, untamed music," a description that was echoed in many of the reviews. But as the tour unfolded, new terms began making their way into the descriptions of the band's performances. The *St. Joseph (Missouri) Gazette* of 15 December 1916 described their style as "ragtime 'blues.'" At their next stop, Cedar Rapids, Iowa, they temporarily adopted a new name, "Alabama Jass Band," apparently a ploy to distract the Cedar Rapids reviewer who had panned the Creole Band the previous year. Under the influence of the new name, the reviewer raved about them:

By their performance a new branch of music was laid open to Cedar Rapids listeners. Jass music has been attempted previously but it has been confined for the most part to trombone moanings and the customary raggy tempo. This is a part of jass—but it is not jass. There is included the squeak of a clarinet and the thrumming of a bass viol, all grouped together in some sort of African time which was evidently the basis of ragtime music.

This must have been real jass, for a group of performers who had finished their work and come to the front of the house to sit across the aisle, writhed in appreciation and shouted approval. Their eastern perception will be accepted.[23]

The reviewer noted that one of the appreciative performers who heard the set was the Chicago songwriter Coleman Goetz, said to be a protégé of Irving Berlin. A search of copyright records in the Library of Congress reveals that publisher Leo Feist of New York had deposited an unpublished song with words by Goetz and music by Leon Flatow on 16 December with the title "Everybody Loves a Jass Band."[24] As the Creole Band worked its way toward Chicago and eventually New York, the words jass, jas, jaz, and jazz appeared more frequently in reviews.

One of the great tragedies of early jazz history is that the Creole Band released no recordings. One of the enduring mysteries is why. By the time that record collectors began seriously investigating the question decades later, Keppard had died and the recollections of other potential eyewitnesses did not gibe. In his masterly summary of the evidence, Lawrence Gushee relates conflicting testimony.[25] Sometime in 1916, possibly during the band's New York run early in the year, they had been approached by the Victor Talking Machine Company with a proposal to make records. According to one oft-repeated account, Keppard told his bandmates: "Nothin' doin', boys. We won't put our stuff on records for everybody to steal." This reinforces the legend of the mystical power of Keppard's playing, which consisted of unconventional techniques that were his own closely guarded secret. Another version has Keppard refusing Victor's proposal to do a test without pay to see if it would be practical to record the band: "Nothin' doin', boys. We've been kicked around so much we don't want to record. We'll do it if you give us money, money right away!" Clarinetist Sidney Bechet, who was not present but was a close friend of Keppard's, simply stated, "Fred just didn't care to, that was all." He amplified this statement by suggesting that making records would have taken the pleasure out of music and turned it into a business venture. Yet another account places the confrontation during intermission at the Winter Garden in New York, where Victor presented a contract for the band to sign. When the seasoned (and well-paid) performers read that Victor proposed to give Keppard twenty-five dollars and the others fifteen dollars each for recording four sides, he shouted, "Take this piece of paper and stick it up your rear. Do I look like a goddam fool? Why, I buy that much whisky a day." The common theme in all of these anecdotes is the leadership of Freddie Keppard. Though bassist Bill Johnson was the business manager of the group, Keppard's personality dominated the band, as his cornet playing must have dominated its sound.

But Johnson's string bass may have been part of the reason the band did not release recordings. There are tantalizing clues that the band *did* make test recordings that were rejected because of poor recording quality. The acoustic recording techniques in use at this time did not have the capability to capture the lower frequencies of the string bass faithfully, but the strength of these inaudible sound waves could sabotage the recording.[26] For one of these reasons or a combination of several, we have no aural record of the sound of the Creole Band in its prime. A successful jazz band recording would need to wait for a band that did not use a string bass.

The call from New York came later than Nick LaRocca had hoped. The Reisenweber Building, an eight-story complex of restaurants and club rooms on Columbus Circle, was closed for renovations, and the jazz band was to be part of the entertainment package that would attract customers who had gone elsewhere during construction. A spectacular advertisement for "the Jasz Band" in the *New York Times* of 15 January (see Figure 2.3) was just a teaser, as the building was not even open yet, and the compositor of the ad does not seem to have had access to the proofreading of the band members. On 17 January, the building was formally reopened with a banquet for several hundred, at which it was announced that the $250,000 renovation had expanded the capacity of the building to 3,500.[27] A 23 January mention of "The Jass Band" in Reisenweber's ad was probably also a teaser, but starting on Saturday, 27 January, the band was advertised daily. That day the ad promised "The First Eastern Appearance of The Only Original Dixieland 'Jass' Band—Untuneful Harmonists in 'Peppery' Melodies," and the following day they were upgraded to "The Famous Original Dixieland 'Jass Band.'"

The time was right for a jazz band to make the jump from Chicago to New York. For nearly a month, agent Max Hart and trombonist Eddie Edwards, the band's de facto business manager, had been sending telegrams back and forth as Hart kept him apprised of the negotiations with Reisenweber's and (for a time) Healy's restaurants. The curiosity about "jass" was so strong in New York that the band received overtures from three other agents while they awaited final confirmation from Hart. On 19 January he sent both a telegram and a registered letter confirming that Reisenweber's would pay transportation plus $350 a week for a guaranteed

Dance to the JASZ BAND. It's New and Gay and It Won't Let Your Feet Behave. First Time In New York at Paradise TO-NIGHT.

Tea Dances Every Afternoon — 4:30 to 6:30
Supper Dances Every Night — 11:30 to Closing

AT

Margaret Hawkesworth's

"PARADISE"

The Smartest, Most Beautiful and Most Modern Ballroom in America

In the New Reisenweber Building, at

Eighth Avenue and 58th Street

Decorations by Joseph Urban and Raphael Kirchner

Miss Hawkesworth announces the Paradise Supper Club for Those Desiring the Advantages of Similar Social Organizations in Europe.

Highest class entertainment every night by well-known artists. Miss Hawkesworth will dance afternoon and evening with Mr. Alexander Kiam. Superb cuisine—best dance music—best dancing floor in town

and

The First Sensational Amusement Novelty of 1917

"THE JASZ BAND"

Direct from its amazing success in Chicago, where it has given modern dancing new life and a new thrill. The Jazz Band is the latest craze that is sweeping the nation like a musical thunderstorm.

"THE JASZ BAND"

Comes exclusively to "Paradise" First of All New York Ballrooms, and will open for a run TONIGHT (Monday). You've Just Got to Dance When You Hear It.

Special Breakfast Served After 1:30 A. M.

EVENING DRESS NOT OBLIGATORY

Telephone 9640 Col.

Figure 2.3 Advance publicity for the Original Dixieland Jazz Band at Reisenweber's Restaurant (*New York Times*, 15 January 1917). There is no evidence that they actually performed before 27 January.

ten weeks, a considerable advance over the $225 they were earning at the Casino Gardens. A follow-up telegram on 22 January read simply, "When are you leaving with band."[28] Their debut took place on Saturday, 27 January 1917.

The arrival of the Original Dixieland "Jass" Band in New York is the stuff of legend, and LaRocca was able to shape the legend through the interviews he gave decades later. As he recalled it, they arrived at the new 400 Club in the Reisenweber Building to find the room dark. The interior decorators, under the direction of eminent architect John J. Petit, had just finished painting brilliant designs on the rough plaster walls, hanging silk-shaded ceiling lamps, and installing dark floor-length curtains on the windows.[29] But the lights were not connected. LaRocca and trombonist Eddie Edwards were both electricians who had honed their musical skills during breaks from their electrical work in New Orleans, so after they helped Tony Sbarbaro carry his drums to the bandstand in the dark, they headed for the basement. There they found the wiring incorrectly installed to the fuse box. Fixing the problem in short order, they turned on the lights in the 400 Club.

The image of turning on the lights is an apt metaphor to describe what they did with their music later that night. After a brief introduction by the manager, who invited diners to leave their tables and come to the dance floor, LaRocca tore into their signature tune, "Tiger Rag." The playing of the five musicians—cornetist LaRocca, trombonist Edwards, clarinetist Larry Shields, pianist Harry Ragas, and drummer Tony Sbarbaro—was so fast and loud that customers who were used to dancing to string orchestras didn't know what to do. After the opening number, the manager again reiterated his invitation: "This music is for dancing." As the band played another number, a few brave souls ventured onto the floor, where they found that the infectious rhythms made their bodies move. Within an hour, the dance floor was crowded, and within a week, customers were lined up outside waiting for a table to come free. Reisenweber's raised its prices and increased the band's pay, with no detriment to the band's popularity. The Original Dixieland Jass Band had turned on the lights to a new era in popular music.[30]

CHAPTER 3

༄

Anxiety

February 1917

The war in Europe drew closer to America on 1 February, when Germany declared the resumption of unrestricted submarine warfare in a large zone of the Atlantic Ocean stretching from northern Spain to southern Norway and encompassing the coastlines of France and the British Isles. The text of the memorandum delivered by Ambassador Bernstorff to the State Department on 31 January stated, "From February 1, 1917, sea traffic will be stopped with every available weapon and without further notice. . . . Neutral ships navigating these blockade zones do so at their own risk."[1] Von Bernstorff's memo framed the decision as Germany's only reasonable response to England's refusal of its peace terms, but the headline of the *New York Times* effectively illustrates American views on this announcement: "Germany Begins Ruthless Sea Warfare; Draws 'Barred Zones' Around the Allies; Crisis Confronts the United States."

The improvement of submarine technology and the development of self-propelled torpedoes had created a potent new weapon for use in World War I. In violation of international law requiring submarines to warn merchant ships and allow their crews to disembark before sinking them, Germany had used the weapon indiscriminately early in the war. The sinking of the luxury liner *Lusitania* on 1 May 1915, with a loss of 1,198 souls, provoked such outrage that Germany suspended this tactic for nearly two years before resuming it on 1 February 1917.[2] The German government claimed that England had used a blockade to starve German women and children, giving them the rationale to create a similar blockade around the British Isles and France. The Allies viewed it as a breach of international maritime law.

This declaration made continued neutrality of the United States nearly impossible. President Woodrow Wilson had successfully run for re-election in 1916 with the slogan "He kept us out of the war," and his administration was determined to avoid entanglements in the war, despite public sympathy for Britain and the outspoken advocacy of former president Theodore Roosevelt and other hawks. He had actively opposed the sort of military preparedness advocated by Roosevelt, with the result that the US military was too small, underequipped, and antiquated to pose any real threat to Germany. As the Kaiser took the calculated risk of provoking the United States, it became clear that the United States did not have an adequate navy to call his bluff. Still unwilling to declare war against Germany, Wilson nonetheless severed diplomatic relations on 2 February and ordered Von Bernstorff home. The ambassador left America on 14 February, and it was later revealed that he had been engaged in a series of plots to undermine US military preparation and sabotage British and Canadian industrial companies.

On 3 February, the American merchant ship SS *Housatonic*, carrying a load of wheat for England, was stopped by a German submarine off the southwest tip of Cornwall. After interviewing her captain, the U-boat commander ordered the crew into lifeboats and sank the ship to prevent the food from reaching England. He then towed the lifeboats toward shore, and they were rescued by a British ship with all lives intact. Coming so soon after the resumption of submarine warfare, this sinking brought the declaration home. Ironically, the SS *Housatonic* had been a German ship (SS *Georgia*) from 1890 to 1914, when it was interned in the United States and sold to an American company.

The dismissal of the ambassador and the sinking of the SS *Housatonic* coincided with a Young People's Concert by Walter Damrosch and the New York Symphony Society in Carnegie Hall. Damrosch began the concert by having his orchestra stand to play "The Star-Spangled Banner," after which he turned to the three thousand children in the audience and said:

My dear young friends: One of the noblest functions of music is to arouse patriotism. Our national anthem symbolizes to us the country we love, the United States of America. This comprises the North and the South, the East and the West; there is no dividing line. Whether we were born here or thousands of miles away, this is the country of our choice, for which you and I must be ready at any moment to make any sacrifice. I want you, my young friends, to remember that what the flag symbolizes to the eye, the national anthem symbolizes to the ear, and through the ear to the heart—demonstrating the great power of music to awaken our deepest emotions and to ennoble us in the awakening.[3]

For the American public, especially for persons with connections to Germany and Austria, these events were a turning point. Though there was no timetable for US entry, it was no longer possible to imagine that the United States would remain neutral. When it did enter the war, millions of American men would be needed for the military. The status of citizens of Germany and Austria—"enemy aliens"—would be altered, but as yet it was not known precisely how. The anxiety was pervasive, particularly among musicians with strong ties to Europe, and this anxiety would have unanticipated effects on music.

On Friday evening, 3 February, a tall woman limped into Roosevelt Hospital in New York with an injured ankle; she was unable to remember who she was or how she had gotten there. In her pocketbook were a ticket from Philadelphia to Boston and papers identifying her as Olga Samaroff, the famous pianist. Her physician, Dr. William M. Polk, was called to the hospital, and he took her to his home to rest. She quickly regained her memory and telegraphed her husband, Leopold Stokowski, who had been conducting a concert in Philadelphia when she left (see Figure 3.1). According to one report, he had been frantically calling the police in Philadelphia and New York in an effort to locate his missing wife. When she finally resurfaced, he urged the papers not to print the story, which would "sound stupid," but it was too late. The story spread, and along with it rumors about what caused her unusual behavior. Her physician released an official statement: "I have tried to get her to stop work for some time. She was nervous and overwrought and her health was endangered by her recent concert tours. She had been through the West and recently played in concerts in and about Philadelphia. When she had a nervous breakdown a short time ago I insisted on her stopping work."[4] The gossip columnist of *Musical America* took the incident as an opportunity to remind readers of how demanding the career of a concert artist could be, but not before rehashing rumors that were swirling about Samaroff and Stokowski. He wrote:

> My own idea of the situation is that Mme. Samaroff lost her memory temporarily from over-work, over-strain, trying to support her husband socially and to further his career and trying, at the same time, to keep up with her own work, giving concert after concert, traveling at night to perform the next day, with little or no rest; having all the discomforts of living in different hotels, sleeping

in a different bed, perhaps, night after night, eating often distasteful, ill-cooked food, poorly served, all the time under a nervous strain with regard to the performance itself; anxious to give her best, finding perhaps, at times, criticism that is unfair. Do you wonder that there come times when human nature revolts, the mind gives way for a time?[5]

Omitted from this list was the rumor that her husband's repeated infidelities were undermining their marriage. Stokowski reportedly joined her in New York on Saturday, but he was soon back at work. On Wednesday, 7 February, his Philadelphia Orchestra performed an all-German concert in Washington, DC, proving that the country's leaders had not lost their taste for German music, even if they had severed diplomatic ties

Figure 3.1 Leopold Stokowski and Olga Samaroff (Library of Congress).

with Germany. The concert opened with Schumann's *Manfred* Overture, followed by Mendelssohn's *Italian* Symphony (no. 4), which was so enthusiastically applauded that the orchestra had to stand to acknowledge the ovation. German mezzo-soprano Elena Gerhardt sang songs by Schubert and Wagner with the orchestra, earning six recalls after this German set. The popular lieder specialist had returned to Germany after the outbreak of the war and had sung for the German troops, but she was called back to the United States for a tour with Karl Muck in fall 1916. The concert closed with *Tod und Verklärung* (Death and Transfiguration), by Germany's most eminent living composer, Richard Strauss. The concert was given rave reviews by the Washington papers, and Stokowski received a hero's welcome from the capacity crowd.

The month of February was a memorable one for Stokowski, as he was granted an honorary doctorate in music by the University of Pennsylvania on Thursday, 22 February. The following day he performed an all-Russian concert in Philadelphia that was repeated on Saturday. On Monday, 26 February, he and Samaroff, now fully recovered, were back in Pittsburgh, where she performed a full recital of works by Brahms, Debussy, Chopin, Liszt, and Wagner for the Twentieth-Century Club. The final piece was a transcription of Wagner's *Ride of the Valkyries*, after which she played an encore by Beethoven. The concert was followed by a luncheon, and as usual, the society pages of the local papers gave a long list of distinguished guests. By popular demand, the orchestra repeated its all-Russian program in the evening at the Shriners' Mosque. During the Pittsburgh visit, Samaroff again played her dual role of conductor's wife and artist in her own right, with no mention of the anxiety that had caused her bout of amnesia at the beginning of the month.

Walter Damrosch also toured during February, when his concerts took him not only to Washington, Philadelphia, and Pittsburgh but also to smaller cities in the Midwest. The advantage of this strategy was that audiences were immensely appreciative. A reporter in Sandusky, Ohio, told readers that the upcoming concert on Saturday, 10 February, which drew ticket reservations from all the surrounding towns, would be "the greatest musical event in the history of Sandusky."[6] The Monday paper included two reviews of the concert: one a serious review by a music critic, and the other a tongue-in-cheek review by a man who "usually reports sporting events or city commission meetings and doesn't pretend to know one note of music from another." This essay followed in a long tradition, going back to the nineteenth century, of American humorous writing in which a country bumpkin writes in innocent yet insightful terms about high culture. Among the observations of the Sandusky rube were these:

> The director, Mr. Damrosch, a greater conductor than whom there is none, never even got a sweat up during the whole show. He took things slow and easy and seemed to be watching every blamed player on the stage. There was not an error made in the whole play, some people said, and it must have been correct for the boss player did not bawl out the musicians once during the show. It was apparent to all in the opera house that the players were old hands at the game. They kept drawing their bows across the strings and blowing their horns without keeping time with their feet. . . . P.S. The drummer was some artist.[7]

As the New York Symphony travelled around the country, Damrosch—described by violinist and critic Winthrop Sargeant as "an inveterate trouper, a sort of symphonic Buffalo Bill"[8]—was at the mercy of railroads, hotels, restaurants, and auditoriums. His correspondence frequently recounts delays or near misses because of railroad schedules, snowstorms, or other inconveniences. In February 1917, the usual challenges of touring were compounded by the political situation. Damrosch's orchestra included players from many of the European countries, along with some American musicians. On 9 February, the day before the Sandusky concert, Damrosch described a recent incident to his wife:

> Darling Mag,
>   Nothing to relate, but poring over the daily papers all the time. I was to rehearse this afternoon but the transfer car was late with the instruments so I gave the men a lecture on gum chewing at rehearsals, on grumbling because rehearsals were called, and—on their patriotic duties towards the country in which they make their living.
>   The last was necessary because a few German members objected to being made to play "America" so often "as if they were an American Orchestra."
>   I told them plainly that that was just what we were.[9]

Damrosch recognized the tensions inherent in American orchestras of 1917. The German-speaking players performed primarily European music for their American audiences, but not all of them were willing to acknowledge their precarious position as guests. Though the disciplinarian in Damrosch could reprimand his players for their behavior, the entertainer in him knew what his audience wanted. For the Sandusky concert he programmed works by German composers Bach, Wagner, and Joachim Raff, as well as selections by Saint-Saëns and two crowd-pleasing numbers from

Edvard Grieg's *Peer Gynt* Suite. Back in New York two weeks later, he played an all-Wagner concert on 22 February, about which the *Tribune* critic commented, "our public can never get too much Wagner." The New York premiere of the symphonic poem *Aphrodite*, by American composer George Whitefield Chadwick, which he played on 25 February, received only cautious praise from the *Times*.

Damrosch's lecture to his orchestra came a day after he was roundly criticized by *Musical Courier* editor Leonard Liebling for playing "America" and "The Star-Spangled Banner" and for making a curtain speech before his New York concerts the previous week. Liebling applauded the conductor's patriotism—and hastened to assure readers of the loyalty of the *Musical Courier* editors as well—but he asserted that a symphonic concert was no place for patriotic songs or speeches. He raised the specter of Caruso, Kreisler, and other foreign artists making similar speeches about their own countries or of Damrosch making a speech in favor of his preferred political candidate at election time. In conclusion, Liebling wrote, "Let us keep symphony concerts free of martial noises. Our national interests are being well attended to in Washington."[10]

On Sunday afternoon, 11 February, baritone Alphonso Grien, performing at an event sponsored by the Labor Forum at Stuyvesant High School in New York, was interrupted by a group of twenty-five Boy Scouts, who marched into the auditorium and forced him to stop singing. Though it was initially reported that he had been singing "Prussian war songs" and "German hymns of hate," subsequent reports clarified that he was actually singing an English song with text by Rudyard Kipling. Liebling again leaped into the fray: "We cannot express too strongly our detestation of this kind of 'patriotism.' . . . All intelligent American musicians will feel heartily ashamed over the happening at the Stuyvesant school, and it is sincerely to be hoped that there will not be a recurrence of such a scandal either in New York or elsewhere in the United States."[11]

The heightened anxiety over the diplomatic situation spilled over into music on many levels; the issue of patriotic music in orchestral concerts was only one of many concerns. For German and Austrian musicians, their status in the event of future hostilities was a primary worry. The board of directors of the Metropolitan Opera issued a public statement reassuring the public and their artists that no change in status was anticipated. *Musical America* reported: "Regardless of the international complications or their outcome, the attitude of the opera house board of directors will remain unchanged. The sentiment prevailing is that the Metropolitan is so large in its artistic purpose and universal appeal that no concession to political partisanship will be tolerated. German operas and German singers will not be slighted nor will the management permit the artists to suffer embarrassment."[12]

Concerns were not limited to German musicians. On 10 February, American soprano Geraldine Farrar neglected to stand with the rest of the audience when a brief snatch of "The Star-Spangled Banner" was heard as incidental music in a play she was attending. Her (in)action was widely reported and much discussed in the following days, as reporters reminded readers of her well-known sympathy for Germany and her previous statements in support of the country where she had gotten her artistic start. Many saw this as an act of disloyalty, but the gossip columnist of *Musical America* saw it merely as an attention-getting ploy.[13] In these days of heightened anxiety, rumors and suspicion were everywhere.

It didn't take long for the Original Dixieland Jazz Band to attract attention after its opening on 27 January. Starting on 2 February, the spelling of the band's name was changed from "jass" to "jazz" in advertisements, reportedly to foil juvenile pranksters who had scratched out the *j* on earlier posters. Within days, the band's popularity exploded, and dancers lined up to try the new steps inspired by this strange music from Chicago that was living up to all the advance publicity. On 9 February, *Variety* reported on the new craze in terms that hinted at much more than musical style:

> The Jazz Band has hit New York at last, but just how popular it will become here is a matter that is going to be entirely in the hands of certain authorities that look after the public welfare. There is one thing that is certain and that is that the melodies as played by the Jazz organization at Reisenweber's are quite conducive to make the dancers on the floor loosen up and go the limit in their stepping. Last Saturday night the Jazz musicians furnished the bigger part of the music for dancing at the 400 Club and the rather "mixed" crowd that was present seemed to like it, judging from the encores that were demanded and from the manner in which the dancers roughened-up their stepping.[14]

The 400 Club was named for the social elite of New York, famously dubbed "The Four Hundred" in Ward McAllister's 1890 book *Society as I Have Found It*. The band members dressed in tuxedos rather than the more casual dress they had worn in New Orleans and Chicago. The *Variety* critic, though, signaled to readers that the new jazz style was upsetting social norms, both by attracting a "mixed" crowd and by encouraging a rougher style of dancing. Part of the appeal of the club was the liberal availability of alcohol, and the critic intimated that if the authorities restricted the sale of drinks, the band's popularity would suffer. For a city anxiously awaiting the declaration of war, this raucous new music provided an ideal escape valve.

Starting on 9 February, Reisenweber's ads began describing the ODJB as "The fad of the hour—an overnight furore," a description that was probably not exaggerated. The band was so popular that imitators sprang up in New York's other cabarets and restaurants. One of the first was Earl Fuller, leader of the orchestra at Rector's Restaurant, ten blocks south of Reisenweber's. As soon as he heard the ODJB and saw the excitement it created, he reduced the size of his own group to five players and adopted the jazz style to the best of his ability. His manager, Ernest Cutting, later conceded that Fuller intentionally reorganized his band to compete with the newcomers from Chicago.[15] Publisher Leo Feist brought out a new song entitled "Everybody Loves a 'Jazz' Band," by Coleman Goetz and Leon Flatow, within days of the ODJB's opening. The music is typical Tin Pan Alley ragtime, and the cover pictures a marching band rather than a jazz band, but the title was enough to sell copies to curious fans.[16]

The escalation of hostilities with Germany affected both Kreisler and Schumann-Heink personally, and each responded with sympathy for those suffering in Europe. In an interview on 1 February, Kreisler endorsed a campaign to convince the US Congress to allocate $100 million for relief to noncombatants in Europe. He stated, "In the world of art there are no national boundary lines, thank God! Art is art, no matter where its place of origin. So also in pity for poor suffering humanity, for the starving and the cold and the ill, there should be no national boundary lines." He went on to describe the suffering of those in rural Galicia and other impoverished regions of the Austro-Hungarian Empire, where, he said, the conditions were even worse than in Belgium and northern France.[17] Meanwhile Schumann-Heink agreed to sing in an upcoming benefit concert for "war sufferers in Germany" on 20 February in Brooklyn. The project was abandoned at the last minute, however, because of "the present strained relations between this country and Germany."[18]

Though their sympathy for citizens of soon-to-be enemy nations was not popular, their musical performances continued to be popular. In February, Kreisler began a midwestern tour that took him through Ohio, Iowa, Kansas, Oklahoma, and Missouri in a little over two weeks. He was then back for a solo recital in Washington, DC (attended by President and Mrs. Wilson), and an appearance with the New York Philharmonic in

Carnegie Hall. Of this last performance, the *Sun* noted, "A few slips in notes showed that he was not entirely in his best form, but as a whole his work offered rich measure in tonal splendor, brilliancy of technic and repose and breadth of style."[19] Throughout his tour, the violinist was welcomed enthusiastically. In Worcester, Massachusetts, the capacity crowd gave him "an ovation such as has seldom been granted an artist in Worcester."[20] The *Cedar Rapids Republican*, reporting on Iowans' love for the violinist and speculating on the possible impact of war on German artists and German music, concluded, "Fritz Kreisler is at the present time an idol of our music-loving public and he will play just as well the day after war is declared, if it should be, as he does now. Kreisler may think he belongs to some country and some of our unthinking people may attempt to separate the man and the musician, but Fritz Kreisler, the musician, belongs to the world."[21]

Schumann-Heink began the month in California, where she was made an honorary member of the California Music Teachers Association. She then returned to the Metropolitan Opera in New York for two appearances. The opera house was packed for her 11 February appearance at a concert where she sang several songs and arias along with other Metropolitan Opera artists. She chose to open her portion of the program with "Ah, mon fils," from Meyerbeer's *Le Prophète*, the heartfelt plea of Fidès for her doomed son, Jean, which called to mind her own son, August, serving in the German navy. On 16 February she made a guest appearance in the role of Erda in Wagner's *Siegfried*. The *Times* welcomed her with the verdict, "Mme. Schumann-Heink was gladly heard as Erda, a part to which she returned last season after an absence of thirteen years from the stage of the Opera House. Erda has only one short scene—that with Wotan at the beginning of the third act. But it is essential that her solemn utterance then given forth, as by an oracle, should be impressively delivered. And few have done this more impressively than Mme. Schumann-Heink."[22] Her appearance was part of a revival of the *Ring* cycle, a major event in New York's cultural life.

The cancellation of the Brooklyn benefit concert on 20 February gave her a few extra days of rest before her next major engagement, headlining a pair of concerts in the St. Louis Symphony Orchestra's annual Wagner festival. St. Louis, with its large population of German Americans, turned out in force to hear the concert planned by conductor Max Zach. On the afternoon of 23 February, she sang in a "surpassing program," of which Shirley Brooks wrote:

It would be impossible to plan an arrangement of selections from the works of this spiritually inspired composer, which would better display the almost-superhuman genius of Wagner; one which would give the symphony orchestra an opportunity to execute and interpret the meaning of his compositions and the audience the pleasure of hearing, under the most favorable circumstances, the most artistic exemplification of vocal art the world knows, from the throat of undoubtedly the greatest and most wonderful living singer—Madame Schumann-Heink.[23]

This effusive sentence was written with the knowledge of what had happened after the concert she was describing. Later that evening, Schumann-Heink and her accompanist, Edith Evans (see Figure 3.2), attended a movie featuring the singer's favorite star, William S. Hart. After the show, around 10:30 p.m., they called a taxicab to return to the hotel. The driver was crossing a streetcar track when he misjudged the speed of the oncoming streetcar and was rear-ended in the intersection. Schumann-Heink suffered two broken ribs, a lacerated wrist, and multiple bruises, and she was forced to cancel not only the second Wagner performance

Figure 3.2 Ernestine Schumann-Heink with her pianist, Edith Evans (Library of Congress).

but fifteen additional dates in Washington, Chicago, New York, and other cities, reportedly at a loss of $100,000.[24] Music critic Brooks went on to express the concern of many by adding, "It is not unlikely that in recovering at her advanced age she may never regain that delicate yet tremendous breath control and power to give her the marvelous execution, technique and tone quality which she has always possessed. . . . It is probable that those who heard the great diva yesterday afternoon will never hear her again nor will anyone in the glorious voice in which she gave utterance to Wagner's masterpieces on this occasion."[25]

The singer, in too much pain to leave St. Louis, was joined there by her personal secretary and lawyer from Chicago. It would be weeks before she could leave St. Louis for her home in Chicago, and weeks more before she could return to her "favorite" home in San Diego. A split-second miscalculation by her taxi driver had been a costly error with the potential to end her illustrious career.

An immediate result of Schumann-Heink's accident was that she could not travel to Camden, New Jersey, to make more recordings for the Victor Talking Machine Company. In recent years recording had become very lucrative for her: she earned a reported $47,000 in royalties in 1914, or about a third as much as her concert earnings.[26] Victor and Columbia, the market leaders, advertised aggressively throughout the country, with a chain of stores that were tightly controlled by the distribution networks of the manufacturers. A short list of classical soloists—led by Caruso, Kreisler, and Schumann-Heink—had proven the popularity of the medium. The record companies had had some success with popular music, but not on the same scale. With the arrival of the ODJB in New York, the time was right for a new genre of music on record.

Two days after their 27 January debut in the 400 Club, the ODJB received an invitation to meet with executives from Columbia. The meeting, which took place on Wednesday, 31 January, at 2 p.m., was in all likelihood only an audition, and there is no evidence that the band made any recordings on that date. Columbia's loss was Victor's gain, however, as the band played a recording session for Victor on 26 February that resulted in the first commercially released jazz record. The sound of this record changed the direction of American popular music, making 26 February one of the most important dates in this momentous year.

Before the introduction of electronic microphones in 1925, the process of making records was entirely mechanical. The recording apparatus was fitted with a large acoustic horn that gathered sound waves and focused them into a stylus, which translated the sound waves into grooves cut into a revolving disk of wax. By 1917, cylinder recordings were practically obsolete, and the preferred format for commercial recordings was ten- or twelve-inch disks, with three to four minutes of music on each side. These disks were mass-produced in Victor's Camden plant from master recordings and then shipped to dealers nationwide.

On 26 February, the band members arrived at Victor's new studio, located on the twelfth floor of 46 West 38th Street in Manhattan.[27] Since the ODJB had never made a record and the Victor engineers had never recorded a jazz band, this historic session involved a great deal of trial and error. As the acoustic recording process was severely restricted in its ability to capture high and low frequencies, the lowest notes of the piano and bass drum were effectively eliminated. The upper overtones of the treble instruments were also attenuated, distorting the tone quality of instruments, like the clarinet, that were overtone-rich. Perhaps most problematic, jazz musicians played louder than many other instrumentalists because they had learned their craft in outdoor parades and noisy cabarets.

The first step was to make a test recording of the five musicians. After the band and the players heard the playback, the Victor engineers, led by Charles E. Sooy, experimented with the configuration of the studio. LaRocca recalled years later that four men with ladders began stringing wires near the ceiling: "I asked them what all these wires were for, and one of the men told me it was to sop up the overtone that was coming back into the horn. The recording engineer at Victor had the patience of a saint. He played back our music until it sounded right."[28]

In addition to stringing wires, the engineers experimented with the distance between each player and the recording horn. If an instrument was too close to the horn, it would overload the stylus and ruin the record; if it was too far away, the clarity would be impeded by unwanted echoes. In the end, the band was arranged something like this:

- Pianist Harry Ragas was closest to the horn, since his instrument did not record well.
- Clarinetist Larry Shields was about five feet from the recording apparatus, with a special horn to supplement the main horn, since woodwind instruments also did not record well.
- Trombonist Eddie Edwards was twelve to fifteen feet from the horn.
- Cornetist Nick LaRocca, an unusually loud player, was twenty feet from the horn.

- Drummer Tony Sbarbaro sat five feet behind LaRocca, but he was instructed to use the bass drum sparingly, as it overloaded the system even at that distance.

Through this expedient, Sooy and his team of recording engineers achieved a balance and clarity seldom matched on later recordings. In particular, the volume levels of trombone, cornet, and clarinet were made nearly identical, an artificial balance that was probably not true to the band's sound in performance but made for a pleasing sound on the recording. Additionally, the musicians were not allowed to tap their feet as they normally did in performance, and LaRocca was not allowed to "stomp off" the tempo to bring the band in together. Instead, they took a visual cue from the recording light—when the light went on, they counted two beats silently and then started playing. After a long day's work, the band had successfully recorded two numbers.[29]

The A-side of the record, entitled "Dixie Jass Band One-Step," was played at a blistering fast tempo typical of the one-step dance it was intended to accompany. The prominent feature of this number is the clarinet embellishment of Larry Shields, which floats above the texture in ensemble sections and has numerous solo breaks as the rest of the band stops for a measure or two. The recording clearly shows Shields to be one of the most important of early jazz clarinetists and one who influenced a long line of later players.

The B-side was a number that the band called "Barnyard Blues," featuring imitations of animal noises. LaRocca imitated a horse's whinny on cornet, Shields imitated a rooster's crow on clarinet, and Edwards imitated a cow's plaintive moo on trombone with a technique known as "freaking." This technique of manipulating timbre through mutes, half-valve techniques, and lip glissandi was famously pioneered by cornetist Joe Oliver in New Orleans; it may be heard as a descendant of African talking-drum techniques that also inspired bottleneck guitar techniques.[30] LaRocca later claimed to have "invented" the technique to attract the attention of a girl in a Chicago club, but it had been actively cultivated in New Orleans before he left town. Both numbers gave the principal melody to the cornet while the other instruments played around it in a polyphonic web of sound. At the end of each piece, the instruments converged in the "Dixieland Tag," a rhythmic formula that brought all the instruments together for a coordinated ending.

The processing of the record for commercial distribution took over a month, which was still a fast turnaround in this era. As they waited for the release of the record, the ODJB continued to draw large crowds at Reisenweber's. The attention led to numerous offers for employment on the side and also spawned a growing number of imitators. These imitators were not an immediate threat because they had only a passing familiarity with real New Orleans music. But there was one band playing authentic New Orleans jazz that was working its way across the country toward New York and would soon be in a position to challenge the ODJB.

As the Creole Band moved east through a succession of vaudeville houses, the term "jazz" was used increasingly to describe their music. A review published in Indianapolis on 26 January (the day before the ODJB opened at the 400 Club) said of the Creole Band, "They are the undisputed originators of the 'Jazz Band' craze now sweeping the country."[31] At McVicker's Theatre in Chicago during the first week of February, the band was advertised as "the original New Orleans Jaz Band, the father and mother of all the jaz bands in the world . . . shows you what a real jaz band is."[32] From Chicago the band made its way to Cleveland and then doubled back to Detroit for the week marking the transition from February to March. There the band was again labeled by the new name but with yet another spelling: "These clever negro entertainers have come to be known in vaudeville circles as the 'Jas' band, 'jas' being a vaudeville word denoting the putting of speed, ginger or pep into an act. And the 'Jas' band well deserves the name for the act is full of music, fun and speed every moment the musicians are on the stage. Ragtime is played as it never was before. That last sentence is true but you will have to hear the band yourself to realize how true it is."[33] Since the band's musicians did not make any recordings, we cannot verify the statement a century later, but when they finally reached New York in March, they were booked for a theater just a few blocks from Reisenweber's, giving New Yorkers an unequaled opportunity for comparison.

The anxious month of February 1917 ended with Schumann-Heink recuperating from her injuries, with musicians debating internationalism in classical music, and with jazz providing a frantic musical metaphor of the unsettled times. Americans sensed that their extended period of neutrality was drawing to a close, and performers stoked the anticipation with patriotic songs and speeches. German and Austrian immigrant musicians had genuine cause for concern as their host country stumbled uncertainly toward a war that could change their status in unpredictable ways. The anxiety of February would soon give way to action.

CHAPTER 4

❧

Noise

March 1917

March began with another bombshell, as President Wilson revealed the text of the infamous Zimmermann telegram, which had been intercepted and deciphered by British agents in January. In this communication, German Foreign Minister Arthur Zimmermann proposed an alliance with Mexico with the promise of support to reconquer territory in Texas, Arizona, and New Mexico that had been lost to the United States in 1836. Zimmermann himself confirmed the accuracy of the decoded message on 3 March, and this admission helped to move American public opinion further away from neutrality and toward entrance into the war. Though Mexico did not accept the German proposal, the audacity of the plan, coupled with strong anti-Mexican sentiment, convinced many Americans that Germany must be stopped.

The next few days brought a quantity of noise in the governmental centers of power, as the congressional session ended at noon on 4 March, the same day that Woodrow Wilson took the oath of office for his second term. In an act labeled by the President as "the most reprehensible in the history of any civilized Nation," twelve pacifist senators succeeded through filibuster in defeating the president's proposal to arm merchant ships for protection against German submarines. The House of Representatives had previously passed a similar bill, dubbed "armed neutrality," by a vote of 403 to 13, but Senate rules allowed a small group of opponents to prolong debate until the session ran out. As the Senate brought legislative action to a standstill, the House of Representatives celebrated its work with a session of songs, including "Columbia, the Gem of the Ocean," "The Star-Spangled Banner," "Dixie," "How Dry I Am," and "The Vacant Chair."[1] Among the last-minute bills enacted in the final days of the legislative session was the Jones-Shafroth Act, granting citizenship to residents of Puerto Rico.

The noise of March was not limited to Congress. During this month, the anxiety of February gave way to noise of all sorts, from shouting to loud music. Patriotic songs were heard everywhere, and as Geraldine Farrar had learned in February, one's reaction to the songs was scrutinized carefully. A music critic for the *Deutsches Journal* was ordered to leave an Aeolian Hall concert in New York when he refused to stand for "The Star-Spangled Banner." Farrar repaired her reputation in March by singing "The Star-Spangled Banner" fervently in public and by denying earlier accounts of being a Germanophile at public events in Boston and New York.[2] Looking back on this noisy time, Farrar recalled in her memoirs, "Between the urge from hoarse-voiced orators to buy Liberty Bonds and the constant din of the Star Spangled Banner that pervaded every place of entertainment, one really had to forego much enjoyment, so hysterically did the super-patriot bedevil us all in places of public patronage."[3]

Jazz became a metaphor to describe the frenzy of the moment, even though most Americans outside New York, Chicago, and New Orleans had never heard the real thing. Whether they called it jazz or ragtime, its noise and audacity captured the spirit of the times. In a letter to the editor of the *New York Tribune*, one writer described the dilemma of March 1917:

Sir: In view of the frequency with which the national anthem is played in New York theaters, moving picture houses, restaurants and cabarets, may I ask you to define the point at which, for a serious-minded person, standing at attention ceases to be an act of devoted patriotism to become something not unlike the applause of an insult?

May I cite a concrete instance? On February 26 the guests at Rector's were cheered near the close of dinner by the performance of a large and beautiful chorus. Any suggestion of frivolity in their costumes—which suggested the possibility of bathing—was corrected by the martial air lent by a fur busby. The nasal announcement set to music by these ladies that "We girlies are going to stop the war" occasioned surprise and some slight incredulity. Thereupon they rendered "The Star-Spangled Banner" (still nasally) to ragtime. In spite of an evident hesitancy, the opinion seemed prevalent, that loyal Americans should stand, silently, reverently (and as steadily as possible) at attention. What, may I ask, would you say constituted a dignified attitude under these circumstances?[4]

Dignity was a scarce commodity this month, which also saw the beginning of a spate of photographs of performers (including some very well endowed opera singers) draping themselves in flags to sell Liberty Bonds or demonstrate their patriotism. Issue after issue of *Musical Courier* featured these photos as space fillers between serious articles on music. In New York, writers in the popular press published a prodigious number of articles on jazz, the new musical genre that seemed to capture the spirit of the times so well.

The Creole Band finally arrived in New York on 4 March for a two-week run at Doraldina's Montmartre on Times Square. This cabaret, connected to the Winter Garden Theatre, was designed to attract playgoers looking for entertainment after the show. It was named for the dancer Doraldina, one of the most popular artists to come out of the Hawaiian craze that had swept the country in 1916. In contrast to its usual vaudeville show, the band played for dancing at the cabaret, a new role for the group that had made a national reputation with a finely honed plantation act. From 4 to 17 March 1917, the Creole Band and the Original Dixieland Jazz Band performed just eight blocks apart from each other. The New York papers featured ads for both, sometimes immediately adjacent, as in the 11 March issue of the *Sun* (see Figure 4.1).

The growing popularity of jazz led to a flurry of verbal descriptions that were humorous in both their colorful language and their contradictions. George S. Kaufman wrote on 11 March, "The latest thing in cabarets is the 'jazz band,' the name of which, presumably, is a contraction of the well-known jasbo, which requires no introduction. The jazz band brings cubistry into music—it plays on mandolins, jugs, tin pans and the nerves of the auditor."[5] S. Jay Kaufman (no relation to George) heard both the Creole Band and the ODJB but chose to write about only the latter. He interviewed trombonist Eddie Edwards, who supplied the following definition:

> The music is a matter of the ear and not of technique. None of us knows music. One carries the melody and the others do what they please. Some play counter melodies, some play freak noises, and some just play. I can't tell you how. You "got to feel" Jass. The time is syncopated. Jass I think means a jumble. We came from New Orleans by way of Chicago. In Chicago a professor told us it was "the untuneful harmony of rhythm." I don't know what that meant, but I guess he was right. Anyhow that's Jass.[6]

Figure 4.1 Adjacent advertisements in the *New York Sun*, 11 March 1917.

Edwards was pulling Kaufman's leg, since he could read music and was often responsible for teaching the other members of the band a new tune that they wished to learn from sheet music. His description does a good job, though, of communicating what the ODJB wanted its patrons to *think* they were doing—playing spontaneous music unencumbered by any training.

The craze gained even more currency through O. O. McIntyre's syndicated column New York Day-by-Day. This daily columnist had begun his career in Ohio, but he was best known for describing the glamour of New York in language that small-town Americans understood. His column appeared in five hundred papers nationwide, and the 22 March 1917 edition introduced the country to this new fad: "After driving nearly everybody in Chicago silly, the Jazz band craze has hit New York. The Jazz band is composed of all brass instruments, and will drive a lot of banjoists and eukalele [sic] players out of jobs. The first Jazz band appeared in New Orleans. In Chicago they have Jazz hats, Jazz soda water, Jazz shoes and Jazz cigars. Because it was so popular in Chicago, blasé New York didn't like to take it up, but one café started it, and now there are about ten Jazz bands in town."[7]

These descriptions were all written to explain the phenomenon to non-musicians, but there were also attempts in the trade journals to clarify the trend for professionals. The Cabarets column in *Variety* on 16 March surveyed the field in New York:

> Music is becoming more and more potent and prominent among the cabaret attractions. Gingery, swinging music is what the dancers want, and it often is looked for by those who do not dance. A group of men the other evening, each knowing only too well all the cabarets of New York, decided the best restaurant orchestras in the city are Rector's, Healy's and the Tokio's. These orchestras get nearer to legitimate "jazz stuff" than any of the others. The genuine "Jazz Band" at Reisenweber's, however, notwithstanding the sober opinion of it, appears to be drawing business there. Late in the morning the Jazzers go to work and the dancers hit the floor, to remain there until they topple over if the band keeps on playing. It leaves no question but what they like to dance to that kind of music and it is "a kind." If the dancers see someone they know at the tables, it's common to hear "Oh, boy!" as they roll their eyes while floating past, and the "Oh, boy!" expression probably describes the Jazz Band music better than anything else could.[8]

LaRocca and his band were the talk of the town, and that meant long days. They began playing afternoons at 4:30 for "Séance Tea Dances" ("Ouija Boards will be provided"), they played for the supper crowd from 6 to 9 p.m., and they played for dancers into the wee hours starting at 11:30 p.m.[9]

Only a few articles cited an African American origin for jazz at this point in its history. An article by "Gill" in the *Ragtime Review*, a monthly journal aimed at players and composers of ragtime, attributed the appeal of the new style to improvisation rather than note reading but also to the natural rhythmic ability of black musicians. The article describes the characteristic interaction of black jazz players that was also present in the playing of the ODJB: "He will almost unconsciously pay as much, if not more attention to the musicians surrounding him than he does to the music. The result is that by each man following this method they soon learn to quickly grasp the other fellow's rhythm."[10] Another article in the *Musical Courier Extra* credits the invention of jazz to musicians in the South who hummed into large, empty lard cans, thus anticipating the saxophone tone that would later be prominent in jazz.[11]

LaRocca was well aware of the competition from the Creole Band, and his recollection was that they flopped. On a copy of the 16 March *Variety* article, he wrote the notation, "This appeared while the supposed great Creol band was playing at Monmartre (Dolodrina Club) [*sic*]. They were unsuccessful 2 weeks—went into vaudeville Pantages time—never was again heard of."[12] By the 1930s, LaRocca felt that his contributions to the popularization of jazz had been unjustly forgotten, and he believed that black musicians were receiving more credit than they deserved. He took every opportunity to belittle the achievements of the Creole Band out of bitterness for his own neglect.

The Creole Band did leave the Montmartre Club after two weeks to be replaced by the Original Frisco "Jazz" Band, but as musicologist Lawrence Gushee's detective work has shown, it may have had more to do with vaudeville labor disputes than with their musical drawing power. A major strike of vaudeville actors (the "White Rats") starting on 8 March left the Loew's circuit of theaters without performers. It seems likely that the Shubert company, which owned the Winter Garden, "loaned" the Creole Band to Loew's for a series of vaudeville engagements that took them from one theater to another for the rest of March and early April. Their cabaret career had lasted only two weeks before they returned to vaudeville, where they were a known commodity but could never achieve the fame of a cabaret act in 1917.[13] A review of the band's performance at Loew's Orpheum, while it may appear negative, was in keeping with the fashionable designation of cabaret jazz as noise: "The Creole Band found it easy going, making a noise that some persons called 'music.' The 'band' consists of a violin, bass, guitar, trombone, cornet, and flute, each vying with the other in an effort to produce discord."[14]

Whatever their reasons for leaving Times Square, the departure of the Creole Band again left the field clear for the ODJB. There was no shortage of imitators, and it may have been at this time that a pianist by the name of Jimmy Durante, whose most notable feature was a nose of such monumental size that he later adopted the nickname "the Schnoz," approached the band to learn their tricks. Like Earl Fuller, Durante recognized that the New Orleans musicians were the ones who held the secret to the new music, and he had often heard the band at Reisenweber's before he invited them to an after-hours snack at his Alamo Café in Harlem. When the five band members arrived at the basement café on 125th Street, they found a feast of food and alcohol set up by their generous host. After eating, they played a jam session with Durante on piano while Henry Ragas sat out.

Responding to Durante's queries, LaRocca gave him a list of New Orleans players who might be willing to join him to give his band an authentic jazz flavor. Durante eventually hired Frank Christian and Achille Baquet (whose brother George played clarinet in the Original Creole Band). The band Durante formed, the Original New Orleans Jazz Band, performed successfully and made several hit records.[15]

Fritz Kreisler began the month of March with concerts in the Midwest, where majority populations of German Americans in St. Louis, Cincinnati, and other cities made him a popular favorite. His Cincinnati concert on 9 March earned ecstatic praise from the *Volksblatt*:

> Fritz Kreisler der Geigerkönig und Fritz Kreisler der Tonschöpfer feierten beide gleich glänzende Triumphe am gestrigen Abend im Emery Auditorium. Es war ein beinahe bis auf das letzte Plätzchen besetztes Haus, welches dem Künstler einen enthusiastischen Willkomm entbot, als er das Podium betrat und nach jeder einzelnen Nummer wurden ihm immer wieder begeisterte Ovationen dargebracht, für die er sich dann durch zahlreiche Zugaben revanchirte und zwar zumeist durch seine eigenen Kompositionen, die von vielen seiner Bewunderer dringend gewünscht worden, nachdem die Veröffentlichung des Programms erfolgt war.
>
> Fritz Kreisler the King of Violinists and Fritz Kreisler the composer both celebrated brilliant triumphs yesterday evening in Emery Auditorium. A house packed almost to the last seat offered the artist an enthusiastic welcome as he entered the stage, and after each single number, ever more enthusiastic ovations were offered, for which he then returned the favor with numerous encores, for the most part with his own compositions, which were urgently desired by many of his admirers since the publication of the program.[16]

The Queen City, as Cincinnati was known, was nestled on the banks of the Ohio River in southwest Ohio. The broad, deep river looked so much like the Rhine at this point in its course that the German-American section of the city just north of the river was nicknamed Over-the-Rhine. Owing to a dramatic influx of German immigrants in the nineteenth century, the population of Cincinnati was predominantly German American, and residents cultivated many aspects of German culture in language, recreation, and civic life. The city's musical heritage was one of the oldest and richest in the West, with a vibrant symphony orchestra, two thriving music schools, and a world-famous May Festival.

In a nation of immigrants, German Americans had been among the most successful of European ethnic groups at simultaneously maintaining strong ties with their homeland while assimilating into the business and political life of the United States. At the start of the European war, most German Americans favored neutrality to avoid a conflict with friends and family in Europe, but swiftly moving events made this position increasingly untenable. Former President Theodore Roosevelt had famously denounced their dual loyalties in a speech delivered on Columbus Day 1915 in New York. In this speech he advocated war as a way to bring together men from all classes and ethnic backgrounds in a common purpose, and he spoke derisively of persons who held onto their ethnic heritage: "There is no room in this country for hyphenated Americans. When I refer to hyphenated Americans I do not refer to naturalized Americans. Some of the very best Americans I have ever known were naturalized Americans born abroad, but a hyphenated American is not an American at all."[17] To Roosevelt, the persistence of German-language newspapers, schools, and social organizations came dangerously close to treason, and the events of February and March 1917 had convinced an increasing number of Americans that he was right. What many failed to recognize, though, was the wide range of opinion among the millions of Americans of German ancestry. Like other citizens, their political views ranged from conservative to progressive, and their ties to Germany ranged from active and current to a vague memory of their ancestors. It would be the goal of propagandists in the coming months to paint a stark "us versus them" picture, thereby demanding that German Americans reject their heritage entirely or fall under suspicion of treason.[18]

Schumann-Heink spent most of March recuperating from her accident in a St. Louis hotel room, but she did not disappear from the news. There was an outpouring of sympathy from around the country along with regular updates on her physical recovery. On 8 March her physician, Dr. Robert Wilson, announced that her voice would not suffer lasting effects from the accident. A week later she was able to get out of bed for several hours a day, and on 24 March it was announced that X-rays showed she was healing well despite having broken three ribs rather than just two, as her physician initially believed. Her strong constitution and positive outlook were credited for her rapid recovery.

Engagements for the remainder of the season were either canceled, filled by replacements, or postponed to the following season. American contralto Louise Homer, wife of composer Sidney Homer, was able to fill several of the engagements on short notice, including Schumann-Heink's heavily advertised 27 February concert in Washington, DC. Concurrent with this performance, the Woodward & Lothrop department store took the occasion to present a "Schumann-Heink Victrola Recital" of fifteen records for those who did not want a substitute for the originally scheduled singer.[19] Throughout March, however, Schumann-Heink's manager was confident enough in her eventual recovery to begin booking dates for summer and the 1917/18 concert season. A full-page ad in the 8 March issue of the *Musical Courier* quoted positive reviews of the 23 February concert in St. Louis and listed contact information for the Wolfsohn Musical Bureau in New York.[20]

As the Boston Symphony visited each of the major cities in the Northeast for the last time in the 1916/17 season, critics waxed nostalgic about the orchestra and its admirable conductor. The Philadelphia concert included Mozart's *Haffner* Symphony, which greatly pleased the reviewer of the *Public Ledger*: "Doctor Muck never illumines his talent so clearly as when he elects to play Beethoven or Mozart. The profound, tragic, spiritual recesses of the master of Bonn are as visible to him as the no-less-profound comic spiritual ones of the master of Salzburg. Some cosmic salt in the veins of each finds response in the conductor. So it is pure delight to hear him read the "Haffner Symphony" as he did last night."[21] The Baltimore concert likewise featured a Mozart symphony, but it was Richard Strauss's symphonic poem *Don Juan* that inspired rapturous praise from the *Baltimore Sun* reviewer; he concluded his review, "it was with much regret that many in the audience realized that Dr. Muck and his splendid organization will not be heard here again until next November."[22]

In New York, the topic of discussion surrounding the BSO season was Muck's decision to play ten concerts in the city without a single star soloist. This detracted from the audience appeal to casual listeners easily swayed by marquee names, but it added seriousness for patrons who appreciated orchestral music in its pure form. Cynical reviewers noted that it also saved a great deal of money in artists' fees.[23] The first of this final pair of concerts was classical in tone, featuring Mozart's *Jupiter* Symphony and the Brahms Concerto for Violin and Cello, with soloists from the orchestra. As in the other cities on this March tour, the New York critics admired Muck's control and polish. The second concert added an eighty-member chorus and tenor soloist for a performance of Liszt's monumental *Faust* Symphony. The edition used for this performance was prepared from the composer's own corrected version, buried for decades in Wagner's Villa Wahnfried in

Bayreuth until Muck rediscovered the score and prepared the parts for performance. Though the differences in this edition were not extensive, they reflected the loving care that the scholarly Muck devoted to the music he admired.

The New York reviewers, who were often the most critical, took the opportunity to reflect on Muck's significance to American musical life. The *Herald* critic called the BSO "the foremost American orchestra" and went on to say:

> The Boston Symphony Orchestra is a national institution. It is one of which the whole country should be proud. By many competent judges it has been pronounced the best concert orchestra in the world.
>
> Naturally local music lovers might be proud if it belonged to New York. Since, however, it does not they should rejoice that it comes here season after season to give them the privilege of hearing its unique playing. It will come again next season and will again be conducted—so far as is now known—by Dr. Karl Muck, to whose skill and industry much of its excellence is due.[24]

The rest of the BSO season, lasting through April and into the first weekend of May, would be mostly in the Boston area, with the exception of a concert in Hartford, Connecticut, and the sixth concert of the season in Providence, Rhode Island.

As yet another season wound down to a successful conclusion, Henry Lee Higginson engaged in some soul-searching. From its founding in 1881, the Boston Symphony Orchestra had been the product of Higginson's will and persistence. During his youth in Vienna, the young man had studied music and become enamored of German musical culture. Returning home from Vienna to fight with the Union Army in the Civil War, Higginson's character was shaped by the military discipline and the thrill of battle, which had left a saber scar across his face (it is visible in Figure 4.2). In the subsequent decades he amassed a sizable fortune, all the while nostalgic for the artistic climate he had reluctantly left behind in Vienna. His goal was to create a concert orchestra of the highest possible quality and stability. To this end he insisted on hiring only European conductors; he forbade orchestra members to moonlight at dances on concert days; and he stubbornly resisted unionization so that he could fire players or conductors when they did not meet his standards. As a civic duty, he kept ticket prices below those of rival orchestras in other cities by agreeing to cover financial deficits every season. He had no board of directors; instead, he retained control of all major decisions, even as he approached his eighty-third birthday.

Figure 4.2 Henry Lee Higginson (1834–1919) (Library of Congress).

Of all the conductors he had hired over the years, Muck was his favorite, perhaps because, as he wrote to the architect of Boston's Symphony Hall, "I always like the severe in architecture, music, men and women, books, &c. &c."[25] He knew that when the United States entered the war, life for enemy aliens would become infinitely harder and that Muck's frank loyalty to the German Empire would come under scrutiny. With the conclusion of the current season, Muck had reached the end of his five-year contract, and Higginson was free to replace him with another conductor. But he admired Muck's musicianship so much that he was willing to overlook the conductor's national origin if public opinion did not turn against him. On 22 March, he wrote to retired Harvard University President Charles Eliot for advice:

> We have come to a strange pass. Our contracts provided for war and other accidents, gave me the power to break up the work at any time if the Orchestra was injured seriously; and it was left for me to decide. We have a dozen nationalities in the Orchestra, and the men have behaved perfectly well toward each other since the war began. Dr. Muck is a hearty German, who wished to enlist and was refused for lack of strength. He has behaved well, and has been

cordial to me since the war began, as before; and he has been most kindly received by audiences here and in other cities. . . . I trust him entirely as an artist and as a man, and he has worked as no other conductor has worked.

Query: Shall I go on with him and the Orchestra? He is the only man I know who can conduct for us. The Orchestra is fine, and has set the pace for the country. . . .[26]

Eliot responded with assurances that he and the public would never doubt Higginson's patriotism and that the orchestra members undoubtedly knew of his sympathies for the Allies. He advised that for the present he could continue to support the orchestra as before. Curiously, Eliot's letter does not mention Muck by name nor address the issue of the conductor but rather addresses the issue of foreign nationals in more general terms:

Have you, or the French members of the Orchestra, had any reason to believe that the German members, or some of them, were what may fairly be called German agents? If no such suspicions have been entertained, I should think it would be safe for you to go on with the Orchestra until war breaks out, and the Government takes measures against Germans resident in this country, confining them or subjecting them to police surveillance. I think our Government will be slow to take any really troublesome action against German residents; but the moment killing, drowning, and wounding begin, our people will probably make the Germans with us uncomfortable and apprehensive. Then you may have to stop maintaining the Orchestra.[27]

This interchange underscores Higginson's role as chief patron of the orchestra. Without his guarantee to cover the financial deficits, it was doubtful the orchestra could survive, making his personal decision crucial. This "national institution," whose annual concerts numbered over a hundred and were heard by hundreds of thousands of Americans, depended to a very great extent on the personal loyalty of an octogenarian Civil War veteran for his talented but aloof German conductor.

Walter Damrosch brought the New York season of his orchestra to a thrilling conclusion with five gala concerts in the second week of March. At a children's concert on Saturday, 10 March, he treated the sold-out crowd of two thousand to a colorful concert enlivened by Russian dancers. For his final subscription concerts, Damrosch took the opposite approach from Muck by featuring star soloists, a sure-fire way to attract large crowds. On the 11th and 13th, the New York Symphony was joined in a performance of the Beethoven Triple Concerto by violinist Fritz Kreisler, cellist Pablo Casals, and pianist Harold Bauer. The reviewer for *Musical America* regretted that so much talent had been expended on what he considered to be one of Beethoven's weaker works, but most critics viewed it as a remarkable opportunity to hear such superstars together. On the 15th and 17th, the orchestra played the Franck Symphony and the *American Negro* Suite, a new work by Chicago composer Thorwald Otterström that incorporated Negro spirituals. The soloist in these concerts was contralto Louise Homer, who sang works by Handel, Schubert, and Verdi. The concert ended with the ubiquitous "Star-Spangled Banner," as reported by the *Times*:

> Mme. Homer stirred the audience to enthusiasm, and there was a still more exciting scene at the concert's close when Mr. Damrosch had his men stand up and play "The Star-Spangled Banner." The entire crowd leaped to its feet and joined first in singing the air and then in applauding and shouting. Pandemonium reigned, from the top galleries down, in a demonstration such as has not been matched for noise in half a hundred symphony concerts this year.[28]

The orchestra had played a total of forty-seven concerts in New York, including five children's concerts. Its popularity with the hometown audience would have allowed Damrosch to extend the season there by a month or more, but instead the orchestra departed the next day on a ten-week tour. This tour, stretching across the country and portions of Canada to the Pacific Coast, was scheduled to include seventy-six concerts, with violin soloist Efrem Zimbalist slated to perform in fifty of them. The members of the orchestra would travel in three railroad cars with two sixty-foot baggage cars for instruments, scores, and luggage. According to advance publicity, the tour was "the most extensive tour the orchestra, or any other such body of instrumentalists, has ever undertaken."[29]

This transcontinental tour was an important musical event that would bring orchestral music to parts of the country that rarely heard performances of this caliber. In the colorful words of violinist Winthrop Sargeant (later a famed critic), "The New York Symphony was a barnstorming outfit. It spent a good deal of its time on the road, often doing one-night stands of symphonic music in prairie towns, mining camps and smaller cities where the local idea of concert music was otherwise represented by the tooting of the town band. . . . His orchestra lived a good deal of its life in Pullman berths, and trudged through blizzards and desert heat to bring the gospel of symphonic music to places that, in those preradio days, had never heard of it."[30] Damrosch loved to perform for audiences in middle America, where the reception was refreshingly different from that of the eastern cities. In this year more than any other, it also afforded him an opportunity to spread his own brand of patriotism and artistic diplomacy. In speeches from the stage and interviews with rural newspaper reporters, Damrosch added his voice to the chorus of political discussions unfolding across the country. Before he returned to New York in May, he would have the chance to make a lot of noise.

CHAPTER 5

༺ঙঌ༻

Explosions

April 1917

In a case of poetic justice—or perhaps a cruel April Fool's joke—ragtime composer Scott Joplin died on the first day of the month when the first jazz instrumental record exploded on the market. Joplin had spent his final decade in New York, far from his home in the Midwest. He began to suffer dementia as a result of syphilis, leading to his admission to the Manhattan State Hospital on 3 February 1917, where he died on 1 April.[1] In a musical sense, the greatest exponent of classic ragtime had succumbed much earlier. Joplin had pioneered a genre in the 1890s that combined the steady beat and rigid sixteen-bar structures of the march with the syncopation of African American music. His original conception of a highly structured genre disseminated through printed scores predominated until about 1910, when the style began to evolve through the influence of faster tempos, blues elements, swing rhythms, improvisation, and small instrumental ensembles like the Original Creole Ragtime Band. Though Joplin began his career as an improviser in popular music, he had staked his reputation on printed music with increasingly higher artistic aspirations. The irony is that while Joplin insisted on moderate tempos and fidelity to the score, the musicians of the Original Dixieland Jazz Band were popularizing a manically fast style of improvised ensemble music. Their brand of "jazz" created a seismic shift in American music when Victor released the recordings made in February.

On the evening of Monday, 2 April 1917, President Woodrow Wilson addressed a joint session of Congress to recommend a declaration of war against Germany. He argued that the country was effectively at war already and that the time had come for the United States to accept formally the role of belligerence that Germany had forced upon it. Characterizing the conflict as one between the autocratic German government and the freedom and self-determination of the United States, he famously urged his audience, "The world must be made safe for democracy." He called for substantial financial support for the Allies to be raised primarily through taxes rather than loans, and he advocated raising an army of 500,000 men through universal conscription. The *New York Times* reported on the reaction to his comments about German Americans: "When he touched on our relations with the Germans there was applause for his promise to those German-Americans who 'are in fact loyal to their neighbors and the Government in the hour of test,' but it was altogether overshadowed by the volume of that which broke out for the antithetical sentence, 'If there should be disloyalty it will be dealt with with a stern hand and firm repression.'"[2] On Friday, 6 April, Congress voted to declare war, and the president signed the declaration at 1:18 p.m.

The declaration changed the country irrevocably. What had previously been known as "The European War" was now a world war. The month of April saw an explosion of patriotism across the country, followed rapidly by Liberty Loan drives to raise money, by military preparations, and by a host of new laws befitting a nation at war. Attitudes and events moved quickly, and millions of Americans were swept along. This month marked a watershed in American history, as the nation committed itself to joining an unprecedented conflict on the other side of the Atlantic. The United States was on the brink of a new era, with no way of knowing how it would end.

The musical world was as unsettled by the war declaration as the rest of the country. Speculation had been rife for months about the fate of German and Austrian musicians, and this issue continued to dominate the music journals. At the time that Wilson addressed Congress, the opera *Canterbury Pilgrims*, by American composer Reginald De Koven, was being performed at New York's Metropolitan Opera House. Copies of the "extra" newspaper with the text of Wilson's address, sneaked into the auditorium, caused a distraction as audience members craned to read it. The orchestra had been provided with parts to "The Star-Spangled Banner" in advance, and the performance was interrupted between acts

III and IV so that the audience could sing the anthem in recognition of the momentous historic occasion. The drama continued as contralto Margarethe Ober, formerly a singer at the Royal Opera House in Berlin, sang her first line of Act IV, then fainted and fell backwards with a thud. She was carried off and attended by a doctor, who would not let her return to the stage. A short time later, German baritone Robert Leonhardt also fainted.[3]

Popular songwriter George M. Cohan, nicknamed "the man who owned Broadway," contemplated the significance of the war declaration on a train ride back to his home in New York on Friday. He spent the following day in his study, and on Sunday morning he showed his family the results of his labor. With a tin pan on his head and a broom over his shoulder, he marched through the house singing what would soon become the most iconic song of the era:

> Johnny, get your gun, get your gun, get your gun.
> Take it on the run, on the run, on the run.
> Hear them calling you and me,
> Every Son of Liberty.
> Hurry right away, no delay, go today.
> Make your Daddy glad to have had such a lad.
> Tell your sweetheart not to pine,
> To be proud her boy's in line.
>
> *Chorus*
> Over there, over there,
> Send the word, send the word over there
> That the Yanks are coming, the Yanks are coming
> The drums rum-tumming everywhere.
> So prepare, say a prayer,
> Send the word, send the word to beware—
> We'll be over, we're coming over,
> And we won't come back till it's over, over there.
>
> Johnny, get your gun, get your gun, get your gun.
> Johnny, show the "Hun" you're a son-of-a-gun.
> Hoist the flag and let her fly
> Yankee Doodle do or die.
> Pack your little kit, show your grit, do your bit.
> Yankee to the ranks from the towns and the tanks
> Make your Mother proud of you
> And the old red-white-and-blue.

His seven-year-old daughter Mary recalled her reaction to the first performance of this hit song: "We kids had heard, of course, that the United States was at war, and now here was Dad acting just like a soldier. So I began to sob, and I threw myself down, hanging for dear life to his legs as he marched begging him, pleading with him not to go away to the war. I kept clinging to him until he stopped."[4]

The enthusiasm over the declaration led to more "Star-Spangled Banner" incidents. In Rector's restaurant on the evening of the declaration, Englishman Frederick Sumner Boyd (a socialist who had previously served time in prison for advocating terrorism) refused to stand during the anthem. A German waiter urged him and his companion (a suffragist who had previously been fined for distributing information on birth control) to stand, but they refused. Their fellow diners were so affronted that they began pelting the pair with salads until they were covered in greens with globs of mayonnaise. He was arrested, but she managed to slip away.[5] In Chicago, three young men were arrested after a symphony concert for refusing to stand during the anthem. They maintained that they had a right to hold their own opinions and do as they pleased.[6]

The prominent German and Austrian soloists who dominated the field of concert music in America were interviewed and closely observed throughout April. Public opinion about them was a bellwether for future developments as the United States made practical preparations for the war.

Fritz Kreisler was on an ambitious tour of California, where he played twenty-two concerts that season.[7] Always popular with audiences, he performed not only in his accustomed roles as solo recitalist and orchestral soloist but also as piano accompanist for baritone Reinhold Warlich. In an article entitled "Fritz Kreisler Is Always Welcomed," the *San Francisco Chronicle* explained that the secret to the violinist's popularity was that his technical and intellectual perfection appealed to the connoisseur, while his passion, fire, and tenderness appealed equally to the unschooled listener.[8]

Kreisler's views on the war were of interest to his audience because of his own military experiences. He had served briefly in the Austrian army in 1914 but was discharged after being wounded in the battle of Lemberg. He subsequently published a book, *Four Weeks in the Trenches: The War Story of a Violinist*, about his brief military career and his abhorrence for war.[9] Interviewed by the *Oakland Tribune* on 7 April, Kreisler walked a fine line. He reiterated his hatred of war and decried the mob passion in warring countries, but he supported President Wilson's speech as "a fine presentation of the case." He expressed the belief that European soldiers were also fighting for democracy and that after the war was over, the United States could add a "much needed force of tolerance and democracy" to the negotiations. The master of romantic violin playing saw nothing romantic about war, which he described as a "dull, sodden, mechanical business—mud, filth, misery and despair."[10]

On the evening of 5 April, Olga Samaroff joined the Kneisel String Quartet for its final concert, which took place in Philadelphia's Witherspoon Hall. Founded thirty-two years previously by Franz Kneisel, the Rumanian-born concertmaster of the Boston Symphony Orchestra, this quartet had set the standard for chamber music in the United States for decades. They had toured throughout the country, enhancing appreciation for chamber music. The reviewer from the *Public Ledger* noted, however, that as public taste for large-scale orchestra concerts and operatic productions had grown in recent years, the audience for the intimate pleasures of chamber music had declined. As the members of the quartet aged, they faced increasing difficulties in attracting an audience. Nonetheless, their final performance of works by Beethoven, Reger, and Franck earned a flowery valedictory: "It would be a work of supererogation to seek to describe the perfections of concerted performance of the four fiddlers, the spiritual communication of the composers' thoughts and feelings and meanings to the hearers, the tonal loveliness, the delicate varieties and values and balance of the program, and the splendid co-operation of Mme. Samaroff, whose piano was integral to the organic artistry of the Belgian mystic's quintet. Sufficient to record that the last of the Kneisel concerts was removed, as pole from pole, from the least."[11]

Ernestine Schumann-Heink was finally able to leave St. Louis in early April, after more than a month of recuperation from her February taxicab accident. She went first to her home in Chicago, where she was interviewed by a reporter after the declaration of war: "Oh, what a day to declare war! Good Friday! Christ was crucified on this day to bring peace to the world. It is a mockery and we mothers must suffer." In tears, she told the reporter that each of her five sons was either in the military or soon to be conscripted. The possibility that her son August, in the German navy, might someday face her other sons in battle was deeply troubling to her.[12] "What can any mother say? O, I love America. It is my home, my country. But I love Germany, too. O, Germany is beautiful. And the German people love America and Americans. O, those people who make war—all of them, all nationalities, all kinds—I hate them!" Coincidentally, the singer received a package from Washington at this time that contained a brooch decorated with a jeweled American eagle. It was a gift from Mrs. Edith Wilson, wife of the president, who included a simple note, "With renewed thanks for the pleasure you gave us last winter."[13]

Eager to return to her home outside San Diego, Schumann-Heink boarded the cross-country train as soon as she was able. On the evening of 10 April, she arrived in the city and proceeded to the Grant Hotel to spend the night before travelling to her Grossmont estate. Upon entering the Palm Court of the hotel, she was welcomed by a large crowd of well-wishers, led by the Twenty-First Infantry Band, which had elected her honorary president of the regimental mess the previous summer. Despite her exhaustion from the trip and with tears streaming down her face, she sang her first public notes since the accident—a rousing chorus of "The Star-Spangled Banner" to the enthusiastic cheers of the audience. She told the crowd again how worried she was and expressed the hope that war could be averted.

During the winter, while James Reese Europe was at the Royal Poinciana Hotel in Palm Beach, Florida, his sergeant Noble Sissle had been advertising nationally for talented black musicians to join the Fifteenth New York National Guard Band. At first he had received many expressions of interest from around the country, but as the drums of war beat louder and some of those persons withdrew their names from the applicant pool, Sissle became discouraged. He hoped that when Europe returned from Florida, well rested and invigorated by the sunshine, his friend could reinvigorate the recruiting effort.

When Europe did return to New York in April, Sissle was shocked at his appearance. He had lost weight, he had dark circles under his eyes, and he was easily fatigued. Although obscured by the glasses he normally wore, Europe's eyes were bulging out of their sockets alarmingly. He confided to Sissle that a physician had taken him aside in Palm Beach and after a brief examination had diagnosed an exophthalmic goiter, now known as hyperthyroidism. The condition was caused by an enlarged thyroid gland that would continue to grow inward until it obstructed his windpipe and strangled him. The only solution was surgery, which the Palm Beach doctor had urgently recommended but Europe believed he was too busy to have. Despite his serious medical condition, Europe resumed his recruitment for the band.

Things moved quickly for the regiment in April. The unit was reviewed by New York Governor Charles S. Whitman on 1 April, reached peacetime strength of twelve hundred the following week, and was transferred from the New York state government to the US War Department on 17 April. On this occasion, the *New York Age* interviewed Col. Hayward about the recruitment standards for officers, as there was great concern in the African American community about the interactions between white and black officers. He informed reporters that black officer candidates had been shown extra consideration in preparing for the examination and had not been discriminated against. Regarding the potential for racial conflict, he said, "When a white applicant comes to me and asks that I nominate him I at once inform him that the Fifteenth is a colored regiment and has colored officers; that if they can come into the regiment and meet men according to their rank as soldiers and not as plain Bill or George so well and good. However, if he intended to take a narrower attitude he had better stay out."[14] He also pointed out that there were white officers serving under black officers without problem because they understood the meaning of rank in the military. Prominent among the black officers was Lieutenant James Reese Europe.

As Europe and Sissle considered the recruits they had already acquired, they identified a glaring weakness. Although their recruitment of brass and percussion players was encouraging, they had been unable to find enough woodwind players of the required skill and experience. Europe presented Col. Hayward with a solution to the problem. He had heard that the island of Puerto Rico had a good supply of talented woodwind players who could be enticed to join the band with the proper financial incentives. Since the Jones-Shafroth Act of March had made Puerto Ricans subject to US conscription laws, the time was right for recruiting there. Hayward quickly arranged for military orders and funds, and before the end of April, Europe was on a boat to Puerto Rico. Sissle, whose memoir is full of dramatic exaggeration, described his feelings about the departure of his friend and commander in a sentence of epic length:

> One of the men in the party that came to see Jim off remarked how bad Jim looked and the anxiety concerning his health which had temporarily been lost during the rush to get him off returned with all its horribleness, and it was with low spirits that I returned to the Armory to start plans to assemble a Band that I had my doubts would ever become a reality, because in my short association with Jim Europe I had learned him well enough to know that he was no quitter nor complainer, and when he told me that he was ill, and what the doctor had told him concerning the seriousness of his condition, I had all the reasons to believe that Jim Europe was a very dangerously ill man, and the fact that he made me promise not to tell anyone, not even his wife, of his condition, made my burdens all the greater because it looked to me like "Suicide" to allow him to

make the journey in his physical condition and me knowing that condition. But, somehow, I just believed that Jim was a sort of superhuman and as long as he believed in himself, he would survive the ordeal.[15]

As the Boston Symphony Orchestra season moved toward its conclusion, Muck and his orchestra stayed close to home. In April and May, the orchestra played the last five weekend pairs of concerts in Boston's Symphony Hall, along with two additional concerts in Massachusetts and the last of the season's six concerts in Providence, Rhode Island. This was the closest of the out-of-state cities where the BSO performed on a regular basis, and the audiences in that city's Infantry Hall were nearly as loyal as those at home. For the concert on 10 April, Muck treated his Rhode Island supporters to Mozart's *Jupiter* Symphony, Rubinstein's Piano Concerto no. 4, with Ethel Leginska as soloist, and Wagner's popular Overture to *Tannhäuser*. Both of the Providence papers raved about the playing of Leginska. They also agreed in their feelings about a planned reduction in the number of Providence concerts for 1917/18: "It is with regret that symphony patrons read of the contemplated change in the orchestra's plans for next season, when the six orchestral concerts will be replaced by . . . but three visits here. . . . The Boston orchestra has been the backbone of the local musical season for the past 36 years, and has been a mighty force for musical culture in this community. It is a pity that the management cannot see its way clear to continue the regular number of concerts."[16]

In Boston, Muck was praised by audience and critics alike for his control of the orchestra and his intelligent interpretations of the musical scores. On those occasions when he also exhibited emotion and rhythmic flexibility, as he did in the Boston premiere of Debussy's *Images* on 13 April, the critics were effusive in their praise. But the recurring complaints about Muck centered on his inconsistent repertoire choices. A week after the brilliant pairing of the Debussy *Images* with Schubert's Symphony no. 9, the conductor was pilloried for offering the premiere of a symphony by German composer Heinrich Gottlieb Noren. Olin Downes characterized it as "hopeless[ly] commonplace and out of date," and he complained bitterly that Muck continually performed "many works by modern Europeans which are palpably worthless" while ignoring the works of talented Boston composers like Henry Gilbert.[17] To his credit, Muck had programmed a concert of American works by Karl Goldmark, Amy Beach, and Charles Martin Loeffler in March, as well as works by Americans Philip Greeley Clapp, George Whitefield Chadwick, and Frederick S. Converse in April.

On 28 April, the classical music world was rocked when *Musical America* reported that a "reliable source" had stated that Henry Higginson planned to withdraw his support from the orchestra unless Muck, concertmaster Anton Witek, and all other German players resigned.[18] This led immediately to rumors about a potential domino effect in American orchestras that would send Stokowski to Boston in place of Muck and Ossip Gabrilowitsch to Philadelphia in place of Stokowski.[19] The rival paper *Musical Courier* contacted symphony manager Charles Ellis for confirmation, who retorted that it was "a —— lie." The *Courier* added, "The word which is represented by a dash is not one which is used ordinarily at Sunday school or at a ladies' seminary."[20] The report was pure gossip, as anyone close to Higginson would have known, but it caused anxiety and called attention to the fact that Muck's contract was expiring. *Musical America*'s editor, John C. Freund, was known for his strong anti-German stance, and the outbreak of war allowed him to express those views to a receptive audience.

As the New York Symphony travelled across the country in April, Walter Damrosch conducted a prodigious number of concerts. From Minnesota he and the orchestra proceeded to Winnipeg and then to Fargo, North Dakota. They played twice in Seattle, twice in Portland, Oregon, and then once in Medford, Oregon, where the concert was called "the greatest musical event in the history of the Rogue River Valley." The orchestra played three concerts in San Francisco (where one reviewer was gratified to note that the San Francisco Symphony did not suffer in comparison to the eastern orchestra) and two in Oakland before turning toward Los Angeles. After playing four concerts there, the orchestra returned to San Francisco for a gala concert with the San Francisco Symphony, Fritz Kreisler, and Efrem Zimbalist. This last concert, performed on 29 April, was an extraordinary feast for the audience. Kreisler and Zimbalist, two of the greatest living violinists, were featured in double concertos by Mozart and Bach. Players from the San Francisco Symphony were used to augment the forces of the New York Symphony, increasing the size of the 80-member touring group to a whopping 125. Their featured work was the *Leonore* Symphony by Joachim Raff, a youthful friend of Walter's father, Leopold, and still a respected composer. After additional works by Debussy and Dvořák, the concert concluded with "The Star-Spangled Banner" played by the 125-member orchestra and sung "lustily" by an audience estimated at over 9,000.[21]

Everywhere he went, Damrosch shared his views on music, the political situation, and anything else that reporters wished to talk about.

In an interview with Mabel Abbott of the *Seattle Star* several days after the war declaration, Damrosch called the notion of a Kaiser "a relic of mediaevalism," stating that it was anachronistic in the modern world. He expressed the view that if the socialists could gain power in Germany, they would oust the Prussian government and create peace. He echoed President Wilson's statement that "our quarrel is not with the German people, but with the German government." He also spoke strongly in defense of German Americans: he believed that 99 percent were "deeply loyal Americans." Abbott ended her interview by asking what he did for recreation. "'Well, I don't need much exercise,' he observed, drawing the rough cloth of his coat sleeve tight, to show a biceps like a melon. 'That's what thirty years of orchestra-conducting does for a man.'"[22]

In a speech before the Commonwealth Club of San Francisco on 21 April, Damrosch's topic was music and patriotism. He used his orchestra as a metaphor for international cooperation, stating that despite hailing from thirteen different nationalities on both sides of the conflict, his men set aside their differences and came together for a common purpose. He spoke of the positive response that his orchestra received to their playing of "The Star-Spangled Banner" and optimistically predicted an important role for the country in the years ahead: "Our first duty now is to our country, to love it greatly and to aid it in every way according to our strength. But the patriotism which is so strong for America will ultimately merge into a greater patriotism that will include a love for all the citizens of the world. We are at war, not with the German people, but with the German government. Race hatred is artificial and is fostered by governments. The great lesson which America is to teach at the end of this war will be the brotherhood of the world."[23]

Perhaps the most fascinating of the month's interviews was written by Jeanne Redman in Los Angeles. She passed lightly over the musical aspects of Damrosch's work and instead delved into his personality and celebrity status. He denied musicians were "unbalanced"; a plumber, he said, with his specialized knowledge of tools, was just as "unbalanced" as a musical genius. He related a humorous incident that had occurred after the gala concert in San Francisco, when he went out to eat after the performance: "He strayed into a café downtown, where four chorus girls, arrayed in American flags, sang 'The Star-Spangled Banner' to ragtime. Damrosch got out as quickly as he could." When questioned about his German heritage, Damrosch told Redman, "I came to America when I was nine years old, and am more of an American than you are, because I am one by choice."[24] Damrosch's interviews were widely reprinted, as he not only had strong opinions on current topics but also had a knack for articulating them memorably. His celebrity status gave him a forum to express his views that few outside politics or journalism enjoyed.

An immediate impact of the war was the announcement on 17 April by New York Mayor John P. Mitchel that starting on 1 May, alcohol would no longer be served in city restaurants, hotels, saloons, cabarets, and roof gardens after 1 a.m. His administration's previous policy had been liberal compared to that of Chicago and other cities, but he tied the new restrictions to the war effort: "Frugality may shortly become a general necessity. It is well to begin its practice voluntarily and before necessity compels it."[25] This restriction had a direct impact on Reisenweber's, where the ODJB entertained patrons after the theatrical shows until early in the morning. In response to this mandate, the starting time of the nightly 400 Club performances was moved to 9 p.m., so that patrons could still enjoy four hours of entertainment before closing time. *Variety* reported that this restriction had a detrimental effect on the income of the club, which had previously stayed open until six some mornings.[26]

The popularity of jazz continued to grow on Broadway, as the ODJB's success spawned imitators of all sorts. The *Sun* reported on 8 April:

> The jazz band, perhaps it should be explained, is a form of Western ruthlessness imported to Broadway from the Barbary Coast. It consists principally of trick cornetists and trap drummers, who play on cowbells, tin cans, washbuckets and other barnyard apparatus. A full Jazz orchestra includes everything except musical instruments. The Jazzbo reign of schrecklichkeit in the Broadway restaurants extends from the Circle to the Square and up most of the side streets. Sagacious restaurateurs during the Jazzbo numbers are now serving ear muffs on request to fractious patrons who insist on retaining their hearing. The difficulties of dinner conversation increased so rapidly after the Jazz bands came in that even tête-à-tête table communication had to be abandoned for a form of sign language.[27]

The article went on to describe a scheme by Justine Johnstone, the twenty-two-year-old star of the hit show *Oh, Boy!*, to open a completely silent after-hours club where patrons could escape the noise. Ironically, though jazz was associated with noise and the ODJB's imitators competed for attention by raising the volume, this was not the ODJB strategy. Their sound featured a range of dynamics, with the most exciting moments coming when the band suddenly got soft. Trombonist Eddie Edwards recalled, "The Original

Dixieland Jazz Band frequently played soft and ratty—pronounced by the boys 'raddy,' so that the shuffle of [the] dancers' feet could be heard."[28]

Just one week after this article, Nick LaRocca and his band decisively set themselves apart from the flood of competition with the release of the first-ever jazz recording, an event that both changed the record industry and standardized the elements of early jazz. The Victor Talking Machine Company was an innovator not only in recording techniques but also in distribution and marketing. The company used these innovations to full advantage to promote the release of the ODJB's first recording. Since early March, the art department had been at work on promotional materials, but the relaxed attitude of the southern musicians delayed the project, as a promised photo did not arrive in time. A 14 March telegram from Victor reads in part: "ARTISTS AND PRINTERS WAITING PLEASE INSTRUCT PHOTOGRAPHERS TO MAIL PHOTOGRAPH AT ONCE FAILURE TO RECEIVE THIS DELAYING ACTION ANSWER." A letter of 29 March confirmed that the advertising promotion was to consist of "a special poster and a special supplement, which will be sent to all Victor dealers all over the country, for display and distribution."[29] The color brochure that was released in April to promote the record featured an action photo of the band all leaning to one side, along with text that reflected Victor's uncertainty about the correct spelling of the new music: "Spell it Jass, Jas, Jaz, or Jazz—nothing can spoil a Jass Band." The promotional copy in the brochure emphasized the fun, hilarity, and unpredictability of jazz as themes for dealers preparing their ad campaigns.[30]

Victor's network of thousands of dealers was tightly controlled. The company set prices as well as distribution dates in an effort to coordinate sales nationwide. The most radical attempt to control the market was the License Royalty Scheme introduced in 1913, which stipulated that Victor machines and records were licensed to the public for use rather than sale and could thus be repossessed at any time. This plan was struck down by the US Supreme Court on 9 April 1917, allowing dealers greater freedom in pricing and sales.[31] The first pressing of the ODJB record, which had been in production for over a month, contains a warning on the label: "This record is licensed in U.S.A. for use only, and only under the conditions printed on the Victor Company's envelope containing it," along with a printed price of $0.75. These conditions were invalidated by the Supreme Court ruling and removed from later labels. Although retailers were not restricted in when and how they offered the record for sale, I have found evidence of only one dealer that offered the ODJB record for sale before its official release date of 15 April.[32]

Starting on 15 April 1917, the new record was advertised nation-wide. Bearing the serial number 18255, the double-sided record featured "Dixieland Jass Band One-Step" on the A-side and "Livery Stable Blues, Fox Trot" on the B-side. In order to clarify the intentions, the label on each side had the words "For Dancing" printed next to the spindle hole. These two numbers introduced the rest of the country to the new musical style that had taken Broadway by storm. The ad published by a store in Lancaster, Ohio (see Figure 5.1) is typical of the layout and content of these ads.

Figure 5.1 Advertisement for Victor record no. 18255 (*Lancaster [Ohio] Eagle-Gazette*, 20 April 1917).

As described in Chapter 3, these two numbers are representative of two of the styles of jazz that the band had popularized in Chicago and New York. The one-step, an extremely fast dance, did not fit any of the previous styles of dancing. Its tempo was infectious, with a manic energy that fit the spirit of the times and inspired spontaneous, improvised dance steps. The fox-trot was a slightly slower dance in which couples held each other close. It was more erotic than the one-step, and in this case it featured elements of the blues. The distinctive feature of "Livery Stable Blues" was the use of barnyard animal sounds as a novelty: LaRocca imitated a horse on his cornet, Shields imitated a rooster on his clarinet, and Edwards evoked a cow's moo with perfectly timed trombone glissandi. It was this side that became the more popular of the two, probably because of the combination of blues harmonies and humorous novelty sounds.

Within weeks the boys were bombarded with praise and offers from around the country. Agent Harry James tried unsuccessfully to entice the band back to Chicago with an offer of $350 a week guaranteed through June 1918. The record was advertised by local stores in New Orleans, and the band was immensely gratified to see ads like the one for the department store Maison Blanche on Canal Street: "Here is positively the greatest dance record ever issued. Made by New Orleans musicians for New Orleans people. . . . It has all the 'swing' and 'pep' and 'spirit' that is so characteristic of the bands whose names are now a by-word at New Orleans dances. It is more proof that New Orleans sets the pace for 'wonderful' dance music—a fact that is recognized and commented upon the country over."[33]

The importance of this first jazz record cannot be overemphasized. Cornetist Bix Beiderbecke was fourteen years old when he heard the record in his home town of Davenport, Iowa. Imitating LaRocca's playing on this record was an important step in his development; it helped him become one of the most influential jazz musicians of the 1920s. Musicians in New Orleans, where the five members of the ODJB had grown up and learned their trade, paid attention to the record and adapted their playing to match this nationwide hit. For the first time, jazz musicians began listening to and imitating a record in addition to basing their styles on musical scores or live performances. The five-piece instrumentation of the band had an immediate impact on other bands. Violinist Manuel Manetta recalled that he was fired from the Joe Oliver / Kid Ory band in New Orleans because the leaders wanted their band to sound like the ODJB.[34] This was vindication for LaRocca, who had not been one of the first-call players when he lived in New Orleans but was now imitated by the very players he had envied as a young man.

The band also received numerous inquiries about the availability of orchestrations of the two numbers on the record. One such letter came from an orchestra leader in Lake Charles, Louisiana, barely two weeks after the record's release:

> Dear sirs:—
>
>   Your "Livery Stable Blues" has taken everybody "off their feet," in this part of the country. I am leader at the "Paramount Theatre" and also have the orchestra at [The Majestic Hotel]. Every day I am hearing calls for your "Livery Stable Blues"—I fail to find it listed with any publishing house. Won't you give me some line on it? Where can I get the orchestration or piano part?[35]

Not being readers themselves, the members of the ODJB had not been concerned with the publication of the music, which had been "composed" and played by ear. The unanticipated success of the record made it necessary to address such issues, which would soon embroil the band in a series of lawsuits to protect their intellectual property. The oral tradition of New Orleans jazz had not prepared them for the complex business of popular music publishing in New York. Years later, LaRocca told historian H. O. Brunn that when the band members left New Orleans, they knew nothing of the ways of the North, but "We sure learned fast!"[36]

The Creole Band was experienced in the ways of the North. Crisscrossing the country for three seasons, they had played in large houses and small from California to New York. They had arrived at the Winter Garden in New York just as the popularity of jazz was cresting in early March 1917, but after two weeks, the Shubert organization sent them on the road again. Working for the Shuberts was the pinnacle for vaudeville performers, and their hard work had earned them this opportunity to be booked by the top agency in the country. But the strike by actors against the Loew's chain of theaters disrupted the world of vaudeville and resulted in the loan of the Creole Band to Loew's. It would have been out of the question for the band to turn down these bookings, even though the lack of control bore an uncomfortable similarity to slave labor.[37]

For the last three days of March, they played Loew's Orpheum on 86th Street. The first half-week of April saw them at Loew's American on 42nd Street, and the second half of the week sent them to Loew's Boulevard Theatre in the Bronx. From there they were kicked to New England, playing first in Boston and then in Springfield, Massachusetts. On Thursday, 26 April, they were announced as the feature attraction at Loew's Theatre in

Portland, Maine: "Here's the Big Shubert Management Act that has made New York sit up—The Creole Band—Sometimes Called the Jazz Band. A Troupe of Wonderful Creole Musicians." But they never showed up.

As with many of the other seminal events in early jazz history, there is no documentation for what happened except the conflicting recollections of the participants, shared decades later. Somehow, the band members missed the train from Boston to Portland, and the resulting fight was the explosion that blew the band apart. Most of the stories, though, state that Keppard was the one who did not show up at the station and that a bottle of gin was the reason. The Portland theater was put in an awkward spot, but a quick phone call to New York secured a replacement act for the following day. In a business that relied on careful coordination of acts moving from theater to theater, the failure of the Creole Band to arrive at the scheduled destination was professional suicide. A few of the band members reassembled for a short (and reportedly successful) run in Philadelphia, but then they dispersed, another casualty of this explosive month.

Two major events of April 1917 would dominate the country for years to come. The first, the declaration of war, caused the United States and its citizens to reassess their position in the world and make logistical preparations for training and equipping millions of soldiers before sending them across the Atlantic to fight. As the preparations began, Americans quickly adopted a new mindset about foreigners in their midst and abroad. The optimistic, generous spirit of reaching out to allies "Over There" was counterbalanced by growing suspicion toward aliens over here. It remained to be seen how these new attitudes would impact the internationalism inherent in classical music.

The second major event was the first jazz record. Arriving as it did just nine days after Congress voted to declare war, the sound of the Original Dixieland Jazz Band's manic, energetic music would forever be linked in the American psyche with the new atmosphere in the country. This genre would have a profound influence on America's musical culture, not just in the war years but in the decades following. The "overnight furore" created by the band on Broadway in January proved to be an even bigger sensation when it swept the country in April.

For a music-historical parallel of equal significance, one has to go all the way back to Mozart's opera *The Magic Flute* of 1791, the first *Singspiel*, or German comic opera, to achieve worldwide popularity with middle-class audiences. In both cases, a genre of music that had previously been considered low-class entertainment was elevated to cultural respectability by one inspired composition. It is perhaps not a coincidence that "Livery Stable Blues" and *The Magic Flute* both combine musical innovation with loopy comedy. The ODJB's publicity photos showed the band dressed in tuxedos for the tony crowd at Reisenweber's, but at LaRocca's feet are the "sugar jar" for tips and the mutes that allowed him to make the horse whinny. This explosion reverberated for generations.

CHAPTER 6

❧

Middle America

May 1917

Jazz music exploded on the national scene following the release of the ODJB's first record on 15 April. The popularity of this record made jazz a household word in every part of the country where records were sold. In Columbia, Missouri, half a continent away from Reisenweber's, an article published on 1 May in the *Daily Missourian* reported on the arrival of what it called "the newest brand of orchestra noise, jazz music":

The craze has struck Columbia. It "jazzed" in a week or two ago. It is the latest from the East, that region east of the Mississippi. In the East, jazz music is blamed on San Francisco, which in turn passes the buck to New Orleans. At any rate, the jazz band has routed the ukulele and bids fair to stay with us for the summer, at least. There is no definition of "jazz." It isn't in the dictionary. The word is as "low-brow" grammatically as the music is harmonically. But a jazz orchestra leader says that it takes a trombone, cornet, piano, clarinet and furious drummer to produce the sounds you hear when listening to a jazz orchestra record. Each musician plays any melody he chooses in every key that he can. The drummer has only one key at his disposal, but he makes up for that handicap by indiscriminately hitting gongs, cymbals and tambourines, shaking rattles, blowing whistles and at the same time keeping up an incessant attack on his drums. The combined efforts sound like a busy day in the foundry. Dancers highly approve of jazz music because of the perfect time. Musicians are said to shudder at the perfect discord. But it's here in Columbia and will have to be tolerated until something worse is invented.[1]

Jazz did indeed last through the summer of 1917 and well beyond. Across the country, jazz bands sprang up in small towns and large cities. The public clamored for sheet music and more records. Almost overnight, the sound of "Livery Stable Blues" and "Dixieland Jass Band One-Step" gave Americans an aural image to go with the new word, allowing writers to conjure up new images of musical mayhem. A *New York Times* review of the Broadway show *His Little Widows*, also published on 1 May, refers to the fad: "Some remote, small-time vaudeville circuit yielded up a strange quartet named the Haley Sisters, who were thunderously applauded last evening, apparently because the tallest of them, who sings third bass or whatever they call the lowest voice in a women's quartette, . . . has a voice like a moose. These four sing rather like a Jazz Band and last evening's audience seemed to like them enormously. It is not known why."[2]

The month of May brought jazz to middle America; it also saw Damrosch and Kreisler touring middle America and saw the country making its first preparations to enter the war in Europe. On 18 May, Congress passed the Selective Service Act, mandating registration of all men twenty-one to thirty in preparation for a military draft later in the year. New restrictions on resident aliens from enemy nations were designed to limit the potential damage of spies and saboteurs. The reactions to music and military preparations illustrate the mood of American citizens across the country in the month following the official entry into World War I.

As soon as the ODJB's record became a hit, the legal troubles began. Jazz to this time had been an improvised music, and the band had no experience with printed music, copyrights, or royalties. The laws on rights in recorded music were still very new, with the first provision in the copyright code dating only from 1909. Two surviving pages from Eddie Edwards's ledger book show what happened with their record. According to the trombonist's notes on page 88, Victor offered the band two propositions for payment. The first was a flat fee of $600 for the record, and the second was a $100 fee for making the record as well as two cents royalty per copy sold. The band's members opted for the second arrangement but almost immediately wished they had taken the cash up front, which enabled Edwards to purchase Sbarbaro's percentage of the royalties for $100 after the fact. On page 89, Edwards wrote: "Two Records made entitled:—BARNYARD BLUES,

ORIGINAL DIXIELAND JASS BAND 1 STEP."[3] The title of the first number was not the title on the label of the Victor record released in April, and this caused most of their subsequent problems.

On 9 April, less than a week before the release of the record, their agent Max Hart took the precaution of filing a copyright claim for the two numbers as unpublished compositions, listing himself as both composer and copyright claimant. His claim was for the title that the band *thought* their record would have: "Barnyard Blues." It is not clear whether this was the band's original title that was changed by the record company, or—as they later claimed in sworn testimony—that their original title "Livery Stable Blues" was supposed to have been changed to "Barnyard Blues" by Victor but was not. LaRocca later gave an elaborate story about Victor executives who felt that "Livery Stable Blues" was too suggestive and that "Barnyard Blues" would be an inoffensive alternative, but this does not pass the common-sense test. "Barnyard," according to the *Oxford English Dictionary*, does indeed have off-color overtones, while "livery stable" does not. Furthermore, the animal sounds that made the record popular—rooster, horse, and cow—are more likely to be found in a barnyard than in a stable for renting horses. In either case, the title on the band's copyright did not match the title on the record label.

The lively interest in the record gave several enterprising persons in Chicago the idea to cash in on its success. The first copyright for the title "Livery Stable Blues" was granted on 12 May to publisher Roger Graham, who filed a claim for the title as an unpublished melody only, with himself as claimant and one May Hill as composer. Another claim was filed on 24 May, again for the unpublished melody only, listing Alcide Nunez and Ray Lopez as composers, with Roger Graham as claimant. The published version of the song was registered on 18 June, with Ray Lopez and Alcide Nunez as composers and Roger Graham as publisher. The common thread in all three copyright claims was the publisher.

Alcide "Yellow" Nunez was a New Orleans clarinetist who had come to Chicago with LaRocca and company in March 1916, when the band started its northern career at Schiller's Café. As the year wore on, LaRocca grew increasingly impatient with Yellow's drinking and tardiness but especially with his propensity to double the cornet line rather than play an embellishing counterpoint. Finally the two had a fight after the band moved to the Casino Gardens. Nunez was replaced by Larry Shields, a much better clarinetist and a key ingredient of the ODJB's later success.[4] But Nunez nursed a grudge against his former bandmates. The discovery that "Livery Stable Blues" had not been copyrighted gave him the opportunity for revenge.

LaRocca hired a New York lawyer, Nathan Burkan, to file an injunction against Graham to stop the sale of the "Livery Stable Blues" sheet music, but it would be months before the dispute came to trial in Chicago. Meanwhile, Victor opted to withhold royalty payments on the "Livery Stable Blues" side of the ODJB record until the court ruling was finalized. In retaliation, LaRocca refused to make more records for Victor. Instead, he took his band to Columbia, which was now interested in working with the ODJB because of the success of the Victor recording.

The two sides that the ODJB recorded for Columbia on 31 May are the least satisfactory of the band's records. In the first place, Columbia insisted that the band play songs that were published by Shapiro, Bernstein, and Company rather than their own original numbers. Side A was "Darktown Strutters Ball," by Sheldon Brooks, and side B was "Indiana," by James F. Hanley. The second number was taught to the band by a staff pianist in the publisher's office, and they hummed it over in their heads as they walked to the recording studio. When they made the recording, LaRocca played the song in his favorite key rather than in the key they had been taught, causing even more cacophony than usual. LaRocca admitted, "I didn't realize anything was wrong until we had finished the number and Edwards and Shields tried to wrap their instruments around my neck!"[5] The Columbia engineers did not take the same care with placing the instruments that Charles Sooy had taken, yielding a muddier sound, with little clarity of individual lines. Because the players were all roughly equidistant from the recording horn, the piano is practically inaudible, the clarinet lacks the brilliancy of the Victor recordings, and the drums are overwhelming. On both numbers, Sbarbaro uses the woodblock extensively, a favorite technique from the old minstrel shows. Especially on "Darktown Strutter's Ball," his masterful lilting swing is the most appealing feature of the record. This number includes stop time techniques that had long been favorites of ragtime players: everyone rests for a measure or two while counting furiously so they can come back in together. This was the first and last record the band did for Columbia.

Meanwhile, the word they had introduced to America was rapidly gaining currency. The appearance of the word "jazz," as such and in variant spellings, in newspapers nationwide increased dramatically during 1917 (see Figure 6.1). The newspapers sampled—those archived in Newspapers.com—are a small fraction of the papers actually published during 1917, but the nearly forty-fold increase from December to November can be assumed to be a representative sample. This graph clearly illustrates the adoption of the word in middle America, with the two largest percentage jumps occurring

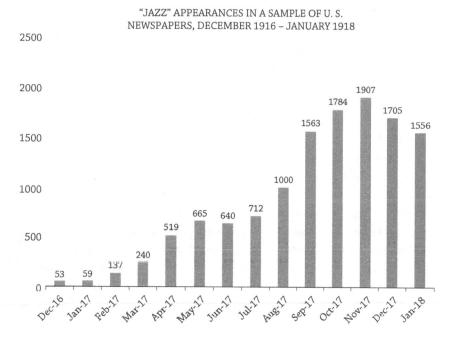

"JAZZ" APPEARANCES IN A SAMPLE OF U. S.
NEWSPAPERS, DECEMBER 1916 – JANUARY 1918

Figure 6.1 Number of print appearances of the words "jasz," "jass," and "jazz" as recorded in Newspapers.com (accessed 23 November 2017).

from January to February, when the ODJB opened at Reisenweber's, and from March to April, when their first record was released.

In the world of classical music, May was the month of music festivals. The return of warmth and fertility had been a cause for celebration in Europe since ancient times, and German culture traditionally celebrated the month with outdoor music festivals. May festivals, a tradition brought to America by German immigrants, had long been important cultural events in midwestern cities with large German populations. It was in Cincinnati, though, that the model was established for a marathon festival where mass choruses sang major choral works with orchestral accompaniment. Since the first Cincinnati May Festival in 1873, this tradition was emulated by communities across the country, and the New York Symphony Orchestra spent the month of May 1917 accompanying one festival after another.

Damrosch and his orchestra began the month at a three-day festival in Greeley, Colorado, followed by three concerts in Denver. Moving east, they played two concerts at the Emporia Festival in Kansas, followed by two more at the Wichita Festival. From there they proceeded to a three-day festival in Bowling Green, Ohio, followed immediately by five concerts in three days at the Spartanburg, South Carolina, Festival and two concerts with the Mozart Society of Asheville, North Carolina. Each of these festivals required the accompaniment of one or more major choral works along with one or more featured concerts by the orchestra. The coordination and advance rehearsals for these mammoth festivals was done by local musicians, and the New York Symphony arrived at the last minute to pull the production together.

The Spartanburg Music Festival (16–18 May) serves as a good illustration. Spartanburg was a small city of three thousand white residents, but it prided itself on being one of the most modern in the region, as reflected in its nickname, "the City of Success." The town was home to Converse College, a women's college with a strong tradition in music. The 1917 event, the city's twenty-third annual festival, was one of the largest ever. Advance publicity urged persons from the surrounding region to band together to attend the concerts: "All roads lead to Spartanburg Gala Week. Form an Automobile Party now and come help celebrate the South's Greatest Musical Achievement."[6] The opening concert on Wednesday evening, 16 May, presented the opera *Samson and Delilah* by the French composer Camille Saint-Saëns. The matinee concert on the following day presented a "popular program" sung by a children's chorus of five hundred voices, along with Princess Tsianina Redfeather, a Native American singer in a chamois beaded dress. She sang a group of Indian songs by Charles Wakefield Cadman to great applause, and the concert ended with patriotic songs. The evening concert brought Flotow's popular opera *Martha*. The final day began with a matinee performance by the New York Symphony that featured the *Irish* Symphony of Charles Villiers Stanford. The grand finale occurred that evening when Metropolitan Opera diva Margarete Matzenauer and baritone Charles Tittman appeared with the orchestra on "Artist's Night." The high level of musicianship and the large crowds throughout the festival enhanced Spartanburg's reputation as a cultural mecca in the Southeast.

Damrosch's performing duties, though demanding, did not prevent him from speaking with reporters, and on the 1917 tour he was especially sensitive to the importance of good publicity. During the early part of the month, he gave several interviews in Kansas that were widely reprinted throughout the country. In an interview headlined "A Music Man Talks Alfalfa," Damrosch gave his views on the nation's food shortage, advocating the addition of alfalfa to bread as a replacement for wheat flour. The interviewer was impressed with his calm, broad-minded discussion of a range of topics, noting that "the nearest he came to an explosion was when the subject of 'jazz' music was cautiously broached." Damrosch retorted, "There is as much difference between real music and that rhythmic noise some people call music as there is between a flower and chewing gum. It is impossible for me to listen to the percussion and jangle of this stuff and then go out and lead a Beethoven symphony."[7]

In Emporia, Kansas, Damrosch earned a vigorous editorial from William Allen White, one of the nation's premiere newspaper editors. White had been instrumental in exposing fraud and corruption during the early years of the century, when he and other "muckraking" journalists supported Theodore Roosevelt's progressive goals and helped call attention to the excessive wealth and power of Gilded Age industrialists. White showed no signs of slowing down, and his editorial is so appropriate to the theme of this book that it bears repeating in full:

DON'T CODDLE US

Yesterday in his program in the Emporia music festival, Walter Damrosch seemed to think, for some reason, that Emporia people would not stand for Wagner. Wagner, during the three years last past when Mr. Damrosch has brought his New York Symphony Orchestra here, has been the soul of his programs. Whatever may be the feeling in the East, here in the Middle West we have no feeling of nationalism in art. We are in this war with no particular hatred of Germany; and certainly with no diminution of our love for every artistic contribution Germany has made to the world. We voted for Wilson here in the West, it is true. But that's no reason why we should be supposed to have no guts. We like Wagner and Tschaikowsky, and have our moments when we can gulp down a strong dose of Brahms without bringing water to our eyes. And we admire Walter Damrosch, largely because he plays music with the innards in it. We are enlisting more than our quota of sailors, here in the West; and are leading the East in the matter of soldiers enlisted. So, for heaven's sake, don't assume that we have to vent our spite in disliking German music. We express our emotions otherwise, and spite is not one of our emotions. Next year, when Walter Damrosch comes to Emporia we want Wagner; we want Brahms; we want Schubert; we want Mendelssohn and all the good old German boys who put the muse in music! We might even stand "Die Wacht am Rhine," arranged as a theme of a fugue with "The Wearing of the Green," "Rule Britannia," and the "Marseillaise" as intertwining threads, and "A Hot Time" as the climax![8]

But the most reprinted article to come out of the Damrosch tour was undoubtedly the one that appeared in the *Wichita Beacon* on 23 May under the title "A Blessing in Disguise?" After opening with the observation that the simultaneous arrival of the war and jazz illustrated the saying that misfortunes never come singly, the author cited Damrosch's characterization of jazz as "rhythmic noise" and went on to describe its wild sounds with picturesque language. The essay ended with an ingenious suggestion that combined jazz with the previous fad in popular music: "There is only one thing worse than jazz, and that is Hawaiian jazz. That is compounding the felony. Each element by itself constitutes a separate offense, and the combination, if used on the Hindenburg line, would easily vindicate the rumor that American ingenuity is about to spring an invention which will make poisonous gas seem like May sunshine and the singing of orioles. The Germans are supersensitive to music. They can almost live on it. Hawaiian jazz played on ukuleles by a picked regiment—you can't beat it! Let jazz do its bit."[9]

Back in the East, there was a notable lack of the midwestern humor found in these articles. When directors of the Metropolitan Opera met to consider dropping Wagner from the repertoire, directing manager Giulio Gatti-Casazza said, "Gentlemen, you may do as you like; but I wish to inform you that if you decide to drop German opera you are at liberty to look for a new directing manager." The directors voted 9 to 6 in favor of retaining German opera. Under intense public pressure, soprano Johanna Gadski, whose husband's views were vocally anti-American, resigned her position with the company. Margarete Matzenauer, in contrast, stated that as an artist she had neither time nor inclination for politics: "A diplomat or a statesman does not attempt to air opinions on the technic of singing. Why then should a singer try to usurp the functions of a diplomat?"[10]

Meanwhile the *New York Tribune* instituted a movement in late April to require that the national anthem be performed only in a respectful manner. In response to complaints from restaurant patrons in the city, Mayor Mitchel issued an executive order on 8 May instructing George Bell, the commissioner of licenses, to warn restaurant and dance hall owners that their licenses would be revoked if their bands were caught playing the national anthems of the United States or her Allies in ragtime style or as part of a medley. The ODJB received a typed note from the management of Reisenweber's informing them of the new rule.

For German citizens living in the United States, May was a crucial month. The federal government announced that no unnaturalized citizen of an enemy nation would be allowed to live or work within a half mile of a federal military facility like an arsenal, a military base, or a navy port without a permit. The permit process opened on 1 May, and the deadline was 1 June. On 16 May the requirement was amended to include armories where troops were stationed. This caused a panic in New York: nearly all the hotels and cabarets were located within a half mile of a National Guard armory.[11] On 26 May, less than a week before the deadline, the "barred zones" were expanded to include any location within a half mile of the coast. This included all of Manhattan below Fourteenth Street. The permit process had started in an orderly fashion in early May, but with the expansion of the zones in the middle of the month, there was a crush of applicants in the final week. As tens of thousands of Germans lined up outside the Federal Building in Manhattan, police reserves were dispatched to the scene to help maintain order. The massive number of impacted persons forced the post office to remain open past midnight during this final week.[12]

Amid this panic, the editors of the New York Times reminded readers of the distinction between enemy aliens and alien enemies. The former were law-abiding citizens of an enemy nation who happened to live and work in the United States, while the latter were subversives who intended to do harm to the country where they were guests. The dividing line, the Times admitted, was not always clear, but they found it unlikely that blanket reprisals would effectively stop alien enemies nor that these persons were likely to call attention to themselves by obvious misbehavior: "The thing to do with an alien enemy is to put him in jail as soon as he can be caught and convicted. The enemy alien is, or at least may be, a bird of quite an other feather, and while it is right that he should be subjected to certain restrictions—restrictions to which, if he be judicious, he will submit patiently—he should not be the victim of useless discriminations or deprived of the privilege of earning an honest living."[13]

In Boston, Muck brought the orchestra's season to a close with a final pair of concerts on the first weekend of May. Reflecting on the season as a whole, Boston's critics agreed that despite some quirky programming choices, their conductor had given the city a diverse selection of music superbly played. Among the most admired works heard for the first time in Boston were the violin concerto of American Ernest Schelling, the Images by Claude Debussy, and the Three Jewish Poems of Ernst Bloch. To quell the rumors spread by Musical America in April, the management announced preliminary plans for the 1917/18 season and began selling subscriptions as usual. There was no indication that Muck's status with the orchestra was in jeopardy. In its summary of the season just concluded, the Boston Globe expressed the esteem of Boston audiences for Karl Muck:

Since the declaration of war by this Government, the audiences at the Symphony concerts have taken particular care to assure Dr. Muck, that whatever his allegiance as a subject of the German Emperor, they respected, admired and warmly acclaimed him for the consistent and unceasing devotion he has given and has continued to give in the administration of the Symphony Orchestra. He has taken his place from week to week with his habitual demeanor as a gentleman, as well as a musical genius, and whatever the embroilment of Nations, there could reasonably be only gratification at the renewal of Dr. Muck's contract, following the one now concluded.[14]

But rumors, once started, take on a life of their own. Higginson confided to his friend President Eliot in July that the public display of goodwill betrayed a private distrust: "Sundry good and friendly people have told me to look out for Dr. Muck and his doings, and some of them are sure that he is making mischief; yet nobody knows anything about it; they simply guess and bid me to dismiss him."[15] If Higginson had been a better politician, perhaps he would have taken the opportunity to replace Muck when his contract expired in May 1917. But he was a businessman used to dealing with facts, not rumors. Moreover, he had a blind spot when it came to the conductor's importance. For some reason, Higginson believed that no one else could do an adequate job of leading the orchestra, and he became more obstinate in this view as the pressure increased. He told Eliot that the "modern men" did not have the same respect for both old and new music that Muck had shown. Higginson admired his work ethic, his honesty, and his uncomplaining attitude. These qualities made him overlook his conductor's prickly, sometimes unpleasant demeanor and the persistent rumors about his loyalty.

Ernestine Schumann-Heink craved publicity as much as Muck shunned it. As she continued to recover, the contralto was often in the news, although she was not yet ready to resume her concert schedule. On 9 May, she was honored with a glowing testimonial at a luncheon by several business and civic organizations in San Diego. Deeply moved, she replied, "San Diego, I pledge you devotion unto the grave. San Diego forever, United States forever!" The crowd of over three hundred responded with deafening applause and shouting.[16]

Two days later, on 11 May, lawyers for the singer filed suit against United Railways for $95,000 damages resulting from the streetcar accident in St. Louis. The suit claimed that she suffered both physical and nervous damage from the accident and that her ability to earn a living was thereby impaired. The sum was estimated to be the lost income from her canceled engagements. This lawsuit was an understandable response to the traumatic experience, but in retrospect it was a mistake. The case would not be resolved until 1926, when the company settled out of court for $3,750.[17]

On 25 May, Henry Schumann-Heink registered with the United States military. His action took place eleven days before the general registration on 5 June and less than a month before his thirty-first birthday on 24 June, when he would have been exempt from military service. His registration card listed his employment as "movie actor" at Universal Film with three months of prior military service as an ordinary seaman in the Michigan Naval Reserve. He also had a wife and child. Among the millions of men who registered for the draft, few were announced in the press. David B. Lyons, registrar of voters in Los Angeles, explained, "It was a dramatic moment when Henry Schumann-Heink registered. It was not without pathos for him to realize that he might be chosen to serve against his brothers."[18]

While on board the ship bound for Puerto Rico to recruit woodwind players for his band, Lt. James Reese Europe received an urgent telegram telling him to wrap up his mission as quickly as possible so as to be back in New York before the regiment left for field training at Camp Peekskill on 13 May. He arrived in San Juan on 2 May, checked into the Hotel Inglaterra, and immediately began hearing auditions. On 5 May, he and twelve Puerto Rican musicians boarded the SS *Caracas* bound for New York. They arrived on 11 May, with just two days to spare.[19] When Sissle saw the new recruits, he laughed out loud: "Their Palm Beach suits were not only of many faded colors, but the trousers were too short for long ones and were too long for short ones."[20] The next two days were so busy with finding blankets to keep them warm, obtaining instruments for them to play, and finding musical scores for the band, that they did not have a chance to rehearse. Sissle recalled that the new band members, whom Europe had placed under his supervision, knew only two words of English. "No good!" was their all-purpose response to the food, the instruments, and the accommodations. They could not understand his instructions, although they paid attention when he shouted profanities.

Just before Europe's return, Sissle had placed the advertisement shown in Figure 6.2 in prominent African American newspapers. It produced a number of crucial acquisitions that would later form the backbone of the band. The cornet virtuoso Frank De Broit from Chicago enlisted on 12

Figure 6.2 Advertisement for musicians for the Fifteenth Regiment, New York Infantry (*New York Age*, 10 May 1917).

May, which was possible only because Hayward agreed to slip him an extra hundred dollars a month to supplement his army salary. Also on 12 May, Francis Eugene Mikell enlisted and was appointed bandmaster. Mikell had extensive experience not only as a cornetist but also as a teacher and band director. He became Europe's second-in-command, and he rehearsed and conducted the band in Europe's absence. On 13 May, the band obtained three students from Hampton Institute in Virginia; they were granted permission to leave school in order to join the Fifteenth Infantry Band.[21] All of these players, along with the Puerto Rican woodwind players, converged on Harlem as the band prepared to entrain for camp in upstate New York, leaving them no time to rehearse together before their departure.

On the bright, sunny Sunday morning of 13 May, the twelve hundred members of the Fifteenth Regiment convened in midtown Manhattan to march up Fifth Avenue and then west on 56th Street to board trains at

60th Street. Col. Hayward had envisioned the regiment marching in military formation to the stirring sounds of Europe's professional bandsmen, but the result was much more ragged. The band had time for only a quick read-through of one number, which sounded fine when they played it standing still but fell apart when the players had to march amid the cheers of friends and family. Sissle reported that the three drummers set three different tempos, and Jim Europe ran alongside trying to get them together. The Puerto Rican musicians were so awestruck by the big crowds and tall buildings that they paid little attention to their music. Nonetheless, the regiment made its way to the trains without disaster, marching past Carnegie Hall and within a few blocks of Reisenweber's Restaurant.

For the next eighteen days, the regiment drilled and practiced on the rifle range at a camp overlooking the Hudson River two miles north of Peekskill. The men were complimented on their deportment, and the mayor of Peekskill told Col. Hayward that his troops had given the local authorities "less trouble" than any previous state regiment that had camped there.[22] Europe spent most of the time in New York, where he selected musical scores and began preparations for a concert in late June. Meanwhile, Gene Mikell rehearsed the band daily and soon began to achieve the sound that Europe had envisioned when so many professional musicians played together. The Puerto Rican players were excellent musicians and adapted quickly to their new environment. Mikell's experience as a teacher allowed him to work out the basics efficiently before Europe stepped in to assume leadership. On Saturday, 26 May, the band gave a concert at Peekskill, the first time the newly constituted group was heard in public.

On Memorial Day, 30 May, the Fifteenth Regiment travelled back to Manhattan, arriving in time to participate in a parade with other New York National Guard regiments. Because they had spent the past eighteen days drilling, they had "the snap of experienced soldiers" and outshone the other regiments. Captain Arthur W. Little later recalled that the "wild reception" they received from their fellow New Yorkers on that day was an inspirational memory that spurred them on through all the hardships of their service during the next two years. He felt that this event was what gave the men "a tradition to support."[23]

The month of May saw Damrosch and Kreisler touring the western United States, Schumann-Heink recovering at home in California, Europe's band training in upstate New York, and the other performers bringing their concert seasons to an end. Concurrent with the predictable annual cycle of the concert season was the new atmosphere caused by the war. Americans across the country prepared for the selective service registration in June, and resident aliens scrambled to adapt to new government restrictions. As these public events took place, private attitudes toward German art and artists were also changing. The discussions about Wagner and other German composers would continue to grow in the months ahead, as would the debate over prominent German musicians on American stages. All of it unfolded to the accompaniment of jazz, which had swept the country and showed no signs of abating. The musical culture of the United States had begun to change, but the extent of these changes would not become clear until the next concert season began in the fall.

CHAPTER 7

⌒⌣⌒

Winding Up

June 1917

During the month of June, performers were winding up the season and preparing for vacation. The growing heat of summer, which made indoor concerts first impractical, then unbearable, gave an annual excuse for an extended break. In 1917, this normal pattern stood in contrast to the US government's preparations for war. The military was "winding up" in a very different sense, with the first draft registration, the establishment of training camps, and the tightening of restrictions on enemy aliens. In June, as the war preparations began to have a genuine impact on the country, musicians were affected as well.

Variety noted in its 2 June issue that with vaudeville managers in the East avoiding acts with German names, performers and their agents were forced to rename their acts or risk cancellation. *Musical America* reported in its issue published the same day that the California legislature had banned the singing of German songs in the state's public schools. This was in keeping with the general mood in the United States that eventually led to the replacement of German street and business names in many cities. By the end of the war, sauerkraut was called Liberty Cabbage, hamburgers were sold as Liberty Steak, the Hackfeld Dry Goods store in Honolulu was renamed Liberty House, and streets named after German cities or persons were permanently renamed in many American cities.[1]

Patriotism continued to be the order of the day, and songwriters across America were eager to "do their bit." George M. Cohan's "Over There," written the day after the war declaration in April, had been copyrighted and published in sheet music form on 1 June. With ironclad agreements in hand, the popular songwriter was ready to introduce the song to the public, and he decided that no one could do that better than Nora Bayes. The popular vaudeville star had been embroiled in a dispute with her manager that led to several months' absence from the vaudeville houses where she was most beloved. Her triumphant return to the Palace Theatre on 11 June was so popular that the standing room section was full to overflowing. The *Brooklyn Daily Eagle* reported that she earned five full minutes of curtain calls and commented, "Biggest of all in her repertoire was a new patriotic song by George M. Cohan, called 'Over There,' which had pep and go to it. Miss Bayes sang it in her best manner."[2] After this auspicious start, the song caught on and became the most popular song of the war, selling over two million copies. Bayes also recorded the new song for Victor, with a release date of 1 October. This song became part of the soundtrack as millions of American men enlisted in the military.

The Selective Service Act, passed by Congress on 18 May, gave the president the power to conduct a draft. It was Wilson's view that volunteers alone could not produce the number of soldiers needed for the war in Europe; he believed that a draft was the most democratic way to raise an army. Consequently, 5 June 1917 was established as the date by which all US men between the ages of twenty-one and thirty were required to register. As the registration cards of millions of American citizens are preserved in the National Archives, it is possible to trace the registrations of individuals and learn significant pieces of information about them.

Henry Schumann-Heink, thirty, had registered early on 25 May, and this fact was reported in the California papers. As noted in the last chapter, when a movie actor who was the son of a beloved opera singer registered for the draft, it was newsworthy. Two of his younger brothers waited until 5 June to register: Walter, twenty-eight, registered in Paterson, New Jersey, and Ferdinand, twenty-four, registered in Wenden, Arizona. All three men were married and thus potentially eligible for exemption because of their family responsibilities. The registration form gave opportunity for a preliminary exemption request, but the middle son Walter wrote "none" on this line. Oldest son Henry wrote "Dependency of Wife & Child," while youngest son Ferdinand wrote "crippled trigger finger & financial obligation wife."

On Friday, 1 June, Dominic LaRocca, twenty-eight, Edwin Edwards, twenty-six, and Lawrence Shields, twenty-three, registered for the draft in

Manhattan. All three men gave home addresses in New Orleans and listed their present employer as Reisenweber's Restaurant. All three claimed exemptions because of dependents: LaRocca for his wife and the other two for their mothers. Henry Ragas, twenty-six, waited until the official 5 June date to register, at which time he listed his home address and employer as Reisenweber's. He had a dependent wife but left the exemption line blank. Anthony Sbarbaro would not turn twenty-one until June 1918, so he waited another year to register. The Creole Band's members were older than those of the ODJB; only Freddie Keppard was of draft age in 1917. His older brother Louis, twenty-nine, registered for the draft in Chicago, where he was working as a musician at the Wilson Theatre. Freddie's registration card has not been found, and it is possible he ignored the mandate to register.

The goal of the Selective Service Act was to raise an army through a combination of volunteers and conscription. Members of the state National Guards were anticipated to be made part of the national army, as were any persons who volunteered to serve in the war. Recruiting had gone very slowly in the two months since the declaration of war, however, necessitating the draft. With the selective service information on file, local draft boards could classify men for eligibility and then conscript as many as needed. Automatic exemptions were rare, applying only to ministers and high government officials. Conscientious objection was not allowed as an exemption, although some form of alternative service was supposed to be offered to noncombatants.

James Reese Europe and his band members did not need to register on 5 June because they had already enlisted as volunteers. The Fifteenth Infantry Regiment (Colored) had reached peacetime strength of 1,200 in April and was leading all the other New York National Guard units in recruiting. The goal was to reach full strength of 2,002 as soon as possible. As recruiting continued, though, the question of the unit's eventual role in the national army remained unresolved. The registration requirements were the same for blacks and whites, and in fact the number of African American registrants exceeded whites in many parts of the South.[3] But the official policy of the War Department was still complete segregation of the races. How exactly the government would use African Americans in the military without integration remained to be decided.

After the Fifteenth Regiment's impressive showing in the Memorial Day parade, recruiting increased markedly. The band also participated in a recruiting parade on 16 June and held its own with all of the other units. Noble Sissle recalled the band's integral role in recruiting:

> Our usual daily procedure was to put the band on top of the bus and ride down in a colored section. Then we would start the band playing the "Memphis Blues" or the "Army Blues," the favorite jazz tune of the Colonel's. A large crowd would gather and it was no trouble to get the men and boys of the crowd to get in the bus to take a ride. Once we got the bus crowded we would make a "bee line" for the recruiting office. As we pulled up to the curb the band would start playing again and as our coup "two stepped" out of the bus they were danced right into the recruiting office—a pen put in their hands and before they were aware of what was going on, under the spell of jazzettes they had raised their right hand and found themselves jazz-time members of Uncle Samuel's army.[4]

With the help of techniques like these, the regiment reached wartime strength of 2,002 by the second week of June. The Fifteenth was the first of the New York National Guard regiments to do so.[5]

Col. Hayward's agreement to supplement the salaries of key band members had facilitated recruiting, but it was quickly depleting the fund donated by Daniel Reid. To replenish the fund, Europe scheduled what he called a Great Military Ball & Band Concert at the Manhattan Casino in Harlem on Friday, 22 June. The proceeds of the event, which was advertised for over a month, were to go to support the regimental fund. For a crowd estimated at seven thousand, the band opened the evening with a selection of concert music that earned plaudits from the audience and critics. Charles T. Magill of the *Chicago Defender* called Europe the "Man of the Hour" and pronounced his band "second to none in the New York National Guard." Lester A. Walton of the *New York Age* affirmed that Hayward's goal, to have the best military band in the country, was within reach: "The dozen or more Puerto Ricans who make up the reed section cannot be excelled, and the brass section is improving daily. Before many weeks the Fifteenth ought to have a well-balanced musical organization and one which should be the pride of New York, irrespective of color."[6]

After the concert numbers, the crowd finally got what they came for when the attendants cleared chairs and sprinkled rosin on the dance floor. Sissle recalled the excitement: "Jim Europe did not disappoint the jazz enthusiasts that had gathered there to pay his band homage. . . . The crowd was no more anxious to hear them play some jazz than they were to play it. . . . I will never forget the yell that went up after Jim had conducted the first dance number. What we thought was a wonderful demonstration of appreciation after each concert number, turned out to be but a ripple on the ocean compared with the mighty roar that followed the last strain of the first jazz tune."[7] Europe's band was unlike any other military band in its ability to play popular music. He had accomplished his goal of recruiting top-notch professional musicians with the versatility to play convincingly in any style, and the June concert was the first indication of how far they could go.

At his moment of triumph, Europe was so fatigued that he slipped out of the building. Sissle found his friend outside, crying and trembling from the exertion. Though Europe was an imposing man physically, his thyroid condition had reached a dangerous stage. On Monday he finally saw a surgeon, who scheduled the first of two operations for Wednesday, 27 June. The bandleader was so weak that the surgeon could not risk a general anesthetic, forcing him to use a local anesthetic only. Europe teased and joked with the medical staff, and the surgeon credited his positive attitude with an improved chance of recovery. The second operation was performed ten days after the first, after which he was ordered to rest for six to eight weeks before returning to work. His assistant bandmaster, Gene Mikell, conducted the band while Europe recuperated.

After working nightly at Reisenweber's for nearly five months, the Original Dixieland Jazz Band took a vacation. The restaurant's ads announced that they would be replaced from 18 June through 1 July by Dunbar's Tennessee Ten, an African American vaudeville act similar to the Creole Band but with more dancers. The act offered plantation humor that was unflattering to blacks; like the Creole Band, they had been earning rave reviews for the jazz band that accompanied them. In May the band had performed in a Nora Bayes show entitled "Two Hours of Song," which she had created as a vehicle for herself while awaiting resolution of her managerial dispute. The show was unusual in that three-quarters of the supporting cast was black. The African American paper New York Age, perhaps in a jab at the Creole Band, called the Tennessee Ten "the best colored act that has appeared on the vaudeville stage in a score of years" with "a jazz band that is the best of its kind that has ever appeared on the stage."[8] A week later, New York Age critic Lester A. Walton applauded her decision to use the group: "The Tennessee Ten has been making a big hit in vaudeville, and Miss Bayes has played a trump card in corralling this energetic and clever bunch. They can sing, dance, create merriment and what's more carry a Jazz Band that is some more Jazz Band. I'll wager it can out-jazz any Jazz Band in these parts."[9] Apparently these and other positive reviews were enough to earn Dunbar's Tennessee Ten a two-week booking at Reisenweber's in the ODJB's absence.

During his vacation, the ODJB's trombonist Eddie Edwards travelled home to New Orleans, as verified by a telegram to him from Max Hart dated 23 June: "Nothing can be done until you arrive New York."[10] This telegram almost certainly refers to the publication on 18 June of the sheet music shown in Figure 7.1. Publisher Roger Graham of Chicago had taken advantage of the ODJB's failure to secure a copyright for "Livery Stable Blues" when the record was released in April. As their agent, Max Hart, had copyrighted the title "Barnyard Blues" on 9 April, the title of the Victor record was left unprotected. Graham secured copyrights for the unpublished melody to "Livery Stable Blues" on 12 and 24 May, following up with copyright number E408051 for the published sheet music on 18 June.[11] When the ODJB learned of this publication, they were furious. Not only

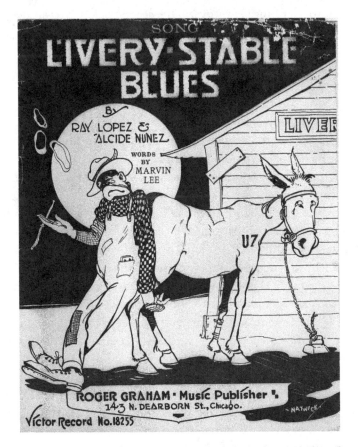

Figure 7.1 Sheet music cover of Roger Graham's edition of "Livery Stable Blues," attributed to Ray Lopez and Alcide Nunez (Rubenstein Library, Duke University).

was their song credited to Ray Lopez and Alcide Nunez as composers, but the cover of the sheet music referred to "Victor Record no. 18255" in the lower left corner. Graham audaciously used the popularity of the ODJB record to sell copies of sheet music falsely attributed to a former bandmate and his friend, whom they had never met. Unable to stop the sale of the sheet music, they filed suit in Chicago against Graham and his colleagues, but the suit would not come to trial until the fall.

Roger Graham was not the only one to realize that imitation is the quickest way to make money in popular music. After the success of the ODJB's April record, other jazz bands hurried into the studio to capitalize on the craze. The Frisco Jazz Band, which had played successfully at the Montmartre Club since the Creole Band's brief run there in March, had four sessions with the Edison Company in the spring and summer of 1917. On 10 May they recorded "Canary Cottage" and "Johnson 'Jass' Blues." On 4 June they recorded "Pozzo" and "Night-Time in Little Italy," followed by the popular "Yah-De-Dah" on 26 July. They recorded three additional sides on 2 August, and their records went on sale the first of October. Earl Fuller of Rector's took his jazz band to Victor, where they recorded "Slippery Hank" and "Yah-De-Dah" on 4 June, followed by further sessions on 13 August and 10 September. None of these recordings approached the driving energy of the ODJB records, but they helped feed the popular hunger for jazz records when they were released in the fall.

The annual meeting of the board of directors of the New York Symphony Orchestra took place on 27 May in the home of its millionaire benefactor, Henry Harkness Flagler. It was reported that the orchestra had performed 150 concerts during the past year, including 70 during the recent nine-week transcontinental tour. The New York concerts had been so popular that the directors voted to move the Friday afternoon series from Aeolian Hall to the larger Carnegie Hall for the upcoming 1917/18 season. This meeting brought the 1916/17 season to a conclusion, allowing Damrosch a well-earned vacation.

The fact that Walter Damrosch was one of the busiest men in American music did not prevent him from taking on another assignment. In mid-June he was offered and accepted the directorship of the Oratorio Society of New York, an organization that had been founded by his father, Leopold, in 1873. In his acceptance letter dated 15 June, he described his feelings at this honor:

I am much touched and appreciate deeply that the old Oratorio Society should turn to me again in its hour of need for such assistance as I might be able to give it. Such a call compels me to put personal convenience and any other considerations aside, and I shall be glad to serve the society as its conductor for the coming season, with the understanding that during that time we shall put our best thoughts together in order to find the right man as permanent conductor. . . .[12]

The phrase "hour of need" alludes to the internal strife that led to his appointment and threatened to split the society as it raged throughout the summer. There is no evidence that Damrosch was involved in the machinations that preceded the change of directors, but there were those who took issue with his use of this loaded phrase. His complicity highlights the politics of New York musical organizations at this time.

When Leopold Damrosch founded the Oratorio Society in 1873, he patterned it after the great choral societies of Germany. The singers who made up the society were all amateurs, and each paid dues for the privilege of singing in the society. Musical standards were high, and the demands for attendance and musical competence rivalled those of professional organizations even though the singers were not paid. Concerts were accompanied by a professional orchestra, and soloists were also paid professionals. The conductor, in true democratic fashion, was elected by the members. For its first forty years, the society was conducted by a Damrosch—first Leopold, then his son Walter, and then Walter's brother Frank. In 1912, Frank had resigned and the position was given to Louis Koemmenich.

The new conductor was popular with the singers and achieved mostly good results, but early in 1917 the board of directors quietly set about changing its bylaws to allow the board's executive committee to choose the organization's conductor rather than put it to a vote of the membership. When they exercised this prerogative by replacing Koemmenich in June, the mostly German members of the society challenged the board, accusing it of autocratic methods that had "out-Kaisered the Kaiser." The membership passed a resolution in favor of Koemmenich by a vote of 116 to 3. The *New York Sun* snidely remarked, "Music hath charms to soothe the savage breast, but it is a fact that the pacifists aren't in it with Music, heavenly maid, for stirring up a real good healthy row."[13] The Cincinnati *Volksblatt* summarized the views of the German American community on the dispute:

Trotzdem sich seitens der Majorität der Mitglieder der Oratorien-Gesellschaft, New York, eine große Opposition gegen das eigenmächtige Vorgehen des Direktorenraths kundgab, der den bisherigen Chormeister Louis Kömmenich ohne weiteres absetzte und an seine Stelle den früheren Dirigenten Walter

Damrosch mit der Leitung des Chors betraute, so bleibt es anscheinend vorläufig bei Damroschs Wiederwahl.

Despite a great opposition announced on the part of a majority of the members of the Oratorio Society of New York against the arbitrary action of the directorship, which simply removed the current choral director Louis Koemmenich and in his place entrusted the leadership of the choir to the former conductor Walter Damrosch, it apparently stands for the moment by Damrosch's re-election.[14]

In common with many of the other musical conflicts in this tempestuous year, the hostile takeover of the Oratorio Society was symbolic of much more than a musical power struggle. The actions of the board were decried as arbitrary, heavy-handed, and autocratic, in opposition to the democratic traditions of the organization. It smacked of Prussian methods, which Damrosch himself had criticized repeatedly. In his speech to San Francisco's Commonwealth Club in April, he had said, "Art is the flower of a civilization. When you think of German glory you do not think of the [Prussian] Hohenzollerns, but rather of Schiller, of Goethe, of Bach and of Wagner. These are the representatives of German greatness."[15] Many of the German Americans were descendants of persons who had left Germany in search of greater freedom in America. For them the notion that all Germans endorsed the militaristic regime of the Kaiser was an unfair generalization. The ouster of Koemmenich over the objections of the rank-and-file singers seemed to undermine the very democratic principles that had drawn their ancestors to America.

While Damrosch added the Oratorio Society to his list of responsibilities, many of his professional colleagues were preparing for a summer vacation. Karl and Anita Muck, Fritz and Harriet Kreisler, and Leopold Stokowski and Olga Samaroff all prepared to relax in comfort for several months. Before the war began, they had often spent their summers in Europe, but for the past two years their destination of choice was Maine. There, in the little village of Seal Harbor, many of America's most renowned musicians relaxed and prepared for the next season's concerts.

CHAPTER 8

⌒

Summer

July–August 1917

The summer of 1917 brought the concert season to an end. Before the introduction of air conditioning, the large crowds and closed spaces of the concert hall and vaudeville theater made indoor events unbearable for at least three months a year. Outdoor performances were possible, but instruments like the violin and piano did not project as well as the brass and woodwind instruments in open spaces. Summer offered ample employment for bands, while orchestral musicians and classical soloists went on vacation.

Vacation did not mean leaving music behind, however. Performers in the competitive and specialized world of classical music generally took a busman's holiday, using the summer to study scores, learn new music, and keep their skills in top shape. The *Musical Courier* poked fun at the typical vacation of a musician with a piece entitled "A Virtuoso's Summer," published in the 2 August 1917 issue:

> Packing six cases full of music to take to the seashore.
>
> Missing nine days of practice waiting for the piano to be freighted from New York.
>
> Finding a spot to move about in after the piano is placed in the cottage parlor.
>
> Neighbor to the left is discovered to have a mechanical voice producing machine.
>
> Neighbor to the right is discovered to have a mechanical piano.

Neighbor across the street is discovered to have two children, one of whom is studying the violin and the other is tampering with the ukulele.

It is too warm to keep the windows shut and shut out the neighboring noises.

On account of the piano, it is too damp to keep the windows open.

Every second day it comes to light that some important piece in the repertoire has been left in New York and a trip to the warehouse trunks becomes necessary.

The pedals and keys of the piano surrender to the sea air and begin to stick.

The piano goes out of tune.

A man comes from town to put the piano in order. He charges $8 and has to be asked to stay for lunch. . . .

The pianist cannot go bathing for fear of catching lumbago.

He cannot play tennis for fear of stiffening his forearm muscles.

He cannot ride horseback for fear of falling off and breaking an arm.

His manager writes him that the dates are filling slowly for the coming season. . . .

The pianist's wife suggests that he does not make any concessions to the public taste, and if he did, could earn more money.

The pianist, in reply, smashes $98 worth of the furniture and bric-a-brac belonging to the hired cottage.

His troubled existence has only one oasis of pleasure—when he receives his MUSICAL COURIER every Thursday morning at 9 a.m.

He discovers at 9.05 that a comma has been omitted from his advertisement, and spends $1.30 calling up ye editor on the long distance 'phone and abusing that wretch loudly and long.[1]

If this tongue-in-cheek account has any truth, it did not apply to Kreisler, Damrosch, Samaroff, or Muck. These elite musicians had the privilege of summering on Mount Desert Island, Maine, home to the villages of Bar Harbor and Seal Harbor and playground of the richest and most powerful families in America. In close proximity to the Rockefellers, the Pulitzers, the Carnegies, and the Vanderbilts, the aristocracy of the classical music world set up a summer enclave where they could rest, socialize, and plan for the upcoming season.

Before the outbreak of the war, many artists had spent summers in Europe. They attended European festivals in Bayreuth, Salzburg, or other cities, they vacationed at spas, and some of them owned property there. All of that changed in 1914, when the declaration of war in July placed many concert artists in vulnerable positions. The assassination of Austrian Archduke

Franz Ferdinand on 28 June 1914 touched off a domino effect prepared by complicated international treaties. Austria-Hungary issued an ultimatum to Serbia, then declared war on 28 July when demands were not met. Russia mobilized in defense of Serbia, and Germany entered the war on the side of Austria. When Germany invaded Belgium and Luxembourg en route to France, the United Kingdom entered the war in their defense. Within days of Austria's declaration of war on Serbia, most of Europe was a war zone, with artists who had planned to perform in America in fall 1914 uncertain of their status. The stories of their escapes became legendary.

Olga Samaroff and her husband, Leopold Stokowski, owned a home in Munich, where they spent their summers before the war. In 1914, Samaroff, with the singer Sara Cahier, was scheduled for a tour of German spa towns beginning in Bad Reichenhall, just over the Bavarian border from Austria. On the day of their concert, it was announced that if war were declared there would be six cannon shots at precisely six o'clock. When the hour arrived, the shots were heard, followed by a band playing "Deutschland, Deutschland über Alles." Not knowing what to expect, the musicians found a full house at the concert hall and performed their program to enthusiastic acclaim. In her memoirs, she recalled, "In a sense the evening was—for all of us—a farewell to the old order of things, and we felt it in a vague way although the full significance of those cannon shots was mercifully hidden from us. From that day on, our cosmopolitan world of music was filled with problems, changes and tragedies."[2] Samaroff, a US citizen, was protected by her country's neutrality, but Stokowski, an English citizen of Polish ancestry, was not. They cancelled the rest of the tour, arranged for the Red Cross to use their Munich home for the duration of the war, and sailed for America from the neutral port of Rotterdam on 15 August.[3]

Ossip and Clara Gabrilowitsch also had a home in Munich, but they spent their summers in the picturesque Bavarian town of Kreuth, just across the border from Austria. There they entertained guests that included the Stokowskis, the New York critic Henry T. Finck and his wife, Abbie, and various German musicians. Born in St. Petersburg, Gabrilowitsch was the conductor of the Munich Konzertverein from 1910 to 1914 and was preparing to take out German naturalization papers. His wife, Clara Clemens, whom he had married in 1905, was the daughter of American author Mark Twain. When the war broke out, Gabrilowitsch was arrested under suspicion of being a Russian spy, and it was only through the intervention of the German conductor Bruno Walter and the papal nuncio to Bavaria that he was released. Clara and Ossip sailed from Naples, Italy, on 11 October 1914, and arrived in New York on the 28th.[4] Like the Stokowskis, they left their Munich home at the disposal of the Red Cross.

Ernestine Schumann-Heink, the daughter of an Austrian army officer but a naturalized US citizen since 1905, was singing at the Wagner Festival in Bayreuth under the baton of Karl Muck during the summer of 1914. The declaration of war was announced at intermission of a performance of *Parsifal*, and the war enthusiasm ran so high that numerous members of the orchestra who were in the military reserves simply abandoned their instruments and left at intermission. Somehow Muck managed to finish the performance with a reduced orchestra, and Schumann-Heink sang her role. The following days brought a mad scramble to leave the country before the borders were closed. She had money in her US bank, but not enough cash in hand to buy tickets for her family and accompanist. Her lawyer contacted the US Secretary of State, William Jennings Bryan, who made arrangements for safe transport through the consul-general in Coburg. With the trains diverted for war use, she found an automobile and began to drive to Coburg, but they were accosted repeatedly on the road. She then took an American flag out of her bag and asked the chauffeur to attach it to the front of the vehicle, which allowed them to pass freely to their destination. She and her entourage eventually reached Rotterdam, where they sailed back home to the United States on an overcrowded liner.[5]

Karl Muck was not in as much of a hurry to leave as Schumann-Heink. Though technically a Swiss citizen, his loyalties lay with Germany, and he returned to Berlin after his duties were complete in Weimar. There he approached the ministry of war about enlisting but met with a disappointing result, as the War Ministry did not accept his offer because of his age of fifty-four. Boston Symphony Orchestra manager Charles Ellis was in Europe to arrange safe transport for the many members who had been vacationing on the continent, and he reported in a letter to Higginson that it was only through appealing to Muck's wife Anita that he convinced the conductor to return to Boston.[6] Karl and Anita sailed from Rotterdam on 27 September, arriving in New York on 7 October 1914.

Fritz and Harriet Kreisler were vacationing at a spa in Ragaz, Switzerland, when war broke out in the summer of 1914. As a former reserve officer in the Austrian army, he was ordered to report for duty on 31 July. The mobilization happened so fast that by 10 August he was on his way to the front. Within weeks his battalion was fighting in the battle of Lemberg, one of the crucial engagements of the first months of World War I. Kreisler later recalled the scenes of horror he witnessed:

> The first man you see die affects you terribly. I shall not forget mine. He sat in a
> trench and suddenly he began to cough—two or three times—like an old man.
> A little blood showed at his mouth and then he toppled over and lay quiet. That

was all. Very shortly none of these things affect you. It has made me mournful when I have thought how quickly we all threw over everything the centuries have taught us. One day we were all ordinary civilized men. Two or three days later our "culture" had dropped aside like a cloak and we were brutal and primeval.[7]

On 7 September, it was reported in the press that Kreisler had been killed, but Harriet had not been officially notified. She was reunited with her wounded, emaciated husband when he limped off the train in Vienna on 10 September. Her letter to her parents in America was published in the *Musical Courier*'s 13 September issue, to the relief of music lovers throughout the country. In October he was declared medically unfit for military duty, and on 24 November he arrived in New York. His memoir, *Four Weeks in the Trenches: The War Story of a Violinist*, gave American audiences a moving account of his ordeal.[8] He returned to the concert stage with a triumphant 12 December 1914 concert in Carnegie Hall. Though he limped slightly and was thinner than before, audiences welcomed him enthusiastically.

These musicians had all seen their old homes, friendships, and artistic connections devastated by the war. Throughout 1915 and 1916 they hoped that it would be short lived, and the pacifists among them hoped that the United States would remain neutral. By the summer of 1917, the country was at war, anti-German feelings ran high, and the artists were more grateful than ever for a refuge. The Damrosch brothers had been attracted to Mount Desert Island long before—Walter and his family to Bar Harbor and Frank and his family to Seal Harbor. By the summer of 1917, there were dozens of musicians summering in the area. Besides the Stokowskis, the Kreislers, the Mucks, and the Gabrilowitsches, there were the pianists Harold Bauer, Leopold Godowsky, Carl Friedberg, Fannie Bloomfield-Zeisler, Josef Hoffmann, and Ernest Schelling; the harpist Carlos Salzedo; and the conductor Artur Bodanzky.

The quaint villages were surrounded by natural landscape. Clara Clemens recalled, "Enchanting paths through the deep woods reminded us of Germany. Colored signs on the trees guided the wanderer, who could now forget the city, even if not the war."[9] In fact it was the desire to protect the rural spaces from overdevelopment that led several of the island's wealthiest residents to donate land and to advocate setting aside most of the island as the first national park east of the Mississippi.[10] The small island, fifteen miles long and ten miles wide, was home to a range of topographies, including wooded mountains up to 1,762 feet high, inland ponds, streams, ocean beaches, and a five-mile fjord that was the only one of its kind on the

Atlantic coast. Automobiles had first been allowed on the island two years previously, and in 1917 the local horses and their drivers were still getting used to the big-city motorists. Fritz Kreisler was notorious for his erratic driving, and Josef Hofmann had a penchant for doing mechanical work on his own automobiles. According to the *Bar Harbor Times*, "It would be hard, indeed, to imagine a more beautiful spot than Mount Desert. Here the traveler can find rest and relief from the sights and sounds of city life. The views from the tops of the mountains embrace an immense extent of ocean, woods and shore. There is a network of wood paths and trails covering the whole island and maintained by the village improvement societies and by private subscription."[11]

The musicians who summered on this Maine island enjoyed the solitude, but they also craved the companionship of professional colleagues. During the concert season, these artists were often too busy touring and rehearsing to relax and socialize together, so a vacation with fellow performers was attractive. Samaroff recalled, "One of the most precious features of the war summers at Seal Harbor was the opportunity for close friendship with congenial musicians. We not only shared pleasant hours of relaxation and stimulating musical experiences, but were drawn close by our interest in world affairs and their effect on our profession. We all knew that whatever the outcome of the war might be, profound changes were taking place in our world of music"[12] (see Figure 8.1). Whereas life in Bar Harbor was very fashionable and governed by strict social rules, the atmosphere in Seal Harbor, nine miles away by the Ocean Drive, was more informal.[13] The village consisted of only one street, with a store, a market, a post office, two hotels, and cottages lining the ocean road. It also had one of two sand beaches on the island.

The "musical colony" had gained national attention in 1916 through the hijinks of its members, described in the *New York Times*, the *San Francisco Chronicle*, and other papers. A full-page article by Clara Clemens in the *New York Times* humorously portrayed their antics through an imaginary conversation between local Maine residents. The accompanying photos showed several of the world's leading concert pianists cavorting with a lawn mower and imitating ballet dancing during a mountain hike. The "long-haired" musicians Gabrilowitsch, Godowsky, Stokowski, and Bauer were pictured with heads shaved on a dare.[14] The high-spirited pranks included practical jokes: Gabrilowitsch was fond of surprising his friends by putting cold things—like a toy dragon for Josef Hofmann— in their beds.[15] With their European friends in mortal danger and their own careers hanging precariously, many of the same musicians returned in 1917, along with others hoping to join the camaraderie. In the words of

Figure 8.1 Clara Clemens Gabrilowitsch, Nina Gabrilowitsch, Ossip Gabrilowitsch, Leopold Stokowski, and Olga Samaroff Stokowski in Maine (Mount Desert Studio).

Samaroff, "The temperament of the artist is inclined to extremes of melancholy and gaiety. In order to relieve the tension of a profound war depression which we all felt very deeply, we resorted to gay frolics which were sometimes so amusing that for a few hours we forgot the woes of the world."[16]

Although Walter Damrosch spent little time on the island in 1917, he and his wife, Margaret, were known as gracious hosts at their home in Bar Harbor. They not only had more social connections than the other musicians, but they also had a larger home and more financial resources. In the summer of 1916, they had hosted a legendary evening of charades described in Samaroff's memoirs. During the summer of 1917, Walter was busy both planning the New York Symphony season and negotiating the politics of the Oratorio Society. In addition, he was called upon to serve on a committee charged by the commissioner of education with preparing an "official" version of "The Star-Spangled Banner" that would reconcile the numerous discrepancies among the various editions in use at this time. The members of the committee—Damrosch, John Philip Sousa, Oscar T. G. Sonneck, A. J. Gantvoort, and Will Earhart—were too busy to meet in person, so they conducted their deliberations by a curious method of voting. Each musician submitted his preferred version of the melody, and the five versions were compared for discrepancies. Each case of disagree-ment (for instance, the rhythm of the opening gesture of the first phrase), was submitted to a vote by strict majority rule. The result was a combina-tion of the five melodies chosen according to a form of popularity contest. When the melody was finalized, Damrosch was delegated to provide a har-monization that would be both easy to sing and appealing to hear.[17]

Even on vacation, the musicians were preoccupied with music. The artists each practiced personal repertoire for upcoming concerts, and they also enjoyed sight-reading duets and trios together as a diversion. Pianists Samaroff, Harold Bauer, and Ossip Gabrilowitsch had been engaged for a series of performances during the coming season of Bach's Concerto for Three Keyboards, and they took numerous opportunities to rehearse to-gether that summer. Samaroff later wrote, "The result made me wish artists could more frequently strive for a perfect ensemble in this manner instead of playing a concerto through once at an orchestra rehearsal according to the prevailing custom. Routine experience and the inspiration of the moment combine to achieve more or less satisfactory results at concerts despite the traditional single rehearsal of the soloist with the orchestra, but our preparation of the Bach Triple Concerto was something very different."[18] Several of the artists gave benefit concerts for local charitable organizations on the island. The conductors were busy studying scores for the upcoming season. Leopold Stokowski, at the suggestion of Alexander van Rensselaer, president of the Philadelphia Orchestra Association, began planning a program of American orchestral works for the season's first concert. When that plan came to fruition in October, it was reported that during his summer at Seal Harbor, Stokowski had evaluated 122 orchestral scores by American composers in an effort to identify works that he could program for the season. Eighteen of the scores met his standards for the Philadelphia Orchestra.[19]

Karl and Anita Muck were new to Mount Desert Island in the summer of 1917. They rented a cottage called "The Lichen," on Ox Hill Road above Seal Harbor, that boasted a commanding view of the ocean and was removed from the noise of the village. This cottage, which had been occupied for at least a decade through 1915 by the amateur wireless enthusiast Dr. A. E. Lawrence of New York, was ideal for the Mucks. It gave him the isolation he needed and gave both of them the sunshine they valued. His time was occupied with planning repertoire for over a hundred Boston Symphony Orchestra concerts for the new season and also with hiking. According to the orchestra's manager, Charles Ellis, he walked ten to fifteen miles a day, rain or shine, and had never been in better health.[20] Unlike Stokowski, Muck made no pretense of considering American music for the upcoming season. An article in the *Musical Courier* of 13 September discussed his deliberations and named some of the composers he was considering— Bach, Liszt, Beethoven, Schumann, Handel, Haydn, Mozart, Raff, Scriabin, Delius, and Svendsen—among whom were no Americans.[21]

The tight-knit community of musicians relished each other's company, but their eccentric habits and standoffishness roused the suspicions of their neighbors. The newly formed Military Intelligence Section, which was organized during the summer of 1917, documented reports of suspicious activity. It was rumored that three of the highest cottages overlooking the ocean had been rented at exorbitant prices by German sympathizers. Agents investigated reports of signal lights being flashed to ships after dark, only to discover that "two elderly ladies and several girls" were reading with the blinds open and had turned the lights on and off when moving between rooms. Lists were compiled of possible German sympathizers for further observation.

Among the musicians on the island was the American pianist and composer Ernest Schelling. The New Jersey native was a piano student of Leschetizky and Paderewski, and his compositions were highly acclaimed. Fritz Kreisler had played Schelling's Violin Concerto with Karl Muck and the Boston Symphony Orchestra in the fall of 1916, and Muck featured Schelling as piano soloist in his *Impressions of an Artist's Life* in early 1916. Unknown to the musical residents of Mount Desert Island, Schelling had recently enlisted in the army and trained as a military intelligence officer. On 21 August he filed a secret report detailing the vulnerabilities of the island to foreign infiltration and listed suspicious persons on the island, including Muck, Stokowski, and other musicians with whom he had worked in the past.[22]

In this time of fear and anxiety, suspicion was everywhere, and no one was immune from its probing gaze. As prominent Americans of German birth, Walter Damrosch and his brother Frank were especially vigilant about any questions of their patriotism. The family members still spoke German at home, but their outward persona was that of a thoroughly American family. During the summer of 1915, their sister Ellie, her husband Harry Seymour, and their children vacationed at York Harbor, Maine, farther down the coast than Mount Desert Island. As Ellie sat on the beach with her children, they were joined by her aunt ("Tante") Marie von Heimburg. Tante began talking excitedly in German about her family members in Germany and her fears for their safety, as Ellie tried to calm her. Within a short while the children noticed that others on the beach had moved away from the family and were whispering among themselves. For the rest of the summer, the children felt ostracized.[23] It was no doubt experiences like these that famously led Walter to begin his 1923 memoir with the statement, "I am an American musician and have lived in this country since my ninth year."[24]

Fritz and Harriet Kreisler spent most of the summer in Seal Harbor, but he travelled often to visit friends and to prepare for the 1917/18 season— in particular, rehearsing for three concerts he had agreed to play with the members of the Kneisel String Quartet. The Rumanian violinist Franz Kneisel, former concertmaster of the Boston Symphony Orchestra, had for decades been one of the world's pre-eminent chamber musicians as leader of the Kneisel Quartet. His announced retirement in 1917 caused such widespread disappointment that Kreisler, who was known as a soloist rather than a chamber player, agreed to take his place in three high-profile concerts to keep the quartet from disbanding.[25] As the summer home of the quartet in Blue Hill, Maine, was less than an hour from Seal Harbor, the four could rehearse regularly. Kreisler also visited the Connecticut home of his friend John McCormack, an Irish tenor whose concerts, like Kreisler's, mixed classical repertoire with sentimental folk songs. Also like Kreisler, McCormack was one of America's most popular concert artists. The two musicians were reported to be avid tennis players, despite the risk to Kreisler's hands.[26]

During this July visit, the two performers decided to perform a concert on 18 August at the Great Auditorium in Ocean Grove, New Jersey. This resort town, which had hosted religious camp meetings since 1869, was a popular summer destination in the early twentieth century. Built in 1894, the Great Auditorium had a capacity of ten thousand. The acoustics were exceptional for a summer venue with such a large seating capacity, making it an attractive destination for concert artists.

The last-minute planning for this concert was unusual in a profession where events are scheduled months if not years in advance. According to publicity for the concert, the two musician friends were visiting each other in late July when they came up with the idea of a joint concert, something they had never done despite enormous popularity in their respective fields. Their managers were able to book the Ocean Grove Auditorium for a Saturday night in August, and the Pennsylvania Railroad agreed to run a special late train from Asbury Park to Newark and New York to allow attendees from those cities to get home after the concert. Ticket sales opened on 13 August; by Saturday the 18th, all had been sold for one of the largest concerts in Ocean Grove history. Despite the addition of a thousand stage seats, three thousand persons were turned away.

The advance publicity told of the only previous performance of the two stars at "a joint private recital." After all the other guests had left a reception, so the story went, Kreisler sat down and began to play the piano, where he was joined by McCormack, who sang all manner of music from symphonic themes to operatic arias, with their wives as the only witnesses. Music lovers were invited to join them for their first public concert, where they would both perform their specialties.[27] Accompanied alternately by piano and organ, the two treated the audience to a program of crowd-pleasers, from arias and violin works by Handel to Irish folk songs and Kreisler's own compositions. A sentimental favorite came when Kreisler sat at the piano to accompany McCormack's singing of Kreisler's song "The Old Refrain." They closed the concert with a request number, the Bach-Gounod "Ave Maria," sung by McCormack and accompanied by Kreisler on violin with the two keyboardists.[28] According to the *New York Times*, the receipts totaled a record $12,000. This report added that, "the great audience made the artists more than double their intended program with encores."[29]

In the summer of 1917, there was no vacation for Ernestine Schumann-Heink, as the fifty-six-year-old contralto returned to performing after her prolonged recuperation. During July and August she toured the country, singing more concerts than any of her colleagues. Most of the events were benefit concerts for patriotic organizations in support of soldiers, their families, or relief agencies that served them. From California, where she performed many times in July, to a benefit concert for "Mothers, babies, and disabled aviators" in the Manhattan Opera House on 30 July, to concerts at Chautauqua meetings in Indiana, Illinois, Iowa, Nebraska, and other midwestern states in August, then back to San Francisco at the end of August, she sang at numerous outdoor venues. The *Musical Courier* review of the San Francisco concert typified her reception wherever she sang:

> Mme. Schumann-Heink was welcomed by a five thousand dollar house at the
> Civic Center Auditorium, San Francisco, the evening of August 30. That is, the
> receipts were $5,000, but Mme. Schumann-Heink sang gratuitously, for the
> benefit of soldiers. She was in superb voice; she had a fine program; she gave
> the best she had—the greatest—and her audience rewarded her with such
> applause as is seldom heard. She wove her spell over their minds and their
> hearts, and they paid the tribute of reverence to genius in a spontaneous and
> whole souled way.[30]

Her concerts and recordings were so popular that it was reported in June that soldiers in the officers' training camp in Plattsburg, New York, asked for opera rather than ragtime records. A much-reprinted poem was attributed to one of the officers there:

> A turkey trot
> Is really not
> The thing that we are after.
>   Our brows are high;
>   We chortle, "fie"
> At brainless song and laughter.
>   "Poor Butterfly"
>   Invokes our sigh
> And only makes us blue, so
>   Give us that queen,
>   Fair Geraldine,
> Schumann-Heink and Caruso.[31]

During the summer of 1917, Ernestine Schumann-Heink had a compelling reason to participate in benefit performances in support of the war effort. As readers throughout the country learned, she was trapped in a parent's nightmare. Among her seven surviving children were five sons of conscription age. Her oldest son, August, was an officer in the German navy, her sons Henry and Walter were part of the US navy, and her son Ferdinand was drafted by the US army in the summer of 1917. In early August, Ferdinand appealed to Arizona Governor Campbell for an exemption from military service because he did not wish to fight against his brother and other German relatives. Governor Campbell had no power to intervene in the matter, and in late August the exemption request was denied, forcing Ferdinand to enlist in the army. Newspapers ran a photo montage of the mother and her five sons (the youngest, George, enlisted later in the year) along with a poignant story by Chicago journalist Howard Mann.[32] In another interview, the singer confided her pain: "Oh, may the good God give me courage. Sometimes I feel I cannot bear it—this tearing of my heartstrings, this frightful conflict of loves! Was ever woman so tortured and so tried? . . . I thank God for my children and for my work. But if my boys are taken from me by this cruel and needless war I think my work and my life will be ended. I love this country. But I love all countries. And so I pray for peace."[33]

In the summer of 1917, both the newly established Military Intelligence Section and the Justice Department opened suspect files on

Schumann-Heink. Both agencies received persistent rumors about her German sympathies, and they were particularly suspicious of one of her employees by the name of Wilhelm Besthorn, who was suspected of being a spy. Despite her frequent public statements of support for the United States, investigators considered her a security risk, and they grew increasingly wary as she performed on military bases where she might have access to information that would aid the enemy.[34]

At the same time that Ferdinand Schumann was lobbying for an exemption to avoid fighting in Europe, the men of the Fifteenth New York Infantry were lobbying for the right to fight in Europe like other American men. The War Office had not decided what to do with black draftees, and Col. Hayward made it clear to his superiors that he wished to see black soldiers included in the army on an equal basis. The draft had not discriminated against men on the basis of race, and the percentage of colored draftees who were granted exemptions was lower than for whites, but the top brass had evidently not considered how to include all these prospective soldiers in a segregated army. Those deliberations stretched out for months in the summer of 1917. An editorial cartoon in the 5 July issue of the *New York Age* (see Figure 8.2) showed a black soldier in uniform urging a pensive Uncle Sam holding a can of paint to "Wipe out the color line."[35] On the editorial page of the same issue, the editors pointed out the discrepancy between the lackluster response among whites to the president's latest call for volunteers and the navy's stated intention to use blacks for kitchen duty and menial jobs only.

If anyone had a justification for requesting an exemption, it was James Reese Europe. His two thyroid surgeries saved his life, but they left him weak and thin. He recuperated for six weeks before rejoining his regiment in mid-August. During his convalescence he was asked by an old friend why he did not apply for a medical discharge, to which he responded, "If I could, I would not. My country calls me and I must answer; if I live to come back, I will startle the world with my music."[36] As he recuperated, the band continued to grow under the leadership of assistant bandmaster Francis Eugene Mikell, who attracted new players and led frequent performances as the band coalesced. Among Mikell's acquisitions were the drummers Steven and Herbert Wright, who quickly became popular with audiences for their ability to play in a variety of styles.[37]

Though the US government had declared war on Germany in April and conducted a draft in June, the country had a woeful shortage of military training facilities. The summer of 1917 saw a mad scramble to

Figure 8.2 Editorial cartoon by Russell (*New York Age*, 5 July 1917).

construct camps for basic training and to order clothing and equipment
for the millions of recruits. On 15 July it was announced that thirty-two
cantonments would be built throughout the country for training the new
national army. Each of the camps was named after a US military hero with
connections to the local area, with several of the southern camps named
after Confederate officers.[38] Southern camps were to be the principal sites
for training during the winter months.

The consolidation of National Guard units with volunteers and draftees
into a newly organized national army illustrated the War Department's
failure to face questions of racial segregation. The New York National
Guard units were combined in early July to form the Sixth Division
USA, scheduled to train at Camp Wadsworth in Spartanburg, South
Carolina. Since a division consisted of nine regiments, four of the thirteen New York National Guard regiments—including the Fifteenth—were

initially unassigned. When it was announced on 21 July that these extra units would probably be attached to those of Louisiana, Mississippi, and Arkansas, the Mississippi congressional delegation lodged an immediate protest against the inclusion of the Fifteenth Regiment's black soldiers in this group. The War Department responded that the other three regiments of white soldiers were intended, not the Fifteenth. A week later, the Sixth Division was expanded to include the four previously unattached regiments, solving the problem temporarily by keeping all the New York troops together.[39]

The New York National Guard units were mobilized into the US Army on Monday, 16 July. The other eighteen thousand troops in New York City continued to live at their armories in the city until orders came for shipping out to one of the southern camps in a grand "Send-Off Day" parade.[40] The Fifteenth Regiment, which did not have its own armory, was sent back to the Peekskill facility, now called Camp Whitman, where the men began training and awaited orders for mustering. Thousands of friends and family wished them well at the train station, as the regimental band led the way playing "Billy Boy," dedicated to Col. Hayward. By late morning they were setting up tents at Camp Whitman.[41]

The regimental band continued to grow in size and fame during its five weeks at Camp Whitman. Three more Puerto Rican musicians who joined the band on 22 July brought it closer to the target size of sixty musicians. The band entertained troops in camp daily, and on Monday, 6 August, the town of Poughkeepsie hosted them in a two-hour concert at Eastman Park. This concert was so popular that the band was invited back on Friday to help send off the men of Poughkeepsie's National Guard Company K in the morning and then play a concert at the Hudson River State Hospital later in the day. When Governor Whitman reviewed the troops on Sunday, 12 August, he declared the band to be "one of the best in the state."[42] Part of the appeal of the band was the catchy new song that had been composed by C. Lucky Roberts to words by Lester A. Walton, music editor of the *New York Age*. "Billy Boy" was the nickname of their commanding officer, Col. William Hayward, but the lyrics so neatly applied the nickname to American soldiers in general that some believed it would be a fitting substitute for the objectionable name "Sammy" that the French were then using for American soldiers.[43]

In mid-August the regiment left Camp Whitman and was split up into smaller units assigned to guard duty at federal facilities throughout the Northeast. The two largest contingents were at Camp Upton, on Long Island, and Camp Dix, at Wrightstown, NJ, outside Philadelphia, where the regimental band was stationed. The soldiers arrived while the barracks were still under construction, and their duty was to maintain order in the camp as construction was completed and tens of thousands of recruits came pouring in.[44] The assignment was relatively easy, since guard duty was not as strenuous as the rigorous drilling of basic training. During this two-month stint the band welcomed Jim Europe back, and he continued the work that Mikell had started.

During the band's first week at Camp Dix, the army's racial tension reached a boiling point because of violent events in another part of the country. A regiment of African American troops stationed in Houston, Texas, had been the targets of constant harassment by the local white populace until they finally responded with violence during the night of 23–24 August. About two hundred black soldiers armed themselves and marched on Houston, resulting in the deaths of five police officers, nine civilians, and four soldiers. To white southerners the Houston Race Riot demonstrated the danger of stationing armed black men in the South; to blacks the riot was a reminder that they were not welcome in the South and could be the target of racial hostility. Throughout the fall of 1917, as the Fifteenth Infantry prepared for the possibility of fighting in France, they followed the news of the court-martials of the soldiers who had rioted in Houston, thirteen of whom were hanged in December.[45]

Despite being commended repeatedly for exemplary behavior, the Fifteenth New York Regiment became the object of scrutiny and suspicion after the Houston Race Riot. On 28 August, four days after the riot, an article in the *New York Times* announced a parade and dinner to be held for the twenty-eight thousand New York troops stationed in the city preparatory to their departure for training at Camp Wadsworth in Spartanburg, South Carolina. It was noted that the parade would not include the Fifteenth Regiment, since they would go directly to Spartanburg. The reaction from South Carolina was swift: though construction on the training camp had not even been completed, citizens of Spartanburg made a pre-emptive protest against the possibility that the Fifteenth would be assigned to their town. According to Mayor J. F. Floyd, the city had requested a training camp with the understanding that African American troops would not be sent there. His threatening words exemplify the world of the Jim Crow South:

> I was sorry to learn that the Fifteenth Regiment has been ordered here, for, with their Northern ideas about race equality, they will probably expect to be treated like white men. I can say right here that they will not be treated as anything except negroes. We shall treat them exactly as we treat our resident negroes. . . . It is a great mistake to send Northern negroes down here, for they do not understand our attitude. We wouldn't mind it if the Government sent us a regiment

of Southern negroes; we understand them and they understand us. But with those Northern fellows it's different. I can tell you for certain that if any of those colored soldiers go in any of our soda stores and the like and ask to be served they'll be knocked down. Somebody will throw a bottle. We don't allow negroes to use the same glass that a white man may later have to drink out of. We have our customs down here, and we aren't going to alter them.[46]

In fact, the New Yorkers understood their attitude all too well. Several members of the regiment had been born and raised in South Carolina, including assistant conductor Mikell. But understanding did not make them compliant. As they anticipated a possible deployment to a camp in the South, the African American members of the Fifteenth Regiment and their white commander, Col. Hayward, began planning their response to racial hostility.

As the impending departure of American troops to the war drew closer, New Yorkers sought recreation of all sorts to fill their evenings. Chief among these was the new fad for jazz dancing. When indoor restaurants and ballrooms grew too hot for comfort, the bands and their patrons moved to the seashore or to the roof. At Reisenweber's, the Original Dixieland Jazz Band returned to the 400 Club on 2 July, after a break in June when they had been replaced by Dunbar's Tennessee Ten ("Playing 'Jazz' Melodies Nightly"). Within a short time they moved from the 400 Club to the Paradise Roof Garden, advertised as the "Airiest Garden Spot—Coolest Place in Town." There they supplied dance music through Labor Day weekend. From 6 to 9 p.m., guests could fortify themselves with a "Special Southern Dinner" for $1.50, reinforcing the connection of jazz music with the South.

For those who could not attend a cabaret, records provided an alternative. The ODJB's record of "At the Darktown Strutters' Ball" and "Indiana," recorded on 31 May, was released commercially in mid-August. The prominence of this recording in the Columbia advertisements that appeared nationally starting on 9 August illustrates the popularity of the band and the genre. On the same advertisements, there was a recording by Rector's Novelty Orchestra of "Cold Turkey" and "12th Street Rag." The first was denoted a "one-step" and the second a "fox-trot," and like the ODJB's records, each side displayed the words "dance music" beside the spindle hole. Though these titles didn't contain the word "jazz," the promotional copy rode the coattails of the ODJB: "The Dixieland Jazz Band and Rector's

Novelty Orchestra (the famous orchestra of Rector's, New York) are so 'just right' for dancing, that they are *bound* to sell out quicker than you think!"[47]

After making hit records for both Victor and Columbia, the members of the ODJB took the opportunity to record for a third company during the summer. The Aeolian Vocalion Company was better known for its pianos and organs but intended to expand into recordings. The company signed the ODJB to a recording contract that eventually resulted in seven records that were released for sale, albeit not until mid-1918. The first session on 29 July produced recordings of "Indiana" and "Ostrich Walk," but the band rejected them. Another session on 17 August yielded recordings of "Barnyard Blues," "Ostrich Walk," "Tiger Rag," and "There It Goes Again," of which the first three were later sold commercially. A third session on 3 September produced the record "At the Jass Band Ball," which the band would record again for Victor in March 1918. This record illustrates a feature of the band's stage act that was often commented on by patrons at Reisenweber's but nowhere else recorded on disc. On the second time through the chorus of "At the Jass Band Ball," they cut the volume in half, which in live performance allowed the sound of the dancers' feet to be heard above the music. In a genre of music known for raucous noise, this delicate touch provided an artistic respite that made the subsequent return of the full sound of the band even more exhilarating.

These recordings were made in the heat of August 1917, but they were not distributed commercially until nearly a year later. When they finally did hit the shelves, their sales were limited by the fact that Aeolian used a vertical-cut technology for its records rather than the much more common lateral-cut technology for which Victor and Columbia owned the patents. As the records could not be played on lateral-cut machines, sales were weak. (These Aeolian recordings can be heard on a CD reissue from 2003.)[48] Of all the Aeolian tracks, "Tiger Rag (Hold That Tiger)" proved to be the most influential. Though initial sales were limited by the vertical-cut technology, the ODJB's March 1918 Victor recording of the song became a national hit and inspired hundreds of cover recordings in the following decades.[49]

Across the country, the summer of 1917 saw a proliferation of jazz bands, though many of them must have been jazz in name only. The entertainment listings of the *Oregon Daily Journal* on 31 July listed no fewer than three jazz bands scheduled to perform at different venues in Portland, and cities large and small across the country advertised "jazz" as part of the summer entertainment lineup. Presumably most of the dance bands supplying this music had simply stolen a few tricks from the records of ODJB and other New York bands rather than learn how to play it firsthand from New Orleans musicians. Even musicians in New Orleans admitted to studying the ODJB recordings to try to replicate their musical style.[50]

In response to the exploding popularity of jazz music, the summer brought a spate of newspaper and magazine articles purporting to "explain" the phenomenon to readers. Most influential (and also most damaging) was an article by Broadway press agent Walter Kingsley in the *New York Sun* on 5 August. Under the headline "Whence Comes Jass? Facts from the Great Authority on the Subject," Kingsley used faux-scholarly prose and quotations from a variety of "experts" to explain the origins and character-istics of jazz. His erudite dissertation on the subject gave an unprecedented list of alternate spellings, attributed the origins of the word to the Gold Coast of West Africa, identified the immediate etymology of its linguistic origin as vaudeville, and described its rhythms in colorful language that betrayed his lack of musical knowledge: "Jazz music is the delirium tremens of syncopation. It is strict rhythm without melody. To-day the jazz bands take popular tunes and rag them to death to make jazz. Beats are added as often as the delicacy of the player's ear will permit. In one two time a third beat is interpolated. There are many half notes or less and many long drawn wavering tones. It is an attempt to reproduce the marvelous syncopation of the African jungle."[51] Never mind that most of his ideas were entirely fabricated. This "authoritative" account was reprinted and cited repeatedly for decades before being debunked.[52] An article entitled "The Appeal of Primitive Jazz," published in the 25 August 1917 issue of *Literary Digest*, quoted Kingsley in its entirety. If Nick LaRocca saw this article he was no doubt furious, for the *Literary Digest* reprint of the article was illustrated by a photograph of Earl Fuller's Famous Jazz Band in humorous poses over the caption "A New York Jazz Band: Where the attitudes of the players per-fectly suggest the nerve-tingling quality of the music their instruments emit."[53]

Many of the articles on jazz still treated it as a humorous novelty, with the word "noise" always figuring prominently. An article in the 19 July issue of the *Musical Courier* purported to give a description of a jazz per-formance from the drummer's perspective, from unpacking his "junk" to pounding mercilessly on each of his "toys" to responding to the adulation of the dancers. His descriptions of the resulting sound grow ever more violent:

> I immediately try to make a boiler factory sound like a group of babies pounding
> marshmallows, in comparison to the amount of music that I get out of my
> "junk." . . . I hammer on the Chinese wood block with a violence that would
> make it difficult for a Chinaman to recognize his native instrument after I have

played a few numbers on it. . . . I am instilled with ambition to do more, so I try to hit the crash-cymbal, bass drum, snare drum and tom-tom, all at one time, on the last beat of the piece, and the effect is similar to that of a few tons of plate glass falling through eight tin roofs and then landing on a charge of dynamite.[54]

This satirical account certainly does not describe the propulsive rhythmic subtlety of Tony Sbarbaro's drumming, but to many listeners in the summer of 1917, jazz represented carefree abandon, wild noise, and physical exuberance. Its energy was infectious as an antidote to the fear and uncertainty of the approaching war. In a July article, commentator Hiram Kelly Moderwell advocated the use of ragtime songs in concerts, and he contrasted popular music with classical music in stinging terms:

> To the professional American musicians, ragtime simply does not exist. They give it no more recognition than if it were the beating of tom-toms outside a side-show. Not recognizing its existence, they cannot distinguish the better from the worse. Because most of the ragtime pieces they hear are feeble (as Heaven knows most American music is feeble) they lump the whole art in one and call it "vicious" or "vulgar." What an argument they use against themselves in that word "vulgar" they never guess. It is an old thought to most of us that the art of the *vulgus*, the people, is the material for national expression. . . . Such distinguished visitors as Ernest Bloch and Percy Grainger are delighted and impressed by American ragtime; foreign peoples accord it a jolly respect. Only the native-born, foreign-educated musician scorns and deplores it.[55]

Moderwell's point was that popular and folk music—like classical music—contained both good and bad compositions, but that the refusal of America's classical musicians to develop sufficient familiarity with this music to judge it knowledgeably was shortsighted. His article challenged these musicians' cultural authority, not their taste or technique. In this hot summer, when the ODJB played every night at Reisenweber's rooftop garden, when the Fifteenth Infantry Band played every day, when the classical musicians rested at Seal Harbor and military intelligence agents quietly investigated them, America's musical attitudes were changing. The fall of 1917 promised to be a season of upheavals that would change forever the way Americans listened to music.

CHAPTER 9

ↂ

Anticipation

September 1917

As Americans gradually reconciled themselves to the idea of sending their sons to fight and die in Europe in answer to President Wilson's call to make the world safe for democracy, militaristic language appeared in unlikely places—including music. Leonard Liebling's Music and Militarism became a regular feature of the *Musical Courier*, and Frederic J. Haskin's syndicated column Musicians and the War was published nationally. The fad for flag-draped opera singers continued unabated, and even the popular American soprano Geraldine Farrar joined in the fun by posing as Lady Liberty in a Liberty Loan pageant.[1] Under the title "Making the World Safe for Music," the always witty editors of the *Musical Courier* called musicians to arms on 20 September:

> Back to the trenches, now that the summer furlough is over! We have enemies
> of all sorts on all sides of us. From one year's end to another we are bombarded
> with vulgarity, gassed with frivolity, blockaded by indifference to music and art,
> attacked by jazz and rag, submarined by card parties and sports. Where can the
> good musician turn for peace and disarmament? He does not possess the wings
> of a dove to fly away and be at rest after the manner desired by the author of the
> fifty-fifth psalm. He must simply dig in, that is all. Throw up the entrenchments
> of good teaching, and use as a base the strong fortress of knowledge and ex-
> perience. Now and then he can make a frontal assault and overcome the foes
> of music with an orchestral concert. This is the heavy artillery of our art. In

the long run, however, the infantry and airplane work of the recitalists count most. Give the enemy no rest. Raid his trenches by night and hammer at his defenses by day. The world must be made safe for music. The junkers and their junk must go.[2]

Whether the "junkers" in question are the Prussian nobility or the purveyors of jazz and rag, the message is clear: music is under attack, and musicians must fight with every tool at their disposal to defend the art they cherish.

Recognizing that one person's hardship is another's opportunity, the call went out to use the wartime restrictions to promote American music and musicians. Pianist Rose L. Sutro pointed out that the declaration of war had made it almost impossible for Americans to study music in Germany, as so many of them had done in the prewar years. She reminded Americans of the excellent schools and teachers in their own country, which she likened to a "giant asleep," whose musical potential would be awakened by the forced isolation from Germany.[3] *Musical Courier* editor Liebling noted that the flood of new works from European composers had slowed dramatically, and he urged American composers to "seize the moment" to promote their works and fight the traditional stereotype against American classical music. In the spirit of the times, he worked himself up to a patriotic frenzy: "Why is this opportune moment not seized for a general offensive against the hosts of obstinate performers, selfish conductors, indifferent opera managers? Why is the appeal not made to our patriotic press, and, through the press, to our patriotic public? American composers, bring forth your best and proclaim that it is available. Bawl out the persecutors who prefer foreign work to yours merely because the other is foreign and yours American; pillory the culprits who stifle our national musical voice and help to make our tonal creations come stillborn into the world."[4] That same week, two conductors, Jacques Grunberg of the Philharmonic Miniature Orchestra and Christian Kriens of the Kriens Symphony Club, issued open invitations for American composers to submit scores for consideration. Louis Koemmenich, the erstwhile conductor of the Oratorio Society, announced some weeks later that he would perform new American choral works with the Mendelssohn Glee Club. It was already too late, however, for the major orchestras and concert series, whose programming had been in the planning phase for many months and was now ready to be publicized. September brought a steady stream of press releases announcing plans for the new concert season that were designed to build anticipation and sell tickets. Despite the changes happening all around, most looked a great deal like previous seasons.

The Philadelphia Orchestra was the sole organization that had anticipated the call for more American music, but this fact was downplayed when the management announced its season with great fanfare on 5 September. The ninety-four members of the orchestra were under the artistic direction of Leopold Stokowski and the management of Arthur Judson. These two men, thirty-five and thirty-six years old, respectively, were near the start of long and influential careers in American music. Stokowski had been appointed conductor of the Philadelphia Orchestra in 1912, and the ambitious Judson had been appointed manager in 1915. They both understood the benefits of responding to public tastes, in the 1917/18 season as elsewhere. In response to audience requests, the orchestra reduced the number of out-of-town concerts in order to give Philadelphia patrons their best performances. Also reduced was the number of guest soloists in order to make room for more concerts featuring purely orchestral music: another change that was said to be in response to audience requests. The initial announcements gave lists of guest soloists—including several of Stokowski's Seal Harbor neighbors—but little information on repertoire. Letters between Judson and Stokowski in the orchestra's archives reflect a strategy to give as few specifics about repertoire choices as possible in order to leave the option to respond to changes in the public's volatile mood.[5] It was promised that there would be concerts devoted to English and Scandinavian music "as well as the usual Tschaikowsky, Wagner, Russian, and all-Beethoven programs."[6] The season preview in the *Evening Public Ledger* highlighted the orchestra's role as a "civic asset" and urged patrons to contribute generously to the ongoing endowment campaign in order to ensure the quality and longevity of the institution.[7]

A follow-up article on 22 September offered more specifics on the Philadelphia Orchestra's season. Because season ticket sales had broken all previous records, it was announced that the boxes in the rear of the Academy of Music's balcony would be removed and replaced by rows of seats, a gesture that not only expanded the seating capacity but was symbolically democratic. The same article tantalizingly hinted that Stokowski had listened to calls for more American music: "While Mr. Stokowski has not made public his program for the coming season, it has been rumored that one program will be made up entirely of the works of Americans, and that the symphony will be Edgar Stillman-Kelley's, while Philadelphia itself will be honored by the inclusion of a work by Philip H. Goepp."[8] This was the first public mention of plans to feature American music, which had been in the works since the summer.

The broad outlines of the season that Walter Damrosch had chosen for the New York Symphony were also announced in mid-September. The orchestra was scheduled to play thirty-two concerts in Manhattan, along with series of concerts in Brooklyn, Philadelphia, Baltimore, Washington, Pittsburgh, and other cities. Unlike the Philadelphia Orchestra, the New York Symphony had scheduled a veritable constellation of stars as soloists, including his Mount Desert Island neighbors Kreisler, Gabrilowitsch, Harold Bauer, and Josef Hofmann. Damrosch announced that because of the difficulty of obtaining new works from abroad, he would bring back some older works by Tchaikovsky, Mozart, and Joachim Raff that he had not played in recent years. He did announce two novelties: a *Symphonie Française* by Théodore Dubois and a symphonic poem entitled *Tam O'Shanter* by the Boston composer George Whitefield Chadwick. September also brought several reminders that an orchestra—which is the closest thing to an army in the musical world—is made up of individuals who sometimes do newsworthy things. Violinist Josef Urdang secretly married the wealthy widow of a soda manufacturer, and two of Damrosch's other players, cellist Engelbert Roentgen and hornist Robert Brown, enlisted in the army. Roentgen had been a citizen of Holland until obtaining US citizenship the previous year, and he informed Damrosch, "Uncle Sam has already done so much for me that I am glad to do something for him in return."[9]

The Boston Symphony Orchestra released its prospectus for the season on 2 September. The management took pains in this initial announcement to remind readers of the uncertainty that had plagued the organization in recent months:

> The prospectus will finally set at rest any few remaining doubts regarding the existence of the orchestra. It will be remembered that last spring the busy gossip-mongers in New York, and Philadelphia particularly, had it quite settled in their own mind that for various reasons the Boston Symphony Orchestra would go out of existence with the end of last season. The rumors were so obviously absurd that the management took no formal note of them but went ahead, quietly, making plans for the coming season. . . . In times of mental stress more than ever is art needed to mitigate and offset the anxieties of the day, and of all the arts, none is so well fitted for this work as music. Boston in its possession of its incomparable orchestra is therefore peculiarly fortunate.[10]

The article went on to state that Dr. Muck had almost completed the selection of music for the concerts but that his repertoire choices would remain secret until the last moment. As in previous seasons, there would be twenty-four pairs of concerts for a total of forty-eight Boston dates, along with a slightly higher number of out-of-town concerts, bringing the total scheduled performances to over one hundred for the 1917/18 season.

The fourteen soloists for the season were announced with great fanfare and photographs two weeks later. The article acknowledged that for many symphony patrons, the star soloists were the main attraction of the concerts. Headlining the season were violinist Fritz Kreisler, pianist Ignacy Paderewski, and tenor John McCormack, three of the most beloved concert artists in America. The Boston lineup featured a number of newcomers to the top echelons of concert performers, including American pianist Frances Nash, American soprano Mabel Garrison, and the twenty-two-year-old Brazilian pianist Guiomar Novaes, who was to become one of the great pianists of the twentieth century.

When the repertoire for the concerts was finally announced, it contained no works by American composers. Muck's specialty was the core repertoire of the German Classic and Romantic eras; new music was not a strong interest of his. According to the Boston Symphony Archives, the BSO played over forty American premieres between 1900 and 1910, just seven in the 1910s with Muck at the helm, and forty in the 1920s.[11] Nearly all of Muck's premieres were of works by European composers; he had not played a new work by an American since 1908. In his isolated cottage on Ox Hill Road, Muck seems to have missed the calls for new American music: his programs for the first four pairs of concerts in fall 1917 did not contain a single American orchestral work, old or new.

Karl and Anita Muck enjoyed the cottage perched above Seal Harbor so much that they extended their stay through the end of September. About noon on 12 September, Ensign Gallatin and Lieutenant Parks, investigators for the US Navy, presented themselves at the Muck cottage. They informed him that they were there to investigate rumors that the cottage was outfitted with wireless equipment. Muck invited them inside, and they made a thorough search of "every room, as well as the garret and cellar."

Wireless technology was such a new phenomenon that the agents admitted they could not tell the difference between wires for radio and wires for doorbells, both of which were in abundant supply throughout the house. They found wires and a dry cell behind a set of drawers in Anita's room, and their report stated, "In an alcove just off his den (a room commanding a very wide view as the house is situated on a high point) we found what had been left of a dismantled wireless plant. The instruments had been removed, but the alcove was filled with wires and so forth."[12] The agents did not believe that the unit was operational, and it was later determined that the wiring and equipment were left by Dr. A. E. Lawrence, who was currently confined to a mental asylum.

Even during this visit, Muck does not seem to have realized the gravity of his position. According to the agents, "When asked if his sympathies were entirely with Germany, he replied that of course they were. In reply to one question, he told us he was a German, but at another time said he was Swiss." Before leaving, the agents informed him that in Germany, no foreigner was allowed to visit the seacoast, and that his living arrangements in Seal Harbor created a very serious situation. The agents questioned him further about a check for $100 and a laudatory poem from his neighbor Leonora Speyer, a known German sympathizer. They took the poem and included a copy in their report as evidence of Speyer and Muck's sympathies.

The Mucks had an invitation for lunch at the Gabrilowitsch cottage, and this unexpected inspection caused them to arrive nearly an hour late. The agitated Muck told Clara Clemens Gabrilowitsch—who was known for her pacifist views—that the agents had asked questions about her as well. Fearing for her safety, she ran upstairs to destroy the check stubs from her contributions to pacifist organizations while her guests ate lunch.[13] This precaution proved unnecessary, since the unauthorized search of Muck's cottage, which one of the agents later boasted about publicly, caused the navy to delay its investigation of the other suspicious members of the Seal Harbor musical colony.

Shortly before leaving the Maine resort, Anita Muck summarized their time at Seal Harbor in a letter written to Ida Chadwick on 29 September:

> We had little time for ourselves recently; everybody is leaving, and entertained and had to be entertained before parting. We musicians kept quite nicely in touch without bothering one another too much. This and the wonderful country here made our summer much pleasanter than we expected. Of course we were not spared lots of gossip and one rather annoying experience of which I will tell you later personally. You will wonder what tricks chance can play; fiction is not more vivid in imagination! Of course Dr. Muck was said to have been arrested nearly daily! I suppose the more we avoided meeting and making any new acquaintances the more suspicious we seemed. . . . Anyhow it is going to be a pretty severe winter for everybody.[14]

The 1917/18 season was shaping up to be a very good one for Fritz Kreisler. As one of a dozen or so artists who were so popular that they could fill a large auditorium in any part of the country, he had all the engagements he wanted, and he could demand fees in excess of $2,000 per performance, about $500 more than the previous season.[15] He began his season earlier than most artists, on 21 September, with a concert in Burlington, Vermont. The season, scheduled to take him from coast to coast, included performances in small Midwest towns and major concert halls of the East Coast. He performed as soloist with large orchestras like Muck's and Damrosch's but also with smaller regional orchestras. The majority of his concerts were scheduled for midsized cities like Atlanta, Detroit, Pittsburgh, and Indianapolis, where his combination of European artistry and audience-pleasing sentimentality were especially beloved. In this era before radio and television, when records were still primitive in tone reproduction, live performances were in great demand. To a city like Pittsburgh, with easy rail access from New York, each year brought dozens of concerts by the greatest performers in the world, enabling audiences and critics to develop a sophisticated familiarity with repertoire and performers. When Kreisler appeared there, the standard of comparison would be last year's concert.

Olga Samaroff also prepared for the concert season ahead, even if she did not command the level of attention Kreisler did. Still at the peak of her pianistic powers, she was nonetheless becoming known more as the wife of the rising conductor Stokowski than as an artist in her own right. This was largely her own doing, for when he was hired by the Philadelphia Orchestra in 1912, she made it her primary responsibility to be the ideal "conductor's wife," cultivating the society ladies who supported the orchestra financially and making sure that their household ran smoothly. She had returned to performing at the instigation of Arthur Judson in 1913, and in addition to playing as a soloist with her husband's orchestra both at home and on tour, she accepted engagements in other cities. As far as the public knew, theirs was an ideal marriage.

But in the privacy of their home, life was not always easy. Two-career families in arts or entertainment are difficult because of the intense commitment required for each career individually. Stokowski was very sensitive to sounds, and they tried everything to keep her practicing from disturbing his concert preparations. Moving the piano to different rooms, muffling it with drapes, even creating a double wall of wood did not solve the problem.[16] Additionally, they were both intelligent, opinionated persons who loved to debate. Ruth O'Neill, executive secretary of the Philadelphia Orchestra, recalled, "There were none who had the comprehensive intellectualism of those two people. Naturally, I would be the interested auditor as

I sat down at dinner with them and there would be an argument about a phrase in a symphony and they would argue it out." She recalled that they would also argue about much more petty things, like clothing, and that these arguments boiled down to fighting for control in the relationship.[17]

In September 1917, as Judson and Stokowski strategized about potential anti-German sentiment, Samaroff practiced for her first performance of the season at the Worcester Festival, in Massachusetts. This annual week of concerts traditionally took place in September, between the summer vacation and the start of the fall concert season, but in 1917 it was held during the first week of October. Since its founding in 1858, the festival had been dominated by Boston conductors and Boston performers, and of course it attracted a Boston audience. But in a sign of the growing reputation of the Philadelphia Orchestra, the 1917 Worcester Orchestra consisted of sixty members of the Philadelphia Orchestra, and the assistant conductor for the event was Stokowski's concertmaster, Thaddeus Rich. He was scheduled to conduct the orchestra when Samaroff played the Saint-Saëns Piano Concerto in G Minor at the matinee concert on Thursday, 5 October. This was the same work that she had played in Pittsburgh the previous winter, but she did not want to take chances with being underprepared.

Ernestine Schumann-Heink was also preparing for an ambitious season of concerts. At fifty-six years of age, she was older than most concert singers, but her voice had held up well, and she continued to perform by adapting her repertoire and audiences. She seldom sang in operas, but instead she toured the country on the Chautauqua circuits. In these venues she often performed as part of religious meetings, and not infrequently she sang in outdoor tents. Her target audience was the rural population, although she could still be heard occasionally in the major urban centers. With the entry of the United States into the war, she found a new mission in entertaining the troops at training camps and in raising funds for the war effort. The story of her sons in opposing navies added an extra ingredient of personal interest to her appearances.

Continuing the brisk pace she had set during the summer, she sang a benefit concert on 9 September for the Red Cross in Wenden, Arizona, near the ranch of her son Ferdinand, who was preparing to ship off to training camp. A magnet for both good deeds and publicity, Schumann-Heink appeared in the news while resting at her son's ranch the week after this concert. While she was there, a nine-year-old boy named Carlos Gonzales was bitten by a rattlesnake. Thinking quickly, the singer sucked the poison from his arm, saving his life. This story was reported in newspapers throughout the country, adding to her legendary reputation for altruism.[18] On 11 September, her youngest son George, who was eighteen years old, enlisted in the navy as a volunteer.

Schumann-Heink joined a group of famous artists in a patriotic concert in Madison Square Garden on 27 September in support of the Humanitarian Cult and Magazine. Hyped as "The Greatest Concert of the Age!" it had the benefit of little competition, since it was very early in the New York concert season. The contralto was joined by violinist Mischa Elman, pianist Percy Grainger, and three stars from the Metropolitan Opera, with the accompaniment of the Russian Symphony Orchestra under the direction of Modest Altschuler. The Australian-born composer and pianist Grainger had moved to the United States in 1914, and in June 1917 he had enlisted in the US Army as a bandsman.[19] The army decided that Grainger was more useful as a concert soloist, however, and he performed in the Altschuler concert wearing a khaki uniform. Each soloist sang a couple of numbers, the orchestra played a generous program, including an arrangement of "The Star-Spangled Banner," and there were speeches by dignitaries. Jeannette Rankin, the first female member of Congress and an outspoken pacifist, served as moderator of the event. The *Musical Courier* said, "Ernestine Schumann-Heink was accorded a real 'Schumann-Heink' reception, and responded with full proof that the advancing years of a long career have in no way dimmed her splendid voice nor her ability to use it movingly."[20]

Nick LaRocca and the other members of the ODJB had spent the summer playing in the Paradise Garden, on the roof of the Reisenweber Building, on Columbus Circle at 58th and Broadway. They had started the craze for jazz in January, and their recordings had made them famous all over the country. In a business where popularity was everything and trends in music and dance were ephemeral, the band could not afford to be complacent. Preparing to move back indoors after Labor Day weekend, they continued to rehearse new numbers and seek new ways to ride the wave of their popularity.

It was clear that the competition from other bands trying to horn in on the New York jazz scene would not let up. Chief among the competitors was Earl Fuller's band at Rector's Restaurant, at 48th and Broadway, ten blocks south of Reisenweber's. Typically, the display ads for these two restaurants were near each other or even adjacent in the entertainment pages of the New York papers. On page 8 of the 31 August issue of the *New York Times*, for instance, Rector's ad boasted "2 Ballrooms, 2 Dining Rooms, 3 Orchestras, Extraordinary Entertainment with the Sensational

Jazz Band that is Town Talk, Featuring Ted Lewis, Champion Saxophone Artist." Immediately below, an ad of identical size trumpeted, "Paradise Roof Garden Atop Reisenweber's: Airiest Garden Spot—Coolest Place in Town with the Original Dixieland 'Jazz' Band Playing Dance-Compelling Melodies—Also Hollander's Orch."

Victor's September catalog of new records included three recordings that capitalized on the popularity of jazz. The titles and descriptions of these recordings were clearly patterned after those of the ODJB, which was not represented in the September list. Collins and Harlan had a record called "Everybody's Jazzin' It (So Let's Start Jazzin' It Too)," Conway's Band offered a medley that included "When I Hear That Jazz Band Play," and Earl Fuller's Famous Jazz Band (which in August had been listed in the Columbia catalog as Rector's Novelty Orchestra) had a double-sided disc with a description reminiscent of the ODJB's publicity of the previous spring: "A terrific wail from the trombone starts 'Slippery Hank' (F. H. Losey) on his glide, and the rest of the Jazz Band noises are in kind. And if you think these are all the noises available for a Jazz Band, turn the record over and listen to 'Yah-de-dah' (Mel. B. Kaufman). The sounds as of a dog in his dying anguish are from Ted Lewis' clarinet. Notice the two little chords at the end of each number. This is how you know for certain that a Jazz Band is playing."[21]

Collins and Harlan were a veteran comedy vocal duo who had been making records for all the major companies and many minor ones since 1902. They had been the first artists to record Irving Berlin's hit song "Alexander's Ragtime Band," a record so popular it was offered for sale by Victor for over a decade.[22] Their loud, belting voices were ideally suited to the acoustic recording medium, and the song "Everybody's Jazzin' It (So Let's Start Jazzin' It Too)" is typical of comedy numbers of the period with its emphasis on clever words and close harmony between the two voices. In deference to jazz style, there are numerous trombone slides, and the percussionist employs woodblock and cowbell. The tempo is slower than those of the ODJB and other jazz bands, however.

The two sides of the Fuller recording are much closer in style to the ODJB. A frenetic tempo, numerous breaks for barnyard sounds, extensive use of the old minstrel-style woodblock, and the clichéd Dixieland tag mentioned in the catalog make it sound very similar to their rival up the street. Clarinetist Ted Lewis, the star of this record, plays virtuosic solos and shows an impressive ability to embellish the melody, albeit perhaps relying a bit too much on trills. The piano is barely audible, and the trombone's repetitive growls and slides are no match for the artistry of Edwards, but the overall sound is surprisingly similar to that of the ODJB.

Jazz historian Gunther Schuller, writing fifty years later, decried the ricky-tick rhythms and structural monotony of the Fuller Band but viewed them as an important transitional group with "a crude sort of excitement."[23] In September 1917, LaRocca and his colleagues must have felt the heat from this band that had managed to copy many of their stylistic elements, especially if they read this blurb in *Variety* on 21 September: "Earl Fuller's Jazz Band is said to have made the best instrument record of a jazz band ever turned out. . . . The sale may run to over 300,000. Fuller, by picture and name, is being heavily advertised on the Victor list and in stores selling Victor records. Rector's is also securing big publicity, all papers announcing the restaurant where Mr. Fuller has his orchestras."[24]

An article in the *Sun* on 23 September noted that all floors of Reisenweber's were in continuous activity because of "the throngs that daily flock there for dining as well as for amusement." At 7:30 and 11:00 nightly, the main restaurant featured a "Girlie Revue" that had been transplanted from its summer engagement at Brooklyn's Brighton Beach. The ODJB's popularity continued to be a big draw both in the afternoon and at the after-hours club: "The Four Hundred Club's original Dixieland 'Jazz' Band continues to entertain the dancers with their syncopated melodies. They have proved such a sensation that now they may be heard at the afternoon teas, a new feature introduced at Reisenweber's daily, from 4 to 6 o'clock."[25] The afternoon tea dances (see Figure 9.1) were hosted by women who fostered an air of respectability and dignity, while an evening in the 400 Club offered liquor, excitement, and danger after the restaurants and theaters closed for the day.

As September drew to a close, LaRocca prepared to deal with the most threatening competition of all. The debate among classical musicians over whether to play American music was not a pressing concern among jazz players. Theirs was an improvised art form, and a composition used in performance was merely a framework on which innovations were hung. These compositions were almost entirely by American composers, most of whom were still living and active in the business. Nick LaRocca was proud to be a non-reader, and he had intentionally built his band with other fakers or, in Edwards's case, with a reader who could pretend to be a faker. But in 1917, LaRocca's naiveté about printed music landed him in trouble with the law. It would take months to sort the trouble out.

When Victor recorded the first ODJB record on 26 February, the two songs were not copyrighted or even (so far as the members of the band knew) written down. In court LaRocca claimed he had composed the piece marketed as "Livery Stable Blues" in 1914 and taught it to his band members at the time. This statement was backed up by the deposition of

ea dances

EVERY AFTERNOON
DIRECTION OF
BETTY SCOTT
(Mrs. Earle Foxe)
with the original
**DIXIELAND
"JAZZ" BAND**

REISENWEBER'S
Columbus Circle &
58ᵗʰ *St.*

PHONE
8640
COLUMBUS

Figure 9.1 Advertisement for Reisenweber's Tea Dances (*New York Tribune*, 27 October 1917).

Edwards. Recognizing that they needed to acquire a copyright to protect their rights, their manager Max Hart arranged for a musician to listen to the band and write down the notes, which he used to obtain a copyright for the music on 9 April. The problem was that the name that the band used for the tune, "Barnyard Blues," was unacceptable to Victor, and so the title was changed to "Livery Stable Blues" for the record. When the record became a hit, their erstwhile clarinetist, Alcide "Yellow" Nunez, attempted to purchase the sheet music, found that it was not available (and had not been copyrighted under the name on the record), and quickly arranged for publication of the music, with himself as composer, by the Chicago publisher Roger Graham. When the ODJB found out in the summer, they signed a contract with Leo Feist of New York to publish their version of "Barnyard Blues" and filed an injunction to stop the sale of the Graham publication. LaRocca claimed that Nunez had learned the piece from the record and published it for spite and personal gain. Nunez countered that he had been one of the composers of the piece when he was with the band and claimed that he had not been given the credit he deserved.

The case, to be heard in federal court in Chicago on 11–12 October, would determine the rightful owner of this copyright. Starting on Friday, 28 September, and continuing into the first week of October, the ODJB's lawyer, Nathan Burkan, with the defendant's lawyer present, took depositions in New York from all the persons who could not travel to Chicago for the "Barnyard Blues" trial. Those who gave testimony in this way were agent Max Hart, several outside musical experts, and all of the members of the ODJB except LaRocca, who was scheduled to appear in court. Their statements give a good sense of the case that Hart and the ODJB were building against Nunez and publisher Graham. Although the band members did not read music themselves, the arguments would revolve entirely around printed musical scores and their bearing on the conflicting copyright claims. This was new territory for LaRocca, and the October trial would place his legal ignorance and his musical aesthetics on display for all to see.

While the *Musical Courier* flirted with military metaphors in its musical articles, American draftees had their first contact with the real thing. The thirty-two camps [cantonments] that had been announced in the summer needed to be built in order to house the recruits who would train there in the fall. Like most of the government's military training cantonments, Camp Dix was built from scratch in a very short time. The camp was located at Wrightstown, New Jersey, not far from Philadelphia. While seven thousand construction workers used one million board feet of lumber a day to construct barracks that would eventually hold sixty thousand soldiers, five hundred troops from the Fifteenth New York Infantry Regiment stood guard.[26] As part of this contingent, the members of the regiment's band were stationed there as well and used the eight weeks to refine their sound through rehearsals and performances. The commanding general ordered a bandstand built so that the band could give nightly concerts as the camp gradually filled up with new recruits. During the weeks at Camp Dix, their reputation steadily grew and spread.

On 8 September, when there were still only about a thousand soldiers in camp, a local newspaper investigated persistent rumors that there had been clashes between black soldiers and white construction workers. These rumors were vehemently denied by all parties, and the commander of the regiment went so far as to state that his guards were doing a service for the skilled mechanics by protecting them from troublemakers among the unskilled laborers.[27] On 7 September, the band played a concert for fourteen hundred recruits. The next day they were called out to play "The Star-Spangled Banner" and "La Marseillaise" for Brigadier General Mark L. Hershey and two visiting French soldiers. His praise of the band and the soldiers was reported in the *New York Tribune*.[28]

As the camp began to fill, the soldiers from all parts of the country formed baseball and football teams for friendly games against other units in camp. Among the officers of the Fifteenth was Captain Hamilton "Ham" Fish, who as captain of the Harvard football team had been a two-time all-American. One of several former all-Americans among the camp's officers, he drilled his men in baseball and football skills when they weren't on guard duty.[29] When the games began, there was no discrimination on the field, as teams from black units competed on an equal footing with those from white units.

The black guards occupied a curious position, detached from yet vital to the functioning of the growing cantonment. They were armed, and they had the authority to arrest wrongdoers, yet they lived separate from the other recruits and did not take part in the marching and combat training that was the purpose of the camp. By 19 September, with the camp population exceeding 42,000, the guards had new disciplinary challenges to face. After initially turning a blind eye to gambling, the army, threatening full military prosecution, ordered a crackdown on craps and other illegal games. When a group of disgruntled laborers was fired from the construction crew in late September, an extra unit of guards was ordered to protect against possible vandalism of the water mains. On 27 September the Department of Justice closed the saloons near camp to discourage drinking. Officers instituted a $1,000 fine for outsiders caught smuggling liquor into the camps, but the guards continued to apprehend persons doing just that. On 28 September, Frank Carson, a guard from the Fifteenth Regiment, spotted flames in one of the barracks and alerted the fire brigade by firing his rifle, saving all the soldiers inside.

The growing reputation of the band contributed to the good feelings about the soldiers of the Fifteenth Regiment. Daily concerts on the bandstand allowed them to refine and tighten their sound, and the band members were confident in the leadership of both Europe and Gene Mikell, the assistant bandmaster who had filled in ably during Europe's convalescence. On 10 September the band played an invited concert for over a thousand persons at the Bordentown, New Jersey, Industrial School, where Mikell had served as music director before enlisting. As usual, Noble Sissle's singing called for special attention from the reviewer.[30]

Music was a constant part of camp life, as the army encouraged singing by the men and gave ample opportunities for band concerts. By 14 September, a "camp song" had been composed by John H. Bolan, an organist from Hackensack, New Jersey, who had been drafted into the army. Its lyrics inspired patriotism in scions of military families, but they did not apply to black soldiers:

> Your granddad fought in '61,
> And met a soldier's fate.
> Your daddy too, was just as brave,
> In eighteen ninety-eight.
> And now in nineteen-seventeen
> It comes your turn. Be true!
> Go pack your kit and do your bit—
> Your mother tells you to![31]

"Billy Boy," the Fifteenth Regiment's song in honor of their commander, had by this time been published and was well known across the country. French actress Anna Held visited Camp Dix on 17 September to tell the soldiers of the devastation to her homeland and lead them in the singing of the two countries' national anthems. On 25 September, fifteen members of the 311th Infantry from South Jersey surprised the camp by forming a band to play a shaky performance of "The Star-Spangled Banner." As the first band to be formed outside of the Fifteenth, they earned kudos from their compatriots. On the last day of September, the camp was opened for 200,000 visitors, who were treated to concerts by both bands. In early October, four pianos were donated to the camp, as the YMCA called for more instruments along with Victrolas and records. Fortuitously, one of the draftees from Monmouth, New Jersey, had been a piano tuner in civilian life and was able to have his tools sent to camp. The arrival of pianos allowed Sissle to perform vocal music accompanied by Europe on piano.

Beneath the music, sports, and guard duty was a constant undercurrent of racial tension. At times it was subtle, part of the teasing that often accompanies male bonding. A Philadelphia paper reported on 19 September: "The negro soldiers of the Fifteenth had a cruel blow handed them this morning, when an order was issued prohibiting the sale of watermelons in the reservation. Watermelon rinds, the doctors say, are breeding places for flies. It is also intimated that the real reason is that it will prohibit the chance of any sly liquor dealers tapping a melon and placing 'booze' inside."[32] But as the population in the camp was swelled by new recruits from all regions of the country, some of the incidents took on a more serious tone. In the first week of October, someone from the Twenty-Sixth Engineers, who considered themselves skilled professionals, posted a sign outside their area that read "For Soldiers Only." They later claimed that the sign was meant to deter the construction workers who were still present in camp. Someone inserted the word "white" before "soldiers," which caused the members of the Fifteenth to tear down the sign in protest. Quick action by the officers of both units averted violence, but the incident underscored how volatile the situation was becoming, even in the North.[33] The men at Camp Dix were spared from violent disturbances of the sort that occurred in Cohoes, New York, and at Camp Upton. At both locations, the black soldiers were attacked by hostile whites; the perpetrators were court-martialled for their actions.[34]

During the eight weeks that the men of the Fifteenth Regiment were divided among Camp Dix, Camp Upton, and other sites as guards, debates continued in the War Department in Washington over what to do with black recruits. Col. Hayward continued to press his case that black men should be included in the national army on an equal basis with whites, a position that was vehemently opposed by representatives of the southern states. Officials in Wilson's administration were not receptive to the proposals, but they were at a loss for a better way to handle the large number of men who had registered for the draft. Those actually drafted would need further training before they would be ready to join the battle lines, and the War Department could not decide where to train them. A rumored plan for a camp outside Des Moines, Iowa, that would train only black soldiers did not materialize. There were those who felt that the path of least resistance would be to send the Fifteenth to France to complete training under French officers, thus avoiding American racial politics altogether. Going abroad was the ultimate goal of the troops and officers, and the proposal would have hastened that result. Captain Little, one of the white officers in the regiment, sent a letter on 25 September to Colonel Edward M. House, a close friend and advisor to President Wilson, urging this course of action. Speaking on behalf of the entire unit, he wrote, "almost every man in the regiment, from Colonel Hayward down to the newest recruit, hoped that that duty may be in France. France is the place where military distinction has got to be won and I want to win some."[35]

September had been a month of anticipation. The promoters of classical music concerts built anticipation through tantalizing hints designed to spur ticket sales. The record companies built anticipation for their new releases with outrageous advertisements. Nick LaRocca and his band members anticipated the Chicago trial that would determine the ownership of "Livery Stable Blues." James Reese Europe and his Fifteenth Regiment Band joined millions of other soldiers in impatient anticipation of shipping off to France. For all of these musicians, October promised a transition from anticipation to action.

CHAPTER 10

⌇⌇

Preparation

October 1917

On 3 October, Colonel Hayward's receipt of orders to prepare the Fifteenth Regiment to move to Camp Wadsworth in Spartanburg, South Carolina, set in motion a potentially inflammatory confrontation between the black soldiers and the white residents who had expressed their opposition in August. Captain "Ham" Fish took matters into his own hands the next morning with a telegram to his friend, Assistant Secretary of the Navy Franklin Delano Roosevelt (the future president):

> My brother officers believe with me that sending northern volunteer negro troops south would cause recurrence of race troubles. This battalion (3rd) could render immediate valuable service in France on line of communications where there is great present need to relieve French troops. Why not solve difficult southern problem by letting these northern negro soldiers go where they can be of immediate use and train for firing line quicker than in the south?[1]

Roosevelt passed the telegram to his superiors, but the army chief of staff did not agree with the recommendation, believing both that the threat of trouble was exaggerated and that sending the unit to France prematurely would be a reward they had not yet earned. The New York papers debated the threat, as the *Evening Sun* printed an article on 9 October entitled "Dixieites Forecast Clash," and the *New York Age* upbraided the *Sun* for attempting to create racial friction. The editor of the *Age*, the city's leading black newspaper, called on Secretary Baker of the War Department to censor news reports coming out of Spartanburg in order to calm racial strife.[2] As the men of the Fifteenth boarded the trains for South Carolina on 10 October, they not only embarked for hostile territory but entered a zone of silence. Newspaper reports during their stint at Camp Wadsworth were brief and superficial; the real story of what happened there would not be revealed until years later.

The Worcester Festival unfolded during the first five days of October, and Philadelphia musicians earned praise for their artistry. The sixty-member festival orchestra was made up of Philadelphia players, and the assistant conductor for the festival was Philadelphia concertmaster Thaddeus Rich. Because all the concerts were sold out, the rehearsals on the first two days were open to the public, allowing even more patrons to enjoy the music. The first concert, on Wednesday, 3 October, opened with the singing of "The Star-Spangled Banner," in which four hundred chorus members, the soloists, and the entire audience "joined with a vigor that made old Mechanics' Hall vibrate."[3] The rest of the evening consisted of a concert performance of the opera *Samson and Delilah*, by the still-living French composer Camille Saint-Saëns.

The presentation of a French work was a patriotic gesture, but the choice of this particular work was ironic. Written over forty years earlier, the first act of the opera was panned by critics when it was performed in Paris in 1875. This initial reaction, coupled with the French public's ambivalence about an operatic setting of a biblical story, made it impossible for Saint-Saëns to find a theater willing to stage the work in France. His friend Franz Liszt, however, was enthusiastic about it and arranged for the premiere to be held at the court theater in Weimar, Germany, in December 1877. The work was thus critically acclaimed in Germany before it was accepted in France.[4]

The second evening's concert extended the theme of patriotism with the premieres of two large choral works. Percy Grainger's *Marching Song of Democracy* elicited extended applause from the capacity crowd for its unusual sonorities and harmonic combinations. This was followed by *Ode to Music*, by the American composer Henry Hadley on a text by Henry Van Dyke, former US ambassador to the Netherlands. The composer stated in the program notes that his intention was "briefly to suggest the whole field of music in the only kind of war which seems to me at all noble or glorious, namely, a war in defense of one's country . . . indicating the idea that the object of the right kind of warfare is to put an end to the passion of military conquest."

The two concerts of the final day were also heavy on music of the Allied nations, but each of them opened with a Wagner composition: The Prelude to *Die Meistersinger von Nürnberg* in the afternoon and "The Entrance of the Gods into Valhalla," from *Das Rheingold*, in the evening. German music was too beloved by American audiences to be eliminated entirely. Samaroff's performance of the Saint-Saëns Piano Concerto in G Minor received high praise from the *Musical Courier*:

> The gifted pianist played the Saint-Saëns piano concerto in G minor with a dash and fire, coupled with a thorough command of her splendid resources which bespoke the finished artist. An anxiety to hear her had resulted in a well-filled auditorium and to judge by the volume, spontaneity and long continuance of the applause which marked the completion of her number, no one left other than completely satisfied with the excellence of her interpretation. A perfection of style and withal a deep sense of the beauties of the work gave to her playing that indefinable something which bridges the chasm between the artist and the audience and makes them one for the time being. After continued recalls, she graciously responded with the "Liebestraum" of Liszt, which served to show another side of this gifted artist and caused the applause to be renewed afresh.[5]

The two works she played are both thoroughly romantic but in different ways. The Saint-Saëns concerto is dramatic, passionate, and serious in tone, while the Liszt *Liebestraum* (or "Dream of Love," as it was often translated in America) is languorously decadent in its lush harmonies, lyrical melody, and sparkling cadenza. In the audience for the performance was her husband, Leopold Stokowski, taking the unaccustomed role of supportive spouse but also keeping an eye on his orchestral players.

While the members of the Philadelphia Orchestra played in the Worcester Festival an hour outside Boston, Karl Muck and his Boston Symphony Orchestra were in Camden, New Jersey, just across the river from Philadelphia. The occasion was auspicious, as reported in the *Philadelphia Evening Public Ledger*: "Heretofore registration on the discs of complete orchestra scores was deemed impossible, but the Victor Talking Machine Company has now perfected its methods for reproducing masterpieces of composition in their entirety. A new sounding room for the purpose has been constructed at the Victor plant in Camden."[6] The word "perfected" was hyperbole, since this recording session and another with the Philadelphia

Orchestra two weeks later involved a great deal of trial and error, but these sessions did break new ground in the history of recording technology.

The problem of acoustical recording, which the engineers had successfully overcome in the ODJB records, was that some instruments registered better than others. With a five-member band, these discrepancies could be minimized through positioning the players at strategic distances from the recording horn. The larger the ensemble, however, the bigger the problems, as the studio became too full for practicality and some instruments were simply too far away to be heard. Victor had been recording "orchestras" for years, including some renowned organizations, but the size had been reduced to thirty or thirty-five players to accommodate the technological shortcomings. On 23 July 1917, Victor's music director, Josef A. Pasternack, along with engineers Raymond and Harry Sooy (whose younger brother Charles had recorded the ODJB), had recorded an orchestra of fifty-one players to their satisfaction in the large eighth-floor auditorium of Building no. 2 of the Victor complex in Camden. The success of their experiments prompted the company to make arrangements to record the Boston Symphony Orchestra between 2 and 5 October and the Philadelphia Orchestra on 22 and 24 October in Camden.[7]

In order to accommodate the ninety-five members of each of these orchestras, the seats of the auditorium were removed, and special equipment was created to focus and direct the sounds of the instruments. The principal innovation consisted of two dome-like structures, placed above the string and wind players, to capture and focus their sound. Because strings did not project well enough for the recording equipment, they may also have used "Stroh violins," which added a metal cone to project the sound toward the recording horn. Soloists were required to move toward the horn when they had a melody that needed to stand out of the texture. This proved especially problematic for the oboe, which resisted all efforts to be heard. Finally, the renowned French oboist Georges Longy was forced to run forward and lean his instrument into the oversized recording horn whenever he had a solo, creating a comical picture for Muck and the other players. In this setting, the conductor was almost superfluous, and it is unclear how much control Muck had over tempo, balance, and other parameters of the performance.

Underlying the challenges of recording so many instruments simultaneously were the limitations in frequency range. Although human ears can perceive frequencies as low as 20 cycles per second and as high as 20,000 cycles, the recording process before the invention of electronic microphones in 1925 could capture only the pitches between 168 and 2,000 cycles per second. This not only limited the audible range of low instruments like string basses, but it also eliminated the overtones that give all instruments and voices their characteristic timbre and richness.[8] The symphony orchestra in particular suffers with the loss of these rich overtones and the depth of the lower instruments. We cannot draw many conclusions about tone quality from these recordings, but we can get a good sense of tempo and any fluctuations from the basic tempo.

The first morning was devoted to recording the Finale of Tchaikovsky's Fourth Symphony in two parts. At the end of the morning, the orchestra had just played the final notes of the symphony when factory whistles all over Camden went off simultaneously to signal the noon lunch break. Muck took the opportunity to let his players take their lunch as well. The following day, Muck, his guest Victor Herbert, and several other persons were returning a bit late to the eighth-floor recording studio when they heard the sounds of the Tchaikovsky coming through the door. Someone said, "What are they rehearsing the Tchaikovsky again for? That's all finished and recorded; they should be rehearsing the *Lohengrin* Prelude." Upon opening the door, they discovered that the orchestra was not rehearsing— they were listening to a playback of the previous day's recording.[9]

The results of these four days of recording were masters of seven different works that the Victor Company intended to release commercially:

Beethoven Symphony no. 7 in A, op. 92: Finale in two parts
Berlioz "Ballet des sylphs," from *La Damnation de Faust*, op. 24
Tchaikovsky "Marche miniature"
Tchaikovsky "Valse des fleurs," from the *Nutcracker Suite*
Tchaikovsky Symphony no. 4: Finale in two parts
Wagner Prelude to Act III of *Lohengrin*
Wolf-Ferrari Overture to *Il segreto di Susanna*

Like the jazz recordings made earlier in the year, the finished records would require several months of processing and manufacturing before they would be ready for sale. They would then be released one or two at a time rather than dumped on the market all at once.

Despite the imperfect conditions, these recordings provide the only surviving aural record of the Boston Symphony under Karl Muck. The complete set of recordings was released on CD (some of the tracks for the first time) by the BSO Classics label in 1995. Regarding this CD, Christopher Dyment has written, "the recordings disclose much of the quality of the Boston orchestra to which Muck's persistent drilling had contributed. . . . Particularly in the wittily inflected Tchaikovsky 'Marche miniature' the superbly full woodwinds shine forth; so much so that the American critic

B. H. Haggin, who revered Muck both in his Boston and in his Hamburg years after his return to Europe, was moved to exclaim to the writer on re-hearing this record some quarter of a century ago, 'Now that's the orchestra I remember!'"[10] Muck himself was quoted in the December 1917 Victor catalog announcing the first release: "Yesterday when I arrived I was feeling very pessimistic. I had heard no satisfactory records of a symphony orchestra. I did not believe they could be made—but today—I am very much surprised. I am very pleased. These records sound like a symphony orchestra."[11]

Far from the East Coast cultural centers, in October Ernestine Schumann-Heink toured the Midwest, where she sang to genuinely appreciative audiences. The *Fargo Farmer* commented on her 10 October performance there in glowing terms: "It is not hard to understand the hold that Mme. Schumann-Heink has on American audiences and the big following that she is able to retain. It might be summed up in one word—thoughtfulness. She radiates a spirit of genuine consideration for her audience that gets over the footlights and creates a friendly feeling for the singer."[12] The critic went on to say that in giving the audience in Fargo, North Dakota, the same difficult program and the same expressive performance as she would in New York, she treated the audience with a respect that resonated in this part of the country.

On 21 October she sang in Chicago for the first time in two years. The *Musical Leader* reported that the box office receipts were over $4,000, the highest amount ever taken for a concert at Chicago's Orchestra Hall. Of the earnings, $2,600 were designated for the Knights of Columbus and the YMCA. She sang a mixed program in German, Italian, French, and English; the English numbers were especially appreciated. The *Leader* reviewer confirmed his North Dakota colleague's assessment of her ability to create a personal connection with her audience, even those regular concertgoers who had seen it all before. As always, patriotism played a central role: "With four sons in Uncle Sam's service, the war has come home very vividly to this great and wonderful woman, but though she has already done far more than her 'bit' for her adopted country, she is so patriotic that she is not only giving many concerts at various forts, but also large sums of money to worthy organizations."[13] After the concert in Chicago, she continued east, as she was scheduled to sing in New York on 1 November.

Nick LaRocca also paid a visit to Chicago in October, but his was not for a performance. He was there for the trial to settle the copyright status of "Livery Stable Blues," the song he had written and recorded—and believed that he owned. That claim of ownership had been put to the test by Alcide "Yellow" Nunez and would be decided in federal court by Judge George A. Carpenter.

The trial was nothing if not colorful, and the Chicago papers made the most of it. Headlines like "'Jazzy Blues' to Moan Lure in Court" and "Blues and More Blues go Blooey in Music Suit" were typical of Chicago's sensationalist newspapers, and the articles did their best to make a sham of the trial. At the heart of the case was whether the two published compositions—"Barnyard Blues" (Leo Feist, New York) and "Livery Stable Blues" (Roger Graham, Chicago)—were the same or different and, more broadly, whether the blues as a genre admitted enough individual expression to be subject to copyright. The plaintiffs kept a jazz band ready in the hall outside the courtroom to prove their points, but the judge chose not to avail himself of their services.

LaRocca appeared in cloth-topped patent leather shoes, a purple striped shirt, and a green tunic. His language was just as colorful:

"I was great on imitatin'," admitted the Kid [LaRocca]. "I was swell on imitating animals. So, you see, I got the idea in 1914, the idea for the Blues."

"May I ask?" inquired the judge, "what are the blues."

The Kid answered, "The blues," said he, "is jazz. The jazz is blues. The blues means to the jazz what the rag means to ragtime, see?"

"Proceed," said the jurist.

"Well," the Kid launched forth, "I came to Chicago with de original Dixie jazz band and we played in the Schiller café. See? Well, one night after the regular piece had been played der was a goil skylarkin' on the floor, see? So I picks up the cornet and lets go a horse neigh at her."

"Did she answer?" inquired the jurist.

"No," said the Kid, "she only smiled. Then Stein [sic], who was the trombone, he says, "Great stuff, kid, put that in a number." "I have," I says, "I got one already and I give them the parts. The drums was to imitate a storm, the trombone was to imitate a jackass or a cow moo, the clarinet was to imitate a rooster and me with the cornet was to be there with the big horse neigh."

"Where did the music come in?" inquired the jurist.

"Them was merely the interplitations," said the Kid. "The music was right along and the interplitations follow within."

"I see," said the judge.[14]

The defendant Nunez took the stand the following day, and impressed the reporter as "one of the most cynical clarinetists that ever tooted." When asked who wrote the "Livery Stable Blues," he testified matter-of-factly:

> You see, nobody wrote "The Livery Stable Blues." Naw. Nobody writes any of that stuff. I invented the pony cry in the "Blues," and LaRocca, he puts in the horse neigh. We was in the Schiller café, rehearsin,' see? And I suggests that we take the "More Power Blues" and hash 'em up a bit. My friend, Ray Lopez, he wrote the "More Power Blues." All blues is alike. They come from a sort of song that all the colored folks sings when they gets lonely. That's what. We hashed up the "More Power Blues" and put in the pony cry and the mule cry and the horse neigh, see? Then we rehearsed it for ten days, steaming it up and getting it brown and snappy. Then we had the piece all finished. . . . I'm entitled to the au-thorship of "The Livery Stable Blues," me and Lopez, as much as LaRocca, that's why I went to Roger Graham and had him publish it. LaRocca done me dirt, so I says to myself, "He's done me dirt and I'll let him out. He goes and has our 'Livery Stable Blues' put on a phonograph record as his'n. Well, ain't that dirt?"[15]

Nunez was followed by a series of experts who testified on the musical qualities of the pieces in question and the genre of the blues in general. The *Chicago Tribune* made merry over the "Prof. Beethoven (Alias Slap) White, Negro jazz hound," whose principal assertion was that "blues are blues."[16] He was followed by May Hill, a "musical expert" who examined a stack of sheet music with blues in the titles and came to the conclusion that they were all the same. She asserted that if played simultaneously they would produce perfect harmony.[17] Not mentioned was the fact that Hill's name had been listed as composer on the first copyright application claimed by Roger Graham on 12 May 1917, less than a month after the release of the Victor record.

In his oral findings at the end of the second day of testimony, Judge Carpenter frankly expressed his disbelief of some of the testimony heard in his courtroom. He also admitted that the music under litigation was so far from his experience that it was difficult to assess. In the end, he agreed that "blues are blues" and threw out the case. His verdict goes right to the heart of the differences between popular and classical music cultures:

> There is a dispute between the plaintiff and the defendant, two publishers, each claiming a right to the monopoly of this song, this musical production. No claim is made by either side for the Barn-Yard calls that are interpolated in the music, no claim is made for the harmony. The only claim appears to be for the melody.

Now as a matter of fact, the only value of this so-called musical production apparently lies in the interpolated animal and bird calls. . . . The cat calls and animal calls were not claimed in the bill and they were not included in the copyright, so we are to exclude them in this question. The only question is, has there been a conceived idea of the melody that runs through this so-called Livery Stable Blues.

I am inclined to take the view of Professor Slap White in this case, that it is an old negro melody, that it has been known for a great many years. . . . The Court is satisfied, from having looked over the manuscripts, that there is a very decided resemblance between the aria—the melody of More Power Blues and the Livery Stable Blues.

The finding of the Court is therefore that neither Mr. LaRocca and his associates nor Mr. Nunez and his associates conceived the idea of this melody. They were a strolling band of players and like—take the Hungarian orchestras, if you will, but with no technical musical education, having a natural musical ear— quick ear and above all a retentive ear, and no human being could determine where that aria came from that they now claim was produced at the Schiller Café for the first time—whatever was produced by the rhythm was the result that pleased the patrons at the place, and it was the variation of the original music that accomplished the result and not the original music itself, and I venture to say that no living human being could listen to that result on the phonograph and discover anything musical in it, although there is a wonderful rhythm, something which will carry you along especially if you are young and a dancer. They are very interesting imitations, but from a musical stand-point it is even outclassed by our modern French dissonances.[18]

His conclusion was that neither party had a legitimate claim to authorship, and therefore both versions could continue to be sold without restriction. The verdict acknowledges a fundamental truth that is so basic that the litigants did not anticipate its importance. In popular music, much of the creativity resides in the performance and its effect on the audience, whereas in classical music, the creativity resides in the composition and the performers' ability to interpret that composition faithfully. In yet another incongruous juxtaposition of this remarkable year in American music, the *Chicago Tribune*'s report of the findings of the trial was printed immediately adjacent to Frederick Donaghey's review of the opening concert of the Chicago Symphony Orchestra's season. Although ample attention was paid to issues of performance, the primary focus of the article was on the repertoire choices of the conductor and the compositional choices of the composers.[19]

LaRocca was advised by his lawyer that Judge Carpenter's disappointing verdict could be overturned on appeal, but he felt he had already spent enough money on the case. He still had two other cases pending. The first was a claim for royalties from the Victor Talking Machine Company, who he said had promised ODJB two cents per copy of the record but had paid only $50. The suit demanded $10,000, and Victor settled out of court for $2,500. (At two cents per copy, this shows that the ODJB estimated the first six months' sales at 500,000 copies, while Victor countered with a figure of 125,000 copies. In either case, the record was a genuine hit.) The other suit had been brought by publisher Joseph W. Stern against the band for interpolating two bars of the copyrighted song "That Teasin' Rag" by Joe Jordan into the trio of "Dixieland Jass Band One-Step." Victor agreed to settle the case by changing the record labels to read "Dixie Jass Band One-Step introducing 'That Teasin' Rag,'" thus marketing it as a medley, which was subject to different copyright laws.[20]

As the Chicago trial descended into low comedy, box offices around the country were busy selling subscriptions to classical concert series. Newspapers ran display ads listing the dates and prices for concerts, and as the performances neared, editors ran articles listing the repertoire to be performed and describing the artists with human-interest stories. In many cases, these were sent by the artist's manager and amounted to "puff pieces," or advertisements masquerading as news. In the more sophisticated markets, like Pittsburgh, though, local reviewers wrote their own articles, which transcended publicity.

Pittsburgh's concert life was dominated by subscription series planned by outside agents or local concert organizers. In the 1917/18 season, the city had four principal series of guest artists that were so important to its cultural life that they tended to discourage local independent concert presenters. These series were the Ellis concerts, the Heyn recitals, the Art Society concerts, and the ten concerts of the Philadelphia Orchestra sponsored by the Pittsburgh Orchestra Association. The Ellis concerts had the highest profile, featuring concerts by violinist Kreisler, soprano Amelita Galli-Curci, contralto Louise Homer, the Boston Symphony Orchestra, and a concert that presented a quartet of soloists from the Metropolitan Opera. In his season preview on 14 October, critic Glendinning Keeble displayed his critical credentials by complaining about the quartet evening as below the expected standard and making snarky comments about the two best-known artists, Kreisler and Muck:

The Boston Orchestra, under Karl Muck, is our greatest orchestra, and Dr. Muck, except on an occasion that may well be forgiven and forgotten, has always presented music of a distinction and significance worthy his great organization. As for Fritz Kreisler, it may be a matter of taste as to whether or not he is the greatest living violinist, but he is second to none, that is sure, and he commands a wider range of style and mood than any other we have heard. Moreover, after giving us trivial programs for a couple of years, he showed a disposition on his last visit to offer music more in keeping with the responsibility which such a magnificent genius imposes.[21]

Two weeks later, by contrast, the announcement of the repertoire to be performed on Kreisler's 8 November concert was so effusive that it could only have been written by a press agent: "The announcement of a Kreisler program is always a matter of great interest, for this celebrated master of the violin seemingly finds nothing in the range of literature for the violin too difficult, abstruse, old or newly fashioned, unworthy of his notice, if he discovers real merit in the works. He infuses new life into many pieces by the warmth and skill of his wonderful art."[22] The audience for classical music was very different from that of jazz, but exaggeration and contrast were the verbal stock in trade of musical promoters in both fields.

On the entertainment page of the 7 October *Boston Sunday Globe*, there was an unfortunate and presumably unintentional juxtaposition of three advertisements (see Figure 10.1). Immediately next to display ads for the Boston Symphony Orchestra season and for Kreisler's first Boston recital was an ad for the movie *The Spy*, with a picture of a menacing mustachioed German in a spiked helmet. Rumors persisted in Boston and elsewhere that Karl Muck was a German spy. During the summer on Mount Desert Island, he had been the target of false reports of his arrest and at least one visit from federal investigators. The visual image of these ads beside each other at the top of the page could not go unnoticed in the charged atmosphere of the fall of 1917.

Opening weekend of the 1917/18 symphony season fell on 12–13 October in both Boston and Philadelphia. The programs of the two concerts reflected the audiences in those two cities but especially the conductors. Muck presented four nineteenth-century European masterworks, and Stokowski played four twentieth-century American works.

Karl Muck planned a program of four heroes. The concert opened with Beethoven's Fifth Symphony, a work with no explicit extra-musical meaning but one that has always been heard as heroic. The progression over the course of four movements from minor to major and from serious to jubilant is inevitably associated with a progression from tragedy to

Figure 10.1 Juxtaposition of advertisements in the *Boston Sunday Globe*, 7 October 1917, 50.

heroic triumph. Next came an evocation of a different sort of hero, the *King Lear* Overture, op. 4 by Hector Berlioz, representing Shakespeare's mad king. Franz Liszt's symphonic poem *Prometheus* represents the quintessential defiant hero from Greek tragedy. The program concluded with the Prelude to Act I of Wagner's *Parsifal*, the religious hero. This final work was Muck's signature piece, the one he had been conducting in Weimar at the moment when Germany entered World War I. The seventy-six-page program booklet contained extensive scholarly program notes by Philip Hale, who was also a reviewer for the *Boston Herald*. Readers had their knowledge broadened with information on the compositional history of each piece, its structure and subject matter, its performance history in Europe and the United States, and its relation to other contemporary works. The hall was filled and the response was enthusiastic, as Boston got exactly what it expected from its scholarly, aloof conductor.

Since the summer, Stokowski and his staff had been considering a concert of American works to open the Philadelphia Orchestra season. It was not mentioned in the initial announcement of the season on 5 September; then, in a press release of 22 September, it was hinted that some American music might be forthcoming; finally, at the last moment it was announced that the entire opening concert would consist of American music. On Friday, 12 October, the orchestra began the concert with an unannounced rendition of "The Star-Spangled Banner," followed by a program of four works by living American composers: the tone poem *Samson*, by Rubin Goldmark, was published in 1916; the "New England" Symphony, no. 2, by Edgar Stillman Kelley, was premiered in 1913 and published in 1915; *Four Character Pieces after the "Rubaiyat" of Omar Khayyam*, by Arthur Foote, were composed around 1900, premiered in 1907, and published in 1912; and the *Heroic March*, by Philip H. Goepp, began as a piano piece and was premiered in its orchestral form in 1904. The program booklet of the Philadelphia Orchestra was very different from that of the Boston Symphony—the program notes by Goepp were a fraction of the length of those by Hale, and in an acknowledgment of the social hierarchy, a page of the program was devoted to a list of proscenium box holders with a chart to identify their locations. The order that Stokowski chose for the four works was not audience-friendly—the first half consisted of two long, serious four-movement works, while the second half offered two works that were shorter and lighter in tone. A more astute program builder might have placed the short march by a local composer (Goepp's *Heroic March*) first, followed by the long symphony. After intermission, the modern work (Goldmark's *Samson*) could have been balanced by Foote's appealing character pieces for a satisfying conclusion.

After the concert, reviews were mixed. The *Philadelphia Evening Public Ledger*, the *Musical Courier*, and the *Musical Leader* were very positive, the *Philadelphia Inquirer* was very negative, and others ranged between. The *Public Ledger* acknowledged apprehension that the concert might be more patriotic than artistic but gushed, "Those who came in trepidation remained to thrill. Mr. Stokowski's program was not only patriotic, but representative of high achievement in the field of music. It was permissible for auditors to be at once loyal and proud of their composer-patriots." The reviewer admired the Kelley and Foote works especially and found only the opening number by Goldmark to be weak.[23] By contrast, the review in the *Inquirer* stated that never in the history of the orchestra had so many patrons left at intermission: "They had listened to all they wanted of an exclusively American programme consisting solely of novelties and they took advantage of the first opportunity to make their escape." In a dig that might have been inspired by a promotional piece for a jazz record, the reviewer castigated the Goldmark as "a noisy, vulgar, pretentious composition throughout which an attempt has been made to conceal the essentially commonplace character of the thematic material . . . by a resort to a number of the various effect-producing devices which the modern composer carries in his bag of tricks."[24] Intriguingly, Goldmark in 1917 was active as a composition teacher in New York; among his students was the teenaged Aaron

Copland. After slamming Goldmark's *Samson*, the *Inquirer* critic admitted that the Kelley was a praiseworthy work but that the topic of New England had led to an unremitting cold, grey, austere mood. Stokowski did not help matters by making disparaging comments about the composers' "absence of exhaustive training as well as of thorough artistic balance, which lack naturally lessens the ability to give master treatment to the subjects involved."[25] This was a remarkable bit of impudence coming from a self-taught conductor who was ten years younger than the youngest of the four composers, but it reflects the prevailing European disdain toward American composers of art music. Stokowski tempered his patronizing comments with a practical suggestion, however: he advocated the establishment of a cabinet-level office for art supervision, along with a federal conservatory where young composers could hear performances and criticism of their works.

American orchestral composers had complained about the lack of performance opportunities for generations, for in the nineteenth century an American work that secured a premiere was seldom repeated. The unfortunate solution to this problem was too often a concert of all American works. I say unfortunate because an entire concert of new music is demanding for players and audiences under any circumstances. The rare opportunity for a full program of American works nearly always led the presenters to include too many works in order to take full advantage of the occasion, thereby defeating the purpose. A movement to present all-American concerts in the 1880s and 1890s had been so widespread that audiences grew tired of so much new music at once.[26] Though American concerts again seemed like the patriotic thing to do in 1917, Stokowski's first attempt was not auspicious. The following week, it was back to Europe.

On the morning of 22 October, Stokowski and his players took the ferry across the Delaware River and spent the day at the Victor studio in Camden, New Jersey. Despite the experience the engineers had gained in working with the Boston Symphony earlier in the month, the first day of recording did not yield any usable masters. The orchestra returned on 24 October, and this time the results were favorable. The orchestra recorded the Brahms Hungarian Rhapsodies nos. 5 and 6, which were ideally suited for both the time limitations of the 78-rpm records and the popular style desired by the company. The experiment was so satisfying to Stokowski that he returned with the orchestra on 6 and 8 November to record the Mendelssohn Scherzo from *A Midsummer Night's Dream*, the Gluck "Dance of the Blessed Spirits" from *Orfeo ed Euridice*, and Grieg's "Anitra's Dance" from the *Peer Gynt* Suite.[27]

Comparing the Muck and Stokowski recordings from October 1917 gives an idea of their contrasting styles. Muck's orchestra is characterized by clarity of textures, rhythmic precision, steady tempos, and consistently transparent ensemble playing—in a word, "discipline." Stokowski's orchestra, on the other hand, has a light and capricious quality, notably in the Hungarian Dance no. 5, with its constant tempo changes. The articulation of the wind parts is not as crisp as those of Muck's orchestra, but the strings are reproduced better in the Philadelphia recordings, perhaps because of adjustments by the Victor engineers. The Philadelphia recordings, particularly the Mendelssohn Scherzo, have greater dynamic range than the Boston recordings, which seem flat by comparison. Stokowski's first foray into the studio was an auspicious start to his sixty-year career as one of the world's most beloved recording artists.

When the Fifteenth Regiment arrived in Spartanburg during the night and morning of 10–11 October, it was preceded by its commanding officer. Colonel Hayward, his adjutant Captain Little, and several other officers had arrived three days early to check out the situation and prepare to keep the men busy when they arrived. The first order of business was to drain a marsh and erect several new buildings to outfit their area of the camp. Also preceding the Fifteenth, the other New York infantry regiments comprising the 27th Division had been in Spartanburg for a month. Among the units already in place was the Twelfth Regiment, a white unit from Manhattan that included soldiers who knew the black members of the Fifteenth from home. Their presence would prove crucial.

The Spartanburg that awaited the Fifteenth Regiment was very different from the one that had greeted Damrosch and his orchestra at the Spartanburg Festival in May. Damrosch saw a vibrant, modern city with excellent hotels and restaurants. The city's music-loving residents generously supported a festival of European music performed by white musicians amid an atmosphere of southern hospitality. The black soldiers from the Fifteenth Regiment found no such cordial welcome. Instead, they were restricted to rundown shops and restaurants, and they were barred from enjoying the hospitality of the city's tourist industry. Their experience was much more sinister.

At 10 pm on the evening of their first day in Spartanburg, according to the *Brooklyn Daily Eagle*, four black soldiers and four white soldiers were walking down the main street of town when "a gang of young fellows standing on a corner made insulting remarks." The black soldiers held their tongues, but their white friends exchanged insults and then blows with the locals before the military police arrived to break things up. According to the report, "News of the disorder spread like wild fire, adding fuel to the already hot resentment against the so-called intrusion of the dusky-skinned soldiers."[28] This would not be the last time that white New Yorkers would take their side in disputes with the locals, but the divide may not have been as clear as it seems. Historians Jeffrey Sammons and John Morrow point out that racial tension had been a fact of life at home as well, and that "perhaps the sentiment of these white northerners was as much anti-southern as it was pro-black."[29]

The day after this incident, Colonel Hayward called his men together and spoke to them from the roof of a shower bath. His words summarized his views on race relations, and are important enough to quote in their entirety. The *New York Age* reported that he said:

> You are camped in a region hostile to colored people. I am depending on you to act like the good soldiers you have always been and break the ice in this country for your entire race. We are about to win the regiment's greatest victory. I want you to promise not to go into town until Monday and then only with permits from me. I want you to stay away from places where you are not wanted. You must keep your temper if you hear the word "nigger," and bring your troubles to me any hour of the day or night. It will be hard, but I want your promise.[30]

After the speech, he asked the men to raise their right hands and promise to do as he asked. The men did so and then cheered their commander. Although support for this tacit acceptance of Jim Crow culture was not universal, all seemed to understand that this test of their self-control would be a deciding factor in the future deployment of the regiment.

Colonel Hayward knew that Europe's band was one of the principal assets of his outfit, and he wanted to make use of it as soon as possible. Consequently, he offered the band's services to the camp's commanding officer for the biweekly concert to be held the following evening, Saturday, 13 October. Before an estimated crowd of 10,000, the band took the stage to the sound of skeptical mutterings, while the white officers circulated through the audience in anticipation of trouble. Captain Little recalled the effect of the band's first performance in Spartanburg:

> Lieutenant Europe conducted, as was his custom, with but a few seconds between numbers, and the program appeared to be short. When the final piece had been played and the forty or fifty bandsmen had filed out of the stand in perfect

order with the "Hep—Hep—Hep—" of the sergeants as the only sound from their ranks, the flower of Spartanburg's citizenry looked at each other foolishly, and one could be heard to say:—"Is that all?" while another would say:—"When do they play again?"[31]

As usual, the program included vocal solos by Noble Sissle, and the talented singer was instrumental in winning the sympathy of the audience. After this event, a group of local businessmen offered honorary country club memberships to the regiment's officers, invited Hayward to speak to the Rotary Club, and asked to hire the band for a dance at the club the following week.

Speculation ran rampant about if and when the soldiers in Spartanburg might be sent to France. When the Fifteenth Regiment began field drills on Monday, 15 October, it was observed that all the men had been issued the most current trench shoes. This fact, "coupled with two or three others," led to speculation in the press that the regiment would be the first to be sent to Europe.[32] Whether or not there was any significance to this item of equipment, it proved very useful on Friday, 19 October, when the regiment was hit by a severe storm about two miles from the end of a ten-mile hike over rough terrain. Despite the buffeting of high winds and heavy rain, the troops stayed in formation, singing all the way back to camp, no doubt aided by their trench shoes.[33] It was also reported in the *New York Times* that the soldiers of the Fifteenth were so far ahead of their white compatriots in rifle training that they would not require additional training in Spartanburg. Their necessary time in camp was cut by more than half.[34]

These bits of news were reported in the New York papers, but there were other, more serious, incidents that never made it into print. Sissle recalled in his memoirs that because of their promise to Hayward, "Our boys had some pretty bitter pills to swallow and all week we had been hearing stories of the ever-increasing insults."[35] One of the black officers, Captain Napoleon Bonaparte Marshall, was insulted and forced to get off a trolley car he was riding despite having paid his fare. A lawyer in civilian life, he knew his rights but chose to accept the indignity in silence because, in the words of Captain Little, "[he] had volunteered to help lick Germany, not to force a social or racial American revolution."[36] When they witnessed such incidents, the white New Yorkers were quick to come to the defense of their black comrades by answering back to those who insulted their fellow soldiers and occasionally fighting with those who attacked black soldiers. The situation grew increasingly tense, as Sissle believed that the men of the Twelfth Regiment were waiting for an excuse "to blow up the town."

Twice during the second week in Spartanburg, violence was narrowly avoided through the self-control of the soldiers and quick action of their officers. In both cases the officers were able to convince all the newspaper reporters—both local and New York papers—to suppress the stories, which did not emerge until years later.

Early in this second week, a local truck driver told some of the black soldiers that two of their men had gotten into a fight with a Spartanburg policeman, after which they had been lynched at the police headquarters. When two soldiers who had been out on passes the night before failed to show up for morning roll call, a group of forty or forty-five soldiers took rifles and ammunition belts and set off toward town. Colonel Hayward learned of their absence too late to stop them, but he raced into town in his car, where he found the men standing at ease near the edge of town. They had sent two men into the police headquarters to inquire about the veracity of the rumor. Hayward went into the station and was cordially informed that there had been no fight or any other misbehavior, which he was allowed to confirm by looking at the police blotter and all the cells. He went out to the street, called the men to attention, and ordered them to march back to camp. By this time a crowd of residents had gathered with no idea of how narrowly they had escaped a riot. When the men wheeled out of the square in formation, the townspeople clapped in appreciation.[37]

The band played a short concert every afternoon in front of regimental headquarters, after the daily performance of "The Star-Spangled Banner." These events became popular with officers, their families, and anyone who was within earshot. Despite frequent performances in the camp and in the town, though, not all the residents of Spartanburg recognized Europe and Sissle, seasoned professional musicians who had long been famous in New York. Near the end of the second week, when Colonel Hayward was in Washington, Europe and Sissle were in town on pass. Europe asked a man where he could purchase the New York papers and was directed to a newsstand in a nearby hotel lobby. Europe asked whether a man of his race would be allowed to go into this hotel and was assured that he would. He said to Sissle, "Go on over 'Siss' and get every paper that has the word 'New York' on it. I never knew how sweet New York was until I landed here."

Despite his apprehensions, Sissle entered the lobby and went directly to the newsstand, where he purchased his papers and was "waited on with all the courtesy of a Boston clerk." Turning with relief to leave, he was suddenly hit on the head from behind by a man who yelled, "Say, nigger, don't you know enough to take your hat off?" The bespectacled singer bent for his hat, saying "Do you realize you are abusing a United States soldier and that is a government hat you knocked to the floor?" He was kicked and cursed by the man (who turned out to be the proprietor of the hotel) all the way to the door.

The lobby was filled with white solders from camp, who had seen the abuse and recognized the chance they had been waiting for to "blow up the town." One of the men ran outside to tell the cohort of black soldiers in the street what had just happened, and the crowd of black and white soldiers turned to face Sissle's assailant.

"ATTEN . . . TION!" called First Lieutenant Europe in a voice so authoritative that all the soldiers of both races stopped in their tracks. He ordered them to get their things and leave the hotel in an orderly fashion. Turning to the hotel owner he asked what Sissle had done.

"That nigger did not take off his hat," the man said defiantly, "and no nigger can come into my place without taking off his hat and you take off your hat."

"I'll take my hat off just to find out one thing," replied Europe. "What did Sgt. Sissle do? Did he commit any offense?"

"No, I told you he did not take his hat off and I knocked it off, now you get out of here."

Europe looked him in the eye from the full height of his six-foot frame and then slowly turned and left the lobby, having saved the man and his hotel from a potentially lethal crowd of angry soldiers. Sissle was humiliated by the incident, especially at being forced to back down without retaliating. After the unit shipped out of Spartanburg, though, Europe quipped to Sissle, "The man has kicked us right to France."[38]

As this incident was taking place, Colonel Hayward was in Washington negotiating a transfer for his regiment. The army faced a quandary, because leaving the Fifteenth in Spartanburg for the winter would almost certainly lead to bloodshed, while moving the regiment to another training camp would be admitting defeat to the racist troublemakers. The only logical alternative was to ship them off to France. General Phillips, commanding officer of Camp Wadsworth, told Hayward, "To my mind, your regiment has established its right to be classed as 'Disciplined.' Having attained discipline, your regiment is fit to represent our country in foreign lands. In France, there is no color line. In France, your regiment can complete its training for modern warfare."[39] His recommendation was crucial in securing the order for deployment.

On the morning of 24 October, two weeks after they had arrived at Camp Wadsworth, the men of the Fifteenth Regiment, New York National Guard, assembled for the last time in the brilliant morning sunshine for review by General Phillips before marching to the train station. Since they would not be taking their tents to France, they left them in place for the next unit of soldiers to use. They had arrived in Spartanburg quietly, converging as separate battalions from their previous guard assignments. When they left, they all marched out together, along a route lined by thousands of cheering New York soldiers. These men, many of whom would eventually follow them to France, sang them on their way with George M. Cohan's iconic song "Over There."

As the Fifteenth Regiment rode the troop trains north to New York, the city's two major orchestras opened their seasons with concerts on the same day (25 October) in the same auditorium (Carnegie Hall). The New York Symphony under the direction of Walter Damrosch performed in the afternoon, and the New York Philharmonic under the direction of Josef Stransky performed in the evening. These concerts were closely observed, not only because of the long-standing rivalry between the great orchestras but also because of the charged political climate in which the two European-born conductors worked. Damrosch had made it clear in his season announcements that German music would not be slighted in his programs, a position that was increasingly coming under scrutiny in the press. The mood of the country was so fluid that what had seemed like a reasonable artistic stance in September or even early October was now questionable in late October.

Damrosch knew the political stakes, and he responded accordingly. Striding boldly to the podium, he began the concert with "The Star-Spangled Banner." Then he turned to speak to the audience. This was not an unusual gesture, as regular patrons were accustomed to his off-the-cuff anecdotes and spontaneous observations on the repertoire to be played. On this occasion, though, he had prepared a written statement, which was afterward shared with the press:

> It is our duty to strike as hard and as quickly as we can until the victory we all hope for is achieved. On this point there can be no temporizing, and our young men are going forth by the hundreds of thousands to prove to our enemies what American determination stands for. To me it would seem unutterably wrong and ethically false to carry our righteous indignation against the German government to the point of excluding the great German masters to whom as a people we owe so much. How can we look upon Bach or Beethoven or Brahms as Prussians when they are great creative artists who have, through their genius, contributed to the development of the world and who no longer belong only to the country in which they happened to have been born, but are a part and parcel of the emotional and artistic life of the entire civilized world? As well might the

Austrian Catholics regret that the Pope was born in Italy, or I, as an American, renounce my Protestantism because Luther was a German. I cannot conceive of now ignoring the great German masters, who form the very cornerstone of all that music has achieved in our country. Rather would I lay down my baton than thus stifle my heart's deepest convictions as a musician and an artist.[40]

His speech was greeted with vociferous and sustained applause, after which the concert proceeded as announced. He opened (as had Muck two weeks previously) with Beethoven's Fifth Symphony. Reflecting the intensity of his feelings, the performance was played, according to the *New York Sun*, "with tremendous earnestness, which occasionally developed into rudeness." The program also included a Bach concerto with pianist Harold Bauer as soloist, along with the popular *Scheherazade* by Rimsky-Korsakov and the early *Burlesque* of Richard Strauss.

The New York Philharmonic concert that evening also opened with "The Star-Spangled Banner" but without a speech. The principal work on the program was Henry Hadley's Symphony in D Minor, *North, East, South, West*, followed by works by French composers Theodore Dubois and Claude Debussy and German composers Richard Strauss and Richard Wagner. Like Hadley's *Ode to Music* performed at the Worcester Festival and the American numbers that Stokowski played on his opening concert in Philadelphia, this symphony was critiqued rather harshly. It was recognized as a worthy patriotic gesture, but Sylvester Rawling of the *World* called it "disappointing" as a symphony. The *Sun* devoted extensive coverage to the work, which it called a welcome addition to the list of American symphonic compositions. The reviewer seems to have been taken aback by the echoes of popular music in the musical style, though, describing it as "a composition of dignified temper, but with no hesitation in frank delineation of those American affections which feed themselves upon 'rag time.'" He described the second movement as "a musical joy ride strongly suggestive of life along the Great White Way." The presence of African American melodies in the third movement led him to call it "an invitation to the clog dance."[41]

It was a sign of the times that despite the playing of "The Star-Spangled Banner" and the earnest avowals of patriotism, Damrosch and Stransky still came under suspicion after their opening concerts. An unsigned editorial in the *Musical Leader* entitled "Are Stransky and Damrosch Making Propaganda?" questioned the motives of the two conductors in presenting music of Richard Strauss, a living German composer, on their first concerts of the new season. In the view of this author, it seemed more than coincidental that both conductors had played Strauss on opening weekend, thereby showing "a great lack of tact, to say nothing else." In a time when all Americans were on the alert for subtle propaganda, the writer warned, conductors should be more careful with programming.[42] The *Musical Courier*, by contrast, drew the opposite message from the two concerts: "Both these events attracted large audiences, who showed by their interest and enthusiasm that music and war seem to have nothing in common, and that symphonic delights are not to be excluded during the trying period through which the United States is now passing."[43]

The busy opening weekend of New York's concert season also featured a recital by Fritz Kreisler on Sunday, his first time in New York that fall. Carnegie Hall was filled to capacity, even the extra seats on the stage. The *New York Times* reviewer gushed with descriptors like "lofty spirit" and "serene spiritual significance." At the same time, the New York Symphony played to a full house in Aeolian Hall. Mindful as always of the political implications of his programs, Damrosch featured pianist Percy Grainger as soloist in Rubinstein's Piano Concerto no. 4 in D Minor. For the New York Symphony concert (as for the Worcester concert earlier in the month), he wore his khaki uniform and his army-style short haircut. The visual image was a potent endorsement of Damrosch's patriotism.[44]

On Sunday, 28 October, the *New York Times* printed a short letter to the editor from one of the attendees of the Thursday concert:

> To the Editor of The New York Times:
>
>   Walter Damrosch began his New York season with a patriotic speech and "The Star-Spangled Banner." Joseph Stransky's program for the Philharmonic had "The Star-Spangled Banner" and an American symphony for its opening numbers. What will the Boston Symphony do when it pays us its first visit this year? No doubt the Boston orchestra is as loyal as our musicians, but it is persistently said that Dr. Muck refuses to conduct the national anthem. That sort of thing may be accepted without question in other places, but not in New York.
>
> MRS. JOHN J. JENKINS.
>
> New York, Oct. 26, 1917.[45]

If Karl Muck read the *New York Times*, it is unlikely that he perused the editorial page that closely on Sunday the 28th. He was playing his second Sunday concert of the year, which placed extra demands on the orchestra after playing their regular concerts on Friday and Saturday. October had been an exceptionally busy month for Muck, and the first week of November was shaping up to be his most grueling endurance test of the entire season. Since its opening weekend on 12/13 October, Muck and his men had played two more paired subscription concerts at Symphony Hall, each with a completely different program: 19/20 October was a modern program of Sibelius, Scriabin, and Enescu, along with the Beethoven Violin Concerto in D Major with Efrem Zimbalist, and 26/27 October offered Brahms, Rachmaninoff, and Debussy. Between these subscription concerts, the orchestra did "run-out" performances in Massachusetts— 14 October in Lynn, 18 October at Harvard University, and 24 October in Northampton—each of which included music not heard in the subscription concerts. November was scheduled to begin with the fourth subscription weekend on 2/3 November, followed by the orchestra's first tour of the season, with concerts in Philadelphia on the 5th, Washington on the 6th, Baltimore on the 7th, Carnegie Hall in New York on the 8th, the Academy of Music in Brooklyn on the 9th, and back to Carnegie Hall on the 10th before returning to Boston for concerts on 16, 17, and 18 November.

Before the November trip could begin, though, Muck had two more concerts in October, the longest and most substantial programs he had tackled this season. On Sunday, 28 October, he offered a program in Symphony Hall that would be repeated with minor changes in Providence, Rhode Island, on Tuesday, 30 October. Muck did not normally perform on Sundays, but this was the first of two annual concerts in support of the orchestra's pension fund. Coming a day after the Friday and Saturday subscription concerts, Sunday concerts presented a challenge, but they were a favorite of working people who could not attend the regular afternoon concerts. In this case the program was one that was close to Muck's heart. The guest soloist—who had volunteered her services for these early-season concerts before her duties at the Metropolitan Opera got under way—was the American soprano Geraldine Farrar, an old friend from his days in Berlin.

Farrar, a Boston girl, had had her first lessons there before finishing her studies in Europe. She had burst on the international stage with her debut at the Berlin Court Opera in 1901, when she was not yet twenty. She sang there under Muck's direction for the next three years while continuing her vocal studies with the German singer Lilli Lehmann. Often a magnet for scandal, she was rumored to be romantically involved with Prussian Crown Prince Wilhelm. She returned to the United States in 1906, where she quickly became one of the biggest box office draws for the Metropolitan Opera. She never forgot her friends in Germany, though, and she did not hide her pro-German sympathies after the war began. She was often invited to be a guest soloist in Boston with her former Berlin colleague Muck, of whom she wrote in her memoirs: "Dr. Muck was a colleague from my early Berlin days. He was never too genial a character and made few friends by reason of a taciturn nature and sarcastic tongue; but he was at all times a fine musician, a splendid figure of restraint upon the podium, and one of the great names that adorned our page of musical history. I need hardly add that many musicians envied him his high position."[46] The singer attracted a large and enthusiastic crowd on Sunday, 28 October, because, as the *Musical Courier* noted in its review of the Boston concert, "Miss Farrar's singing is always as pleasant as she is to look at."[47] Indeed Farrar was so attractive that she had recently expanded her résumé to include starring roles in silent films. Two of her films were showing in Boston at the time of this concert: *Joan the Woman* was an epic retelling of the story of Joan of Arc, and *The Woman That God Forgot* cast her as an Aztec princess at the time of the Spanish conquest.

The program for Sunday afternoon the 28th in Boston was devoted primarily to Richard Wagner's music. After the orchestra opened with the dolorous Tchaikovsky Symphony no. 6, Farrar sang the joyous "Dich teure Halle," from Wagner's *Tannhäuser*, followed by a group of piano-accompanied songs by Franz, Schumann, Grieg, Mussorgsky, and Gretchaninov. The orchestra played excerpts from Wagner's *Parsifal* and *Lohengrin*, and then Farrar returned to sing three of Wagner's *Wesendonck Lieder* with the orchestra. Symphony Hall was so full that persons were standing in the aisles, and many latecomers were unable to buy tickets. The *Boston Post* noted that, "The superb music of Tschaikowsky, the masterpieces of Wagner—all music which is well known to the orchestra, and in which it excels—made a deep impression on the audience, which applauded the conductor and his men to the echo."[48] Farrar was recalled "times without number," but the *Boston Globe* commented, "It was a marked and curious thing that, although pressed even to insistence by her audience, Miss Farrar did not sing an extra number nor in English. Her texts were in German."[49]

The program for the Providence concert on Tuesday the 30th was essentially the same as the pension fund concert, with the substitution of Liszt's *Prometheus* and Beethoven's Overture to Goethe's *Egmont* for the two Wagner orchestral excerpts. Providence was the closest of the cities that the BSO visited on a regular basis, and in recent years, the orchestra had played five or six concerts there each season. The friendly Providence audience in the familiar surroundings of Infantry Hall should have been a good way to prepare for the coming tour, but Muck was preoccupied with the demanding series of concerts scheduled for the first ten days of November.

Muck's absentmindedness was well known to all who worked with him, and his wife was often in the position of apologizing for his missed appointments or inadvertent scheduling conflicts when his mind was in his music. Perhaps this was why the symphony's manager, Charles A. Ellis, chose not to bother him with a minor annoyance that arose on the morning of the Providence concert. He received a telegram from Thomas H. West Jr., the chairman of the Rhode Island Liberty Loan committee, and eight prominent women leaders of musical clubs requesting that the orchestra play "The Star-Spangled Banner" at the concert in Providence. Ellis shared the telegram with Higginson, and when they discovered that none of the signatories of the request was a concert subscriber, they chose to ignore it. As precautionary measures, though, they refused press passes to all reporters except those from the two Providence newspapers, and they stopped selling tickets at 3:30 on the afternoon of the concert in order to keep out last-minute troublemakers. Since Muck had bigger issues on his mind, they did not inform him, and the concert took place without incident. The fallout from that concert would set off the most stunning chain of events in this eventful winter.

CHAPTER 11

☙

Implosions

November 1917

By Thursday morning, 1 November, a tidal wave of indignation had swept from coast to coast. The *Los Angeles Times* headline was splashed across the entire width of the front page: "'Star-Spangled Banner' Slighted by Boston Symphony Orchestra. Cacophony in Boston" (see Figure 11.1). The accompanying article ran a full column on page 1 plus nearly an entire column on another page. Hundreds of editors across the country weighed in with patriotic invective, much of it based on incomplete information and inaccurate quotations. How did this happen?

From the BSO perspective, the incident was straightforward. On the instructions of the Boston Symphony management, the box office of Infantry Hall in Providence was closed at 3:30 on Tuesday, 30 October, to prevent the last-minute purchase of tickets by troublemakers. Three hundred persons who wished to attend were reportedly denied entrance. The concert took place without incident, except for some "faint hissing in several parts of the hall" after Geraldine Farrar's German arias.[1] The symphony players returned to Boston on a special train, and when they arrived at Back Bay Station, Manager Ellis was asked by a reporter if Muck had refused to conduct "The Star-Spangled Banner" in Providence. Ellis retorted, "He did not refuse to play it. He was not asked to play it. He knew nothing about the matter. I received several telegrams this morning from persons who were not subscribers, and who were not there this evening, but as they were not subscribers, I paid no attention to them."[2]

Figure 11.1 Front page of the *Los Angeles Times*, 1 November 1917.

Providence residents saw it differently. In fact, the texts of the telegrams had been printed on page 1 of the *Providence Evening Bulletin,* which went to press several hours before the concert began. The signatories may not have been known to Mr. Ellis, but they were among the most prominent leaders of local music societies in Providence. As in many other American cities, musical clubs were an important part of women's society life in Providence, which boasted a Chopin Club, a Schubert Club, a MacDowell Club, a Chaminade Club, a Monday Morning Club, and others. The clubs met for performances, educational programs, and refreshments. The telegram sent by the eight club leaders was brief and to the point: "The undersigned earnestly request that 'The Star Spangled Banner' be played by the Boston Symphony Orchestra this evening, Oct. 30, at Infantry Hall."[3]

That evening, the officers of these musical clubs arrived at the theater dressed in their evening wear ready to purchase tickets. The scene was an affront to Providence society: "Scores of prominent men and women who went to Infantry Hall, expecting to buy tickets at the door, were met with a blunt refusal on the part of the management to accommodate them, although there were several vacant rows at the back of the hall. Many of them appealed to Mr. Ellis, only to be met with the statement, 'We have sold all the seats we care to sell.'"[4] As the concert began, a reporter for the *Daily Journal* offered to pay the admission price to sit in a dressing room adjacent to the stage but was told this was "an impossible request."

"Will the orchestra play 'The Star-Spangled Banner'?" he asked Mr. Ellis.

"I think not," Mr. Ellis replied. "The Boston Symphony Orchestra played it every night for 10 weeks during the pop concerts in Symphony Hall, Boston, where it was appropriate. We have announced our programme for tonight and people have purchased their tickets to hear this programme, and I think it will be well worth hearing. I received the telegrams requesting 'The Star-Spangled Banner' this afternoon . . . not one of these names appears on our list of subscribers for the season."

"You say the orchestra played the national anthem in the pop concerts," the *Journal* representative continued. "Did Dr. Muck lead that?"

"He does not lead the pop concerts," was the answer.

"Has he ever led 'The Star-Spangled Banner'?"

"I do not know."[5]

The enterprising journalist tracked down the senders of the telegram to confirm that they were not subscribers to the current year's BSO series and learned that many of them were long-time subscribers who had cancelled their subscriptions the previous year because of Muck's rumored disloyalty. They were nonetheless affronted at being denied admission to the concert, and some were insulted that Ellis had not recognized their names from previous seasons.

The day after the concert, the spurned clubs condemned the actions of the orchestra and its conductor. The Chaminade Club adopted the statement: "Resolved, that the Chaminade Club of Providence, R. I., will not support the Boston Symphony Orchestra or any other musical organization which refuses to play 'The Star-Spangled Banner' and otherwise recognize and honor the flag of the United States of America." The Schubert Club advocated that the national anthem be played at all concerts and that the flag be displayed in all public places of entertainment. The Providence Art Club passed a stronger, if less grammatical, resolution: "Until the Boston Symphony Orchestra and its leader prove to the American people that they are not inimical to what this country stands for, they would better not appear in this city."

Ignoring the protestations of Ellis that the decision had been his rather than Muck's, many in Providence blamed the conductor. *Providence Journal* editor John Revelstoke Rathom, one of the country's most avid spy hunters, used the incident as vindication of his warnings against enemy activities in the United States, fanning the flames of indignation in the community.[6] The Rhode Island Council of Defense "unreservedly condemns the conductor of the Boston Symphony Orchestra for his deliberately insulting attitude and respectfully urges the Police Commission of the city of Providence to refuse permission to the Boston Symphony Orchestra to give concerts in the city of Providence during the present war when conducted by the said Karl Muck." The following day the War Council of the Providence Chamber of Commerce requested that the Police Commissioners refuse permission to *any* organization conducted by "one 'Dr. Karl Muck.'"

In the face of such opposition, Higginson cancelled the remainder of the BSO's concerts in Providence, a move that was applauded by the editor of the *Providence Journal* on 2 November. He stated that his city would not tolerate the Boston Symphony Orchestra "so long as Dr. Karl Muck continues in the post of conductor. The place of that insolent German music master is not on the American concert stage but in an internment camp, under strict guard."[7] The change in mood since April, when both Providence papers had lamented the reduction in the number of BSO concerts scheduled for 1917/18, reflects the changing mood across the country.

Back in Boston, Higginson and Ellis released statements correcting the reports coming out of Providence that Muck had "refused" to play the anthem. Higginson stressed his obligation to protect the livelihoods of the players who were under contract to the orchestra, but his indignation was also personal:

> When a man or a woman—for many of them are women—sends me an anonymous letter accusing some man, it is like sticking a dirk in a man's back. They have a notion they are going to test my loyalty. I'm under contract with these men, and owe them an obligation, knowing that they have no other way of supporting their families or of earning their living. For several decades I have given my time so that Boston might have this orchestra, but when Dr. Muck goes, the orchestra will go, and Symphony Hall, which it costs me $13,000 to $18,000 a year to maintain, may be sold.

Higginson's commitment to Muck was so strong that he was willing to risk the future of the orchestra to keep him. But he went on to state his views about the place of the anthem in a concert of classical music:

> Now as to "The Star-Spangled Banner," why should they play it? It has no place in an art concert. If it did it would be played. Last Summer during our Summer concerts with the two-thirds orchestra we played that and "America" every night, and those who went there know it. Another man was leading the orchestra, but there was no dodging—it was because our contracts have arranged for Dr. Muck to conduct at the Winter concerts. Those were popular concerts. These are not—they are art concerts and "The Star-Spangled Banner" has no place at them.[8]

Muck weighed in on the artistic issue with even less tact than Higginson. The *New York Tribune* attributed to him the statements:

> Why will people be so silly? Art is a thing by itself and not related to any particular nation or group. Therefore it would be a gross mistake—a violation of the artistic taste and principles, for such an organization as ours to play patriotic airs. Does the public think that the Symphony Orchestra is a military band? or a ballroom orchestra? No! The Symphony Orchestra is a classical musical organization, composed of the finest musicians, with varying temperaments and cultivated tastes. To ask them to play some compositions would be almost an insult.[9]

This was too much. Instead of quelling the controversy, Higginson and Muck's statements about the artistic merit of the anthem only inflamed it. Boston Mayor James Curley announced that Muck would not be allowed to conduct the orchestra in Symphony Hall unless he played the anthem. Former President Theodore Roosevelt fumed, "I am shocked, simply shocked that anyone can apologize for him on the ground that the music is not artistic, but a patriotic work. No man has any business to be engaged in anything that is not subordinate to patriotism. If the Boston Symphony Orchestra won't play 'The Star-Spangled Banner' it ought to be made to shut up."[10] Residents of Boston debated whether the anthem should be played at the concerts scheduled for the 2nd and 3rd, as did residents of Philadelphia (5th), Washington (6th), Baltimore (7th), New York (8th and 10th) and Brooklyn (9th).

In the face of this criticism, the orchestra librarian hurriedly searched for a score to the anthem. At this time there was still no official arrangement, and time was too short to order parts from a music dealer. The score that he found was the final two minutes of Victor Herbert's *American Fantasy* of 1893, which would have to do in a pinch. Designed as the grand finale of a much longer work, Herbert's setting gave the melody to the brass, while violins played ornate figuration around it. The triangle, cymbals, and snare drum played throughout. Muck asked the librarian to sing it for him so that he could learn the correct tempo and hear where it was customary to hold ("free") and retard the tempo ("and the home of the brave").[11]

The capacity audience for the afternoon concert on Friday, 2 November (predominantly women at this time of day) arrived early at Boston's Symphony Hall in order to talk about what they were about to hear. The applause of those who could see the stage entrance signaled the beginning of the concert, but it was not Muck who stepped to the front of the stage; instead it was Henry Lee Higginson, the orchestra's founder and veteran of thirty-six seasons of symphony concerts. The audience rose and applauded loudly before he read a prepared statement:

> I have asked Dr. Muck and the orchestra to play "The Star-Spangled Banner," and they have complied. They have never refused. Last spring, at my earnest request, Dr. Muck consented to remain in charge of the orchestra, because I considered him essential to the continuance of these concerts. He has placed his resignation in my hands, because he does not wish that any personal feeling towards him should prejudice the welfare of the orchestra. To lose him would be a disaster. Therefore the matter rests with me, and will have my earnest consideration.[12]

When Muck came on stage a few supporters stood and applauded while, as reported in the *Post*, "the rest of the audience, silent and undemonstrative, remained seated." Muck coolly bowed and conducted the program as printed. As he reached the end of the final piece, the audience did not gather their belongings for the usual rush to the door but waited expectantly. After a polite bow, he turned to the orchestra and began to conduct. With orchestra and audience on their feet, he led "The Star-Spangled Banner" for the first time in his life. Gradually a few women began to sing along, joined by more, and eventually by the men in the audience until the sound filled Symphony Hall. Wild applause drowned out the orchestra's final chord. The *Post* reporter wrote: "Hundreds of eyes and opera glasses stared at the conductor. If anyone thought that he would fail himself, they were doomed to disappointment. They could have searched for a line that was changed in that face, for a movement or a tremor that would tell what Dr. Karl Muck, persona grata above most other musicians in Germany at the court of the Kaiser, was feeling. A strange destiny, indeed for such a man. And a man capable of meeting the day without a quiver."[13]

Muck had acceded to the demands of the public, Higginson had affirmed that the original omission was his fault rather than the conductor's, but the story was much bigger than two men and an orchestra. As the outrage grew and spread in the first ten days of November, it was clear that this was bigger than music. The reason for this explosive reaction to the Providence concert is that this series of events coincided precisely with the moment when the United States entered World War I.

When Congress voted to declare war on 6 April, the Allies were disappointed to learn that American troops would not be joining the fight anytime soon. The United States had not fought a major military battle since the Spanish-American War in 1898. The country's commitment to neutrality had kept it from making preparations for military escalation. Before any men could join the combat in Europe, officers needed to be recruited, soldiers needed to be drafted, camps had to be built, equipment had to be manufactured, and the first recruits had to be trained and outfitted at home, shipped through submarine-patrolled waters to Europe, and then trained further in France. Despite the enthusiastic show of patriotism, it took over six months before American men reached the front lines in late October.

On 27 October, the day before the pension fund concert in Boston, American artillery units finally reached the front and fired their first shells at the German lines. The following day American infantry soldiers entered the trenches on the front lines, where they were hugged and kissed on both cheeks by the French soldiers. The event was noted in a political cartoon in the *Baltimore Sun* showing a muscular Uncle Sam confronting a flabby German (see Figure 11.2). On successive days that

Figure 11.2 Political cartoon, *Baltimore Sun*, 28 October 1917.

week, as the Providence patriotic groups formulated their demands, American snipers registered their first kills, and American infantrymen first joined the French in patrols into no man's land. And then, early on Saturday, 3 November, between the two BSO concerts in Symphony Hall, a small unit of American soldiers was surprised by a German shock troop that swarmed into their trenches and engaged them in hand-to-hand combat. After a brief skirmish, the Germans withdrew, having killed three Americans, wounded four, and captured twelve. Adding insult to injury, the victory was announced by the German War Department in Berlin before it was acknowledged by the American government. In a psychological sense, this was the day the United States truly entered the war, or in the words of the *Brooklyn Daily Eagle*, "It marks the line between preparation and action. It signalizes our crossing of the Rubicon of war."[14] For the duration of the war, millions of American families hoped and prayed they would not receive the dreaded telegram from the military. As they waited anxiously, there was little they could do but buy Liberty Bonds, knit warm clothing for the soldiers—and watch for signs of enemy activity in their midst.

In Baltimore, where Francis Scott Key had penned the words of "The Star-Spangled Banner" during the War of 1812, former Maryland Governor Edwin Warfield took umbrage at Muck's intemperate belittling of the anthem: "Our national anthem is particularly dear to Baltimoreans and to Marylanders generally. It is the pride of Baltimore, for it was inspired, composed, printed, and first sung here. Men like Muck, who do not realize their obligation to their adopted country, should be interned. Is he not making money here to support his government in fighting our soldiers?"[15] One of the most common accusations against German and Austrian artists at this time—with no proof—was that their income was being funneled toward the war chests of the enemy.

Walter Damrosch joined the chorus of comment, but because his statement was so long it was abridged in many papers, causing him much frustration in trying to get them to reprint his entire statement. He was initially quoted as saying "It seems to me that it would be an injustice to Dr. Muck to expect him to conduct 'The Star-Spangled Banner' in this country at the present time. He is a loyal citizen of Prussia and is in this country not by his own desire but at the request of Major Higginson. . . ."[16] Muck was actually a citizen of Switzerland who had been born in Bavaria, and this statement seems to be supporting his right to flaunt the anthem.

Damrosch's subsequent statement tempers his characterization of Muck but still presumes to speak on his behalf:

> If Dr. Muck had spoken up like an honest man and said: "How can you expect me, as a loyal citizen of Germany, to conduct 'The Star-Spangled Banner' when you know that my sentiments in this war are in sympathy with my own country?" fair-minded Americans would have accepted this attitude. I, myself, would certainly not have enjoyed hearing him conduct our national anthem under such circumstances. But the explanation that he gives to this morning's papers is cowardly and evades the real issue. . . . He chooses to ignore the fact that the national anthem is the symbol of our patriotism and loyalty at a time when our nation is at war, and even though he is an "enemy alien" the Boston Symphony Orchestra is, or should be, most decidedly an American organization and ready to play our national anthem on any occasion when the patriotic emotions of its public demand it. . . .[17]

On 4 November, Richard Aldrich of the *New York Times* summed up the discussion in a lengthy essay that touched on patriotism, loyalty, nationalism in music, and the unique situation that prevailed during wartime. He advised Higginson and Muck to set aside their aesthetic objections to the anthem at this highly charged historical moment:

> The national hymn takes only a very few minutes out of the evening. Its shortcomings as music do not infect or invalidate the rest of the program in the slightest degree, in the minds of an audience accustomed to hearing it as a prelude to any important undertaking of the spirit. Neither Dr. Muck nor Major Higginson will have found any general demand in New York for the elimination of German music because it is German. In that sense Dr. Muck is right when he says that art is not related to any particular nation or group. Dr. Muck has made up his programs very much as he did before the war began. There is no chauvinism in them. He has played German music in larger proportion than that of other nations, for the simple and undeniable reason that there is more and better German music than music of other nations. But he has not hesitated to play French, Russian, Finnish, and Rumanian music. All these nationalities are represented on the two programs that he announced for this week in New York. To these it was necessary that one piece be added closely identified with the United States, though composed in England by an Englishman. Its name is "The Star-Spangled Banner."[18]

Higginson again declined to accept Muck's resignation, and the Boston Symphony Orchestra departed on its tour to what had always been friendly territory in past years. Advance publicity assured patrons that "The Star-Spangled Banner" would be played at every concert in every city. The orchestra's Philadelphia concert on 5 November came off as planned, but critic H. T. Craven described the performance of the anthem as "void of soul and overweighted with astonishing embroidery,"[19] evidently unfamiliar with the Victor Herbert arrangement used by the orchestra. In Washington, the local musicians' union passed a resolution on 4 November that *all* concerts in the city should include the national anthem. At the concert in Washington on 6 November, Muck dispelled the tension immediately by opening the concert with the anthem. The concert was enthusiastically received, but several subscribers stayed away in protest.[20]

The tour was scheduled to continue in Baltimore on 7 November, but the atmosphere in that city had grown increasingly hostile. Ex-Governor Warfield took it upon himself to stir up his fellow citizens by stating on 4 November, "Karl Muck shall not lead an orchestra in Baltimore. I told the Police Board members that this man would not be allowed to insult the people of the birthplace of 'The Star-Spangled Banner.' I told them that mob violence would prevent it, if necessary, and that I would gladly lead the mob to prevent the insult to my country and my flag. I told them that I knew of a thousand others who would gladly aid in leading the throng."[21] The explicit threat of mob violence caused the Baltimore police to cancel the concert.

The movement against German music and musicians was instigated and carried out by a small group of persons in high society whose financial support was crucial to orchestras and opera companies. Their plans and ideas were shared in a monthly journal entitled *The Chronicle*, which had begun publication in March 1917. Printed on luxurious paper with (at first) no advertising, the journal cost a hefty one dollar per issue and was available to invited subscribers only. The editor, Richard Fletcher, who claimed to be a recently arrived Englishman but was in fact an Ohio native named Richard Fechheimer, wrote most of the content and employed no trained journalists. Other authors were the subscribers themselves, who shared their views regardless of qualification and with little or no prior experience in publishing.[22]

The November 1917 issue of *The Chronicle* contained an article by Mrs. William (Lucie) Jay, the only woman member of the executive board of the New York Philharmonic. An editor's note stated that in this article she "writes for the first time for publication." Her maiden voyage as an author was entitled "German Music and German Opera." In this article she spoke approvingly of the classic German orchestral works, despite the fact that audiences did not enjoy them as much as the more emotional works of Tchaikovsky and Wagner: "I believe that true musical appreciation can only be cultivated through the study of the works of Bach, Mozart, Haydn and the others. When trained to love and understand these, the public will be brought into a closer sympathy with and a more intelligent understanding of all good music." Her main point, though, was that German opera was inappropriate at this time. She personally would miss operas like *Tristan und Isolde* and *Die Meistersinger* but was willing to give them up as "almost a matter of self-denial" because "Given as they must be in the German language, and depicting in many cases scenes of violence and conflict, they must inevitably draw our minds back to the spirit of greed and barbarism which has led to so much suffering." Editor Fletcher praised Mrs. Jay, who "valiantly fires the first shot against the menace of this insidious German propaganda," adding that "German art is literally the mortar in the crumbling structure of Pan-Germanism."[23] This was indeed only the first shot, as during the next year, *The Chronicle* and its subscribers launched increasingly vitriolic attacks on all things German in the world of music.

On 3 November, the Metropolitan Opera announced with little fanfare that it was dropping German repertoire and singers from its programming for the remainder of the season. The vote by the board of directors was unanimous, but the board chair refused to comment on the action. General manager Giulio Gatti-Casazza distanced himself from the decision: "I have no vote on the directorate board. Personally I have always held that reason and fairness should rule in these matters, but of course one must expect that at a time like this, emotion is a much stronger force than reason. My duty merely is to carry out the wishes of the directing board."[24] Johanna Gadski and Otto Goritz were fired, while Frieda Hempel, Margarete Matzenauer, and other German singers were allowed to sing in French and Italian operas as needed.

This crazy weekend saw yet another important musical event. On Sunday, 4 November (a day after the Metropolitan Opera announcement and a day before the BSO's Philadelphia concert), the *New York Sun* published a half-page article on jazz by F. T. Vreeland, the most complete and technically precise description of the new genre to date. The author, a recent graduate of Cornell University, interviewed composers and performers, and he also visited Reisenweber's Restaurant, where he paid close attention to the music he heard:

> The young man with a face that seems to have grown florid from blowing his cornet to the point of apoplexy looks around at his handful of fellow players

commandingly and begins thumping earnestly with his fashionably shod feet and instantly the whole pack is in full cry. The musical riot that breaks forth from clarinet, trombone, cornet, piano, drum and variants of tin pan instruments resembles nothing so much as a chorus of hunting hounds on the scent, with an occasional explosion in the subway thrown in for good measure. It is all done in correct time—there is no fault to be found with the rhythm of it. Even though the cornetist is constantly throwing in flourishes of his own and every once in a while the trombonist gets excited about something and takes it out on the instrument, their tapping feet never miss step. The notes may blat and collide with a jar, but their pulses blend perfectly. In fact, they frequently inject beats of their own between the main thumps just to make it harder for themselves, yet they're always on time to the dot when the moment arrives for the emphatic crash of notes.[25]

Vreeland's word picture not only gets at the essence of jazz, but it also highlights the contrast between this new popular style and the orchestral music that was under fire. The "musical riot" is loud, raucous, and jarring in its timbres and melodies, and its strength lies in its rhythmic precision.

This was not only a new sound; it was also a new attitude toward musical inspiration. Muck's appeal lay in the authority of his interpretations—he drew on his intimate association with the great German composers to present their works in faithful interpretations of their intentions. But LaRocca told Vreeland that his music defied authority: "We don't know the least thing about notes, and we don't aim to either. It might spoil us—and we can't take a chance on losing our ear for music. We don't want to become regular musicians." At precisely the moment that American soldiers were challenging German military authority, jazz musicians were challenging German cultural authority. Like the coincidental release of the first jazz recording a week after the war declaration in April, the New York Sun article coincided precisely with reports of the first American casualties in Europe.

Vreeland's article quotes from an impressive number of popular musicians. Irving Berlin told him, "Jazz is all counterpoint. Its distinctive feature consists of the variations in time and not in different melodies. All jazz performers play by ear. Like ragtime, jazz is another of the contributions of the negro race to American music." Raymond Hubbell, composer of the hit song "Poor Butterfly," explained why jazz was so appropriate to this historical moment: "These are strenuous times. The world's turned upside down. The minds of the people are so upset by the happenings around them that they want to get away from their thoughts. They don't want to think about such things as melodies. Jazz has something wild about it that fits in with their mood. That's why it's so popular with dancers."[26]

During their unexpected day off, the members of the BSO prepared for the real test of their November tour—the three concerts in the New York metropolitan area. The New York papers had reported extensively on the controversy in other cities and assured readers that the concerts would go on as scheduled, unless Higginson chose to accept Muck's resignation in the middle of the tour. At a speech in the Brooklyn Academy on 3 November, Prof. William Starr Myers of Princeton addressed the issue of the anthem by saying, "To my sense of things the 'Star-Spangled Banner' is good music, it expresses one of the noblest of the human emotions, patriotism, and I feel that that is a higher emotion than any that may be expressed in the Ninth Symphony of Beethoven."[27] This comparison is reflective of the nation's mood, when Schiller's call for universal brotherhood in the last movement of Beethoven's Ninth—"Alle Menschen werden Brüder" (All men become brothers)—was deemed less noble than patriotism.

Anticipating trouble at the first New York concert of 8 November, the New York Police Department stationed plainclothes policemen throughout the crowd, but they were not needed. The audience applauded Muck's entrance "mildly," "warmly," or "with hearty applause," depending on which critic one believes. The orchestra immediately played "The Star-Spangled Banner," which was applauded enthusiastically, and then the concert proceeded as usual, with praise for the disciplined and intelligent playing and complaints about programming choices. New Yorkers proved unruffled by the controversy that raged in other cities.

The Brooklyn reception on the evening of 9 November was not so cordial. Before the concert, Higginson met with a committee of trustees from the Brooklyn Academy to hear their concerns and to convey a statement reiterating his views on how the controversy arose in Providence and how the orchestra and its conductor had since responded. This statement was published in the *Brooklyn Eagle* the following day. Higginson reiterated the announcement that "The Star-Spangled Banner" would open that evening's concert. The review of the concert noted that the auditorium had more empty seats and boxes than ever before at a BSO concert, where demand always exceeded supply. The *Eagle* described the opening minutes of the concert in dramatic fashion: "When Dr. Muck appeared, a little very emphatic applause was heard, and the leader turned to bow to it. Then subdued hisses began and the director turned sharply, brought the orchestra to its feet and started the anthem. With the first bar, of course, the audience arose. They heard the notes and nothing else. The audience applauded vigorously and kept on until the orchestra began that preternaturally solemn opening phrase of Tschaikowsky's Sixth Symphony."[28] Always on the alert for negative publicity, Higginson wrote to the editor of the *Eagle* to deny that he

Figure 11.3 Political cartoon by Greene, *New York Evening Telegram* (reprinted in the *Philadelphia Evening Ledger*, 7 November 1917).

heard any hissing and to state that in his view, the house was "almost full." Meanwhile, political cartoonists had a heyday with the controversy (see Figures 11.3 and 11.4).

The patriotic organizations of Pittsburgh were as outraged by the reports of Muck's behavior as their colleagues to the east. H. H. Bengough, retired adjutant general of the Grand Army of the Republic, requested that city authorities deny a license for the Boston Symphony Orchestra's scheduled performance on 30 January and ban the New York Symphony Orchestra as well because of initial reports that Damrosch had supported Muck's refusal to play the anthem. When the Pittsburgh police declined to act on concerts that were so far in the future, local patriots turned their attention to Fritz Kreisler, who was scheduled to perform in the area during the coming weeks. On 4 November, the *Pittsburgh Post-Gazette* published an article detailing the local complaints under the title "Hot Protests Made Against Fritz Kreisler: Caustic Shafts Are Aimed at Austrian Army Officer Musician."

IT LOOKS LIKE A HARD WINTER FOR STUBBORN GERMAN PUPILS

Figure 11.4 Political cartoon by Hungerford, *Pittsburgh Sun* (reprinted in the *Philadelphia Evening Ledger*, 15 November 1917).

The Women's Club of Sewickley Valley, just north of Pittsburgh, cancelled his planned concert in their town, which was then rescheduled for Pittsburgh. Meanwhile, the Daughters of the American Revolution, the Daughters of 1812, and the Daughters of the Confederacy joined the GAR and local Red Cross chapter in calling for the cancellation of Kreisler's two Pittsburgh concerts in the second week of November. The announcement on 5 November that one of the three casualties in the German raid two days earlier was a Pittsburgh man intensified the chorus of complaints against Kreisler. On 7 November, the day before his first concert, public safety director Charles Hubbard denied permits for him to appear in Pittsburgh. Kreisler and his wife Harriet were escorted by police through a rear entrance of the train station, where they boarded the overnight train for New York.

The violinist who had always been a favorite of Pittsburgh audiences was now branded an Austrian army officer on furlough while he recovered from an injury, a financial contributor to weapons destined to kill American soldiers, and a spy who was sending American military plans and secrets to his masters in Europe. These "fake news" stories proved as difficult to counteract as the false reports about Muck coming out of Boston, as they were repeated and embellished before they could be contradicted. The personable violinist, famous for his ability to make connections both on and off the stage, was deeply wounded. That night, as Harriet Kreisler rode the sleeper car through the Pennsylvania mountains to New York, she heard cackling laughter from the upper bunk, and she was sure that her famous husband had finally cracked under the strain.

> "Fritz, are you all right? Are you sick?" she called.
> "What's the matter? What makes you think so?" he replied.
> "You are laughing like a madman."
> "Oh, that. I've just been reading one of the funniest books I ever laid my hands on. It's by Alexander Moszkowski, and full of excellent jokes."[29]

Despite his ability to divert himself with light reading, Kreisler took seriously the charges that were leveled against him, and unlike Muck, he wrote a thoughtful and detailed answer to critics that countered the false rumors about him and also gave his philosophy of art and its value to human civilization. The statement, published in the Pittsburgh papers on 8 November and reprinted throughout the country, began by refuting the assertion that he was associated in any way with the Austrian army and continued with a detailed listing of the charities to which he donated the bulk of his earnings. He closed with his thoughts on art and its relation to the war:

> During every minute of my three years' stay in this country, I have been conscious of my duty to it in return for its hospitality. I have obeyed its laws in letter and in spirit and I have not done anything that might be construed in the least as being detrimental to it. Not a penny of my earnings has ever, nor will it ever, contribute to the purchase of rifles and ammunition, no matter where and in whatsoever cause. The violent political issues over the world have not for an instant beclouded my fervent belief in true art as the dead center of all passion and strife, as the sublime God-inspired leveler of things, as the ultimate repacifier, rehumanizer and rebuilder of destroyed bridges of understanding between nations.

It is to the cause of crystallizing and purifying this true vocation of art and to the preservation and marshalling of its forces, the priesthood of artists all over the world, against the coming day of their mission, that every penny of my earnings has been and shall be devoted as long as I shall be permitted to exercise my profession. No sordid consideration of my material welfare enters for a moment into my mind. After four years' successful tour of this country, I have less money to my name than many a prosperous bank clerk. I have no personal interests at stake. I shall serve the cause I am devoted to undismayed by personal attacks as long as I shall be permitted to and so long as the deep sentiment and feeling I bear this country will not be thrown into conflict with the fundamental and unalterable principles of my honor as a man and artist. I make no appeal for sympathy, but for justice and respect.

But come what may, my deep gratitude for past kindness, hospitality and love shown me by the American public will be forever engraved in my heart.[30]

The statement was published in all of the English-language papers in Pittsburgh and was later republished in New York. Kreisler's words were published in German in the pages of the *Pittsburg Volksblatt und Freiheitsfreund* under the headline "Ewig schade! Geigerkönig Kreisler tritt nicht in Pittsburg auf. Seine Erwiderung auf Protest der Ueberpatrioten" (A Shame Forever! Violin King Kreisler does not perform in Pittsburgh. His response to the protest of the superpatriots). Thanks to stringent new regulations of the Alien Act that took effect on 15 October, German-language papers were required to file translations of all potentially subversive articles with the local postmaster, which served as a damper on editorial criticism.

In the remaining weeks of November, Kreisler saw a string of concert cancellations in New Castle, Williamsport, Harrisburg, and Lancaster, Pennsylvania; in Youngstown, Ohio; Morgantown, West Virginia; and Buffalo, New York. He played concerts in Baltimore, Washington, Brooklyn, and New York, but the empty seats and continued press attacks made it clear that the time was not right for the subtle delicacy of his playing or for his message of universal culture. In New York, where he played three concerts in late November, the wildly enthusiastic audiences—including a large number of soldiers and sailors—refused to leave even after the lights were dimmed. Though his popularity there was as great as ever, he announced on 26 November that he was retiring from the stage, and asked to be released from his remaining concerts of the year, except for his charity performances, at a reported loss of $85,000.[31]

Muck and Kreisler reacted in opposite ways to the implosion of their careers. Kreisler defended his record passionately and eloquently, but when it became clear that his arguments did not resonate, he withdrew with dignity from the stage. Muck continued to conduct all scheduled concerts, silent and detached, for as long as he could. Providence and Baltimore did not allow him to perform there, and enhanced security starting in late November made it illegal for aliens to perform in Washington. The weekend concerts in Boston were the principal venue for his performances. True to form, Muck continued to offer a broad range of repertoire, with an emphasis on German music. He programmed Edward MacDowell's Second *Indian* Suite, op. 48 and his Second Piano Concerto, but American music was otherwise absent. The *Musical Courier* remarked that there was no sense in Boston that the orchestra was weathering a crisis, and in fact, "Dr. Muck seemed unchanged—his customary dignity, serenity and concentration upon his music have been unimpaired by the storm that has centered about him these past few weeks."[32]

Elsewhere, the authority of German music seemed in danger of imploding during this month. The Philadelphia Orchestra's concert in Pittsburgh on 29 October had contained so much German music that the patriotic citizens protested. The ever-malleable Stokowski agreed to eliminate all German repertoire from his Pittsburgh concerts for the duration of the war, and his 19 and 20 November concerts consisted entirely of music by composers of Allied nations. Other orchestras, opera companies, and soloists followed suit, but strangely, the new chauvinism did not create a boom for American composers; instead, the music of Russian and French composers enjoyed a heyday, while British and Belgian music was featured occasionally for variety.

But American tastes were difficult to change, and the large Eastern cities refused to give up German music entirely. On the last day of November, the Philadelphia Orchestra introduced Bach's Concerto in C Major for three keyboards, featuring Harold Bauer, Ossip Gabrilowitsch, and Olga Samaroff as soloists. They were three of the most eminent pianists active in America, and their extensive rehearsals during the summer in Seal Harbor had prepared them to give an unusually polished performance. H. T. Craven raved, "Their combined endowments of dazzling technique, sound authority, personal magnetism and discriminating taste ennobled a composition written nearly 200 years ago."[33] Recognizing a good thing when he heard it, Stokowski featured the work with the same soloists at many of his out-of-town concerts that season.

In New Orleans, there was an implosion of a different kind when the prostitution district known as Storyville was closed at midnight on 12 November 1917 under pressure from the US Navy. Protesting the decision,

New Orleans mayor Martin Behrman famously said, "You can make it illegal, but you can't make it unpopular." The closure of "the District" ended a twenty-year era in which New Orleans became famous for its laissez-faire attitude. It also changed the musical opportunities in the city, eliminating an important venue for ragtime and jazz musicians.

New Orleans Alderman Sidney Story had written the rules and guidelines for the District in 1897, and his name came to be associated with it through its familiar nickname, Storyville. The concept was based on legalized prostitution districts in German and Dutch port cities, where vice was contained in tightly regulated sectors. In New Orleans, a sixteen-block area was established in which prostitution was not technically legalized but was monitored and regulated in order to keep it confined to a small section of the city. Especially through the publication of "blue books" advertising the services of establishments in the District, Storyville developed into a tourist attraction and a symbol of hedonism and permissiveness. The famous motto "Honi soit qui mal y pense" (Shame on him who thinks badly of it) summed up the non-judgmental spirit of the District and by extension of the city that established it.

Music was essential to the operation of brothels throughout the District. Because of the close proximity of so many different establishments, musicians mixed freely, learned from the playing of others, and developed new styles of music from the raw materials of ragtime, blues, gospel, and classical music. Such jazz pioneers as Buddy Bolden, Joe Oliver, and Jelly Roll Morton played in Storyville during its heyday. Though it would be an overstatement to say that jazz was born in Storyville, its early history was intimately connected to this unique place.

With the preparation for war, the military established new rules and regulations both for the health of the soldiers and also for their moral protection. Specifically, brothels were forbidden within five miles of a military installation. After four soldiers were killed in separate incidents in Storyville during 1917, military officials demanded its closure over strenuous objections from New Orleans officials. After 12 November, the District continued to be a popular area for restaurants and dance halls, while prostitution dispersed to underground locations throughout the city. Contrary to popular belief, the closing of Storyville did not lead to a mass exodus of jazz musicians to the North, but it did bring to an end an important phase of New Orleans history.[34]

There was no denying the popularity of jazz music in the North, as Victor, Columbia, Pathé, and other companies advertised new jazz records in

November. The ODJB continued its successful afternoon tea dances and nightly performances at Reisenweber's, and the players also filled as many extra engagements as they could squeeze into their off hours. The band was booked for private parties at the home of Al Jolson and other celebrities, they played weekend concerts in the city, and they played occasional benefit performances. In November they also jumped into the lucrative vaudeville circuit. *Variety* reported that they were backing up dancers Frank Hale and Signe Patterson at Keith's Colonial Theater, where they "took up the pace with a flying start."[35]

The band was hired to appear in a scene of the silent movie *The Good for Nothing*, directed by Carlyle Blackwell, who also played the starring role. The film involved a footloose young man named Jack who was kicked out of his home by his exasperated father but made good through his winning personality. The crew from Peerless Productions filmed a scene in Reisenweber's 400 Club featuring the members of the ODJB playing in the background. When the movie opened nationally in the first week of December, jazz fans could see the band on screen, even if they could not hear it.[36]

Although none of the Aeolian Vocalion records that the ODJB had cut in August and September had gone on sale, the band returned to this company's studio three times in November. The two tracks they recorded on 9 November were rejected, but on 21 and 24 November they made three successful recordings that were released in 1918. "Look at 'Em Doing It Now" was cut on the 21st, while "Reisenweber Rag" and "Oriental Jazz" followed on the 24th. "Reisenweber Rag" was a new version of "Dixie Jass Band One-Step" with a new trio in place of the one based on "That Teasin' Rag." "Oriental Jazz" was a tune they had learned for the vaudeville act of Hale and Patterson. Accompanied by a steady tom-tom beat and featuring chromatic descending lines in the clarinet, the principal melody of "Oriental Jazz" does not sound much like jazz, but the trio slips into a more familiar jazz style accompanied by woodblock before returning to the main melody.

The nationwide popularity of jazz also led to the unexpected resurrection of the Original Creole Band. Following their breakup in Boston in April, the players had scattered to different parts of the country, but in late October they had reassembled with most of the original members for a tryout at Chicago's Logan Square Theatre. After playing at the Winter Garden in New York and touring the East under the management of the Shubert organization and Loew's theaters, this engagement was a serious demotion. But as Lawrence Gushee points out, the band had probably earned a bad reputation with its Boston debacle, and this was the way to come back. For the rest of the year, they played split weeks in small-time houses in Indiana and Michigan.

As they toured, critics made snide remarks about the tired plantation act that was still the source of their comedy routine. But the real attraction was their association with jazz music. During their six-month absence, jazz had become a household word throughout the country, and their advance publicity called attention to their role in the genre's development. A promotional blurb in Kalamazoo made the bold claim, "There has been much contention as to which has been the original 'Jazz' band, but there is not very much room for argument when one sees the original New Orleans band which headlines the bill."[37] The band was still a hit with audiences, but we have no recorded evidence of how they sounded.

Ernestine Schumann-Heink sang her first formal New York concert of the season on Saturday, 3 November, on the day of the first American casualties and the weekend that Muck added "The Star-Spangled Banner" to his programs. Carnegie Hall was filled to overflowing, with extra seats added on the platform. Among the audience were sailors from the US Navy, including one of her sons. The *New York Times* reviewer assured readers that she had fully recovered from the accident earlier in the year: "Mme. Schumann-Heink's art is as it has been for the many years in which she has been acquiring admirers. There are the powerful voice, the rich and vibrant lower tones, the expressive and clear enunciation, the often dramatic turn of phrase, and through it all the whole-heartedness, the all-inclusive amiability that are irresistible."[38]

Despite being the daughter of an Austrian military officer who still spoke broken English after years in America, Schumann-Heink's loyalty was seldom publicly questioned. The military service of her sons was constantly mentioned in the news, and many of her concerts were for the benefit of soldiers and the organizations that supported them. She announced her intention during November to curtail her concert season the following May in order to perform for troops in Europe. Her concerts and records were more popular than ever, owing to her remarkable ability to please her audiences both artistically and patriotically. She was welcomed as enthusiastically in Harrisburg, Pennsylvania; Rochester, New York; and Indianapolis, Indiana as she was in Washington, DC. Nonetheless, even she had to make concessions to the current war hysteria, as she was asked to replace the sets of German songs she had planned with songs in English when she performed in Louisville and Rochester. Anxiety about her sons in opposing armies was heightened when a rumor of her eldest son's death reached her during a concert in Cleveland. After the concert she was relieved to learn that the rumor was false, but she was chagrined when an audience member asked her, "Did you love that son more than the others?"[39]

On 27 November she sang in Washington, DC, to great acclaim. In a scene that was all too familiar, the management placed over a hundred chairs on the stage to accommodate more patrons after the auditorium was sold out. She was assisted by cellist Vladimir Dubinsky and her accompanist, Edith Evans, who had been with her in the car crash in St. Louis. The audience especially loved her rendition of Beethoven's "Ich liebe dich," they requested that she sing "Silent Night," and they recalled her repeatedly after she closed the program with "My Country 'Tis of Thee." The *Washington Herald* reviewer stated that she "has lost none of the volume and power that has distinguished her so greatly in the past."[40]

Belying her outward appearance, the singer was quite ill, and she collapsed immediately after the concert. On 29 November she announced that all engagements through the middle of January had been cancelled and that she would soon return to California to recuperate from a severe case of bronchitis. The *Post* reported,

> Her secretary said last night that Mme. Schumann-Heink, following a lifelong custom, had refused to see a doctor, even though she was suffering from fever and was weakened as the result of a racking cough which comes upon her at times. There is another reason for the great singer's sudden determination to cancel all her engagements. Physically ill, she is also broken-hearted. As she puts it herself, "When I try to sing the tears choke my throat."[41]

The article went on to describe her anguish at having sons fighting on both sides of the war. The writer compared her plight to that of mothers in the American Civil War, reporting that it was her prayer that if her sons were ever forced to meet in battle they would not realize it. The article closed with her poignant words, "When will it end?"

As the controversy surrounding German music and musicians continued to rage throughout November, Walter Damrosch proved himself to be a consummate politician. His outspoken comments on Karl Muck had the effect of casting him as "the 'good' German against the 'bad,'"[42] and he was constantly sought out for comment by newspaper reporters. He reiterated frequently his view that the current German government was Prussian and that the great German musicians of the past had come from regions oppressed by the Prussians. He argued that Schumann had been secretly subversive and that even Wagner had not been well treated by the

Prussians, despite their current admiration for his heroic works. He also used this viewpoint as a justification for denigrating the works of Richard Strauss, Arnold Schoenberg, and other "neo-Straussians."[43]

Damrosch had effectively insulated himself from criticism through his words and actions of the previous year. He had been among the first to include patriotic music in his concerts, and he had defended this practice on political rather than artistic grounds. On the afternoon of 3 November, the day after Muck's first performance of "The Star-Spangled Banner," Damrosch's orchestra opened its concert at the Brooklyn Academy of Music with the anthem:

> That "The Star-Spangled Banner" can be played by a symphony orchestra with inspiring effect and without in the least detracting from the classical program to follow was demonstrated yesterday afternoon at the Academy of Music when with Walter Damrosch conducting, the New York Symphony Orchestra played the national air as it had seldom been played before. The vast audience was stirred to unwonted enthusiasm, and round after round of applause burst forth as the last notes of the patriotic song ran out. Hundreds of voices joined in the song and as the instruments of the great orchestra swelled the volume of sound, the crowd throbbed and thrilled with patriotic fervor.[44]

But Damrosch was also one of the country's most ardent champions of German orchestral music. His argument that the music of Beethoven, Brahms, and even Wagner remained acceptable during the war with Germany was a risky one that he was able to defend because of his un-impeachable patriotic credentials. In mid-November, his orchestra again took to the road, and he again walked a fine line between patriotism and cosmopolitanism.

Before leaving on tour, the New York Symphony participated in a novel experiment in mechanical sound reproduction during its Aeolian Hall concert of 17 November. The Aeolian Duo-Art was a latecomer to the reproducing piano market that had been introduced in March 1914. The mechanism was similar to other "player" pianos in employing a pneumatic system of holes punched into a paper roll. The sophisticated system made thirty-six hundred perforation rows per minute, resulting in an accuracy of one-sixtieth of a second. Dynamics were added manually after the first pass of the roll.[45] For the unusual concert on 17 November 1917, Damrosch conducted the New York Symphony in a performance of the Saint-Saëns G Minor Piano Concerto with a Duo-Art piano roll of the solo part recorded previously by Harold Bauer. On the same evening, Bauer played a solo recital in Chicago as his previously recorded piano roll took the stage in

New York. Among the audience members for this remarkable event were Fritz Kreisler, Ignacy Paderewski, and Ossip Gabrilowitsch.[46]

During the following week, Damrosch played in Altoona, Harrisburg, and York, Pennsylvania, before appearing in Washington, Baltimore, and Philadelphia. Advance publicity promised that the Altoona concert on Friday, 23 November, would be "assuredly the greatest musical treat that has ever occurred in Central Pennsylvania," as Damrosch appeared with the young pianist Ethel Leginska. The British-born Ethel Liggins had studied in Frankfurt and Vienna and, like Samaroff, had adopted a Slavic stage name on the advice of her agent. The Polish-sounding name led to her popular nickname "the Paderewski of Lady Pianists," which was how she was marketed to the Altoona audience. The orchestra played two concerts on Saturday, 24 November—the afternoon performance in Harrisburg featured Leginska as soloist, while the evening concert in York presented a concerto performance by American pianist Wynne Pyle. All three of these Pennsylvania concerts opened with "The Star-Spangled Banner" and featured explanatory comments by Damrosch on the music to be performed.

For the concerts in Washington on Monday, 26 November, in Baltimore on Tuesday, 27 November, and in Philadelphia on Wednesday, 28 November, Damrosch called on pianist Percy Grainger, who again appeared in khaki. The Australian-born pianist-composer had enlisted as a bandsman in the US Army in June, but starting in late summer he had performed often as a concert soloist, since his fame as a musician made him much more useful to the military on stage than in a training camp. All three concerts presented an all-Tchaikovsky program, with the somber Symphony no. 6, *Pathetique*, on the first half and the powerful Concerto no. 1 in B-flat Minor, op. 23, on the second half. The combination of familiar music by the favorite composer of America's ally Russia with a piano soloist in an army uniform, preceded by a rousing rendition of "The Star-Spangled Banner," spoke volumes about Damrosch's patriotism and political savvy.

The Fifteenth Infantry Regiment of the New York National Guard had left Camp Wadsworth in Spartanburg, South Carolina, to the cheers of their fellow New Yorkers on the morning of 24 October and boarded trains for home, where they would be shipped to France as soon as possible. Because of the danger of crossing the Atlantic, transport ships sailed in convoys escorted by destroyers, and Captain Hamilton Fish wrote to his father in confidence that they had orders to sail for France with a convoy on 27 October. When they arrived at Camp Mills on Long Island on the morning of the 26th, they learned that their departure had been delayed, and they would need to wait for the next convoy.[47]

They also learned that they had not left racial discrimination behind. Upon their arrival in Camp Mills, they were immediately harassed by a group of soldiers from the 167th Alabama Infantry. These men insulted the black soldiers, who because they had made no promises to accept the abuse as they had in Spartanburg, fought back. Twenty or more fights ended with the Alabamans beaten, and their provocation of black soldiers made headlines around the country. White officer Hamilton Fish offered to fight any five soldiers of the 167th at once, either officers or enlisted men. When Colonel Hayward received a formal apology from the Alabama regiment's Colonel Screws, he graciously replied: "The white troops of any command are always welcome to enjoy our music or our mess if they care to participate in it. All that we ask is decent treatment. We have no quarrel with any but the Germans. We are ready to meet them, and our one object is the defeat of Germany."[48]

The situation was so volatile that after only two nights at Camp Mills, the Fifteenth was moved again, this time to be housed in four different armories in Manhattan. On Friday, 2 November, the regiment was reviewed in Central Park by Brigadier General Eli D. Hoyle, commander of the Eastern Department. Europe's band figured prominently in this ceremony, playing a variety of music for the parade.[49] As they continued to wait for more than a week to join the next convoy, the band participated in recruiting to replace soldiers lost to attrition. The *New York Age* advertised a "Monster Farewell Dance" on 9 November featuring the music of the band and an exhibition drill.

Finally, on 11 November, the regiment was ordered to the port of Hoboken, New Jersey, where they boarded the transport ship *Pocahontas*. They sailed the next day, ready at last to leave America behind and make the voyage to France. Again the ill-fated regiment was thwarted, as the ship blew an engine rod 150 miles out, leaving them with insufficient power to keep up with the rest of the convoy. The *Pocahontas* turned around and limped back to Hoboken, as Captain Seth McClinton observed Colonel Hayward shedding tears of disappointment on the bridge.

The regiment was sent to Camp Merritt in New Jersey to wait for the repairs to be completed. There they immediately encountered trouble from a group of Louisiana officers who did not want to share quarters with black officers from the Fifteenth. Camp Merritt turned out to be the worst accommodation of all the camps where they had been stationed, with substandard food and inadequate heat during a bitter cold snap. The camp was still under construction and did not offer proper fields for drilling. The men were bored and homesick, and hundreds began to go AWOL to see their families and sweethearts. The officers were constantly busy rounding up the men and keeping them out of trouble. In the midst of this frustrating time, one of the men shot and killed a fellow soldier over a gambling debt.[50] By the end of November, the morale of the regiment was at a low ebb, with no word on when or if the *Pocahontas* would be repaired. Like so many other American institutions, the Fifteenth Regiment seemed to be imploding as the devastating month of November 1917 drew to a close.

In retrospect, the month of November can be seen as a watershed in American musical history. At precisely the moment when the American army reached the battle lines in Europe, public opinion at home turned decisively against German music and musicians. Although aided by propaganda like Richard Fletcher's magazine *The Chronicle*, it symbolized much more than wartime patriotism. This month reflects a tipping point when nationalism took precedence over internationalism.

For much of the nineteenth and early twentieth centuries, American audiences had viewed Austro-German music and musicians as a standard toward which the country was striving. American musicians studied in Germany, American concert organizations favored Austro-German repertoire, and the culture of classical music in the United States aspired to emulate the model of central Europe. The principal American composers of art music had for generations sought to be accepted into the mainstream of European musical repertoire, though only MacDowell and Chadwick had come close to succeeding in this aspiration. The underlying assumption that American music could participate fully in international musical culture was at the heart of concert life in the United States.

The events of November 1917 changed that fundamental assumption. The Metropolitan Opera proved that it could survive without German repertoire, an example that would soon extend to symphony orchestras as well. As concert managers discovered that Austro-German artists like Muck and Kreisler were not indispensable, they began to consider new directions in booking. Audiences, rebelling at the notion that the concert hall was immune from the political turmoil of the outside world, demanded instead that concert organizations show loyalty or cease performing. The new genre of jazz, which had seemed so exotic at the beginning of the year, was recognized as perfectly attuned to the chaotic, anxious mood of wartime. The November experiences of the musicians we have followed reflect the changes that were transforming music in America.

CHAPTER 12

❧

Fallout

December 1917

New York Sun critic W. J. Henderson summarized the events of November in "Rising Tide of Sentiment against German Music," an article published on Sunday, 2 December. He suggested that the root of the problem stretched back years earlier, when arrogant German musicians openly celebrated the sinking of the *Lusitania* and attempted to sway the opinions of "stupid Yankees" to support the Central Powers. He lamented that "the simple, devout soul of Sebastian Bach" and the universal beauty of Mozart and Haydn had been tainted by the machinations of enemy aliens. He applauded the directors of the Metropolitan Opera for eliminating German opera and the German singers who had been among the worst offenders of American values, but he regretted that Kreisler had been swept up in the hysteria: "It has been shown in no uncertain manner that this great artist is to suffer in most places for the sins of the propagandists, who have transformed the mildest of music lovers into determined foes of all things Teutonic."[1]

Henderson acknowledged that it was not the "blundering of the Boston Symphony Orchestra people" that had caused this hostility. Rather, "the explosion touched off by the Providence incident was of powder waiting for the touch of the match. Now the fire burns." He astutely summarized the change in American attitudes that had transpired since the spring of 1917 and could not for the moment be reversed:

In short there are evidences that since the latter part of last season the entire situation has changed. At that time there was apparently no question as to the acceptability of the offerings of Teutonic musicians or the enjoyment of Teutonic musical compositions.

At this writing there is incontestably a deep feeling about it in the hearts of a large number of American-born people and it is impossible to foresee just how powerful the influence of this feeling may grow to be. But regrettable as it may be, there is ground for fear that sooner or later everything German in music will have to be temporarily retired and all the German interpreters or conductors permanently removed from the stage.[2]

Throughout the month of December, events confirmed Henderson's assessment that America's musical landscape had been irrevocably altered. Each of the musicians whom we have followed through the turbulent year dealt with the fallout in different ways, and none would enter 1918 unchanged.

On 2 December, the same day that Henderson's article appeared, the *New York Times* announced that American violinist Maud Powell would take over any of Fritz Kreisler's cancelled tour dates that her schedule allowed, with the fees to be donated to the American Red Cross. A lengthy article in the *Tribune* examined the reasons for his retirement and reprinted many of the editorial comments on the opposition to the violinist.[3] Kreisler was scheduled to perform that evening in the New York Hippodrome with a host of other stars for the benefit of the New York American Christmas Fund. The advertisement read, "You remember how good it was last year!! This year your fondest expectations will be surpassed and your most sanguine hope outdone." Kreisler withdrew at the last moment because of illness, but the event still raised $9,480 for poor children in New York.[4]

The prospect of an indefinite retirement from the stage was daunting for the consummate performer Kreisler, and the following week he seized an opportunity for another benefit performance. On the morning of 6 December, the French cargo ship *Mont-Blanc*, fully loaded with a cargo of high explosives, collided with another ship in the harbor of Halifax, Nova Scotia, causing the largest man-made explosion before the introduction of nuclear weapons. It killed two thousand, injured nine thousand more, and flattened buildings within a half mile of the blast site, including a village of Mi'kmaq people. Throughout the Northeast, relief agencies sent aid to the stricken community.[5] On the day of the disaster, the Boston Symphony Orchestra was performing a concert with soprano soloist Nellie Melba in

Brooklyn. A group of players suggested to Muck and Melba that the orchestra perform a benefit concert for the Halifax victims, to which they readily agreed. Fritz Kreisler was in attendance at the Brooklyn concert and offered his services as well. The impromptu concert was approved by Henry Higginson and scheduled for Symphony Hall on 16 December. When ticket sales opened on 11 December, the concert sold out within a day, breaking all previous box-office records.

In his last Boston concert for the foreseeable future, Kreisler did not disappoint. Olin Downes wrote, "Mr. Kreisler played with a freshness and enthusiasm and felicity rare, even with him. He made no attempt to give a new interpretation of the suave and poetically colored Mendelssohn concerto, but played the music as it was written, without undue sentimentality, without unnecessary speed in the pyrotechnics of the finale, and with incomparable tone, sentiment, and taste." Downes added that both Melba and Kreisler showed the maturity of their years of experience, calling it "a quality which cannot be gained by mere talent, or voice, or enthusiasm, or callow youth, but must be earned and paid for by years of thinking and living." The critic reserved his most lavish praise for the orchestra's performance of Rimsky-Korsakov's *Scheherazade*, waxing poetic about picturesque imagery and orchestral finesse: "It has never been played with such spirit, such imagination, such inimitable and fascinating mastery of detail, within the memory of the writer, at any concert in this city. It thrilled the most hardened concertgoer. . . . With due respect to Mr. Kreisler and Mme. Melba, violinists may come and singers may go, but one such impression of the magic of a great orchestra with a master of the baton at its head will outlast the memory of them all."[6] The next day, BSO manager Ellis sent a check for $10,539.26 to the Halifax Relief Fund.

Kreisler's final concert took place on 21 December, the day of the winter solstice, in Aeolian Hall. This was the first of three scheduled concerts with the Kneisel Quartet's remaining members, whom he had agreed to help when their leader retired earlier in the year. The house was full out of curiosity, but reviewers agreed that Kreisler dominated the other players and that both the balance and the intonation would benefit from further practice as an ensemble. And so on the darkest day of 1917, the world's favorite violinist slipped into retirement.

On the first day of December, record stores throughout the country began selling the first of the recordings the Boston Symphony Orchestra had made in October. Advertisements trumpeted the technological feat of capturing a full orchestra on disc, and the Victor publicity materials raved about the musical qualities of the performances. The records featured the Finale of the Tchaikovsky Symphony in F minor on two discs and the Prelude to Act III of Wagner's *Lohengrin*. Curiously, although the record labels contained the name of the orchestra and its conductor, most advertisements omitted Muck's name. An advertisement from the *Great Falls Tribune* (Figure 12.1) shows how artfully the writers could promote the record without admitting that the ensemble was directed by the disgraced conductor.

The first of December was also the day that new enemy alien regulations went into effect. President Wilson had proclaimed in late November that for security reasons, all citizens of enemy nations would be barred from the District of Columbia, and so Washington's restaurants and hotels had been forced to replace their German waiters with Italian, Greek, and Swiss

Figure 12.1 Advertisement for Boston Symphony records (*Great Falls Tribune*, 30 December 1917).

waiters from New York. As the nation's capital scrambled to implement the new rules in late November, it became clear that theatrical troupes and musical groups would need special permission to perform in the District of Columbia. Also included in the proclamation was the new rule that aliens were forbidden to travel within three miles of the shoreline.[7]

The Boston Symphony Orchestra was scheduled to play another East Coast tour in the first week of December, but there were twenty-two unnaturalized enemy aliens among its players, in addition to the conductor Karl Muck. Despite furious lobbying by Higginson and Ellis, the authorities refused to grant an exception, forcing the orchestra to cancel its performance in the District of Columbia, as well as those in Baltimore and Philadelphia, which were within three miles of the shoreline. It is hard not to read frustration in the notice Ellis placed in the Washington papers on Tuesday, 4 December: "The regulations concerning aliens which have recently been promulgated by the Department of Justice at Washington affect twenty-three members of the Boston Symphony Orchestra and make it impossible properly to give the concert which has been announced for this afternoon at the National Theater. . . . The management regrets that this notice could not have been published earlier, but owing to the holidays, definite information concerning the effect of the regulation was not received until late Saturday afternoon."[8]

Exceptions were granted by the Justice Department for performances at the Brooklyn Academy of Music on 6 December and Carnegie Hall in New York on 7 and 8 December. The Brooklyn concert opened with "The Star-Spangled Banner," which was applauded so vigorously that the orchestra repeated the anthem. At this concert and those in New York, reviewers were happy to report that the ornate Victor Herbert arrangement that had been so criticized during the November tour had been replaced by a more sedate version. Muck showed no other signs of modifying his programming tastes, though, as the Brooklyn concert featured Beethoven's Fifth Symphony, Wagner's *Tannhäuser* Overture, a Berlioz selection, and arias sung by Nellie Melba. The following day's concert in New York featured the long and ponderous Rachmaninoff Second Symphony and some ethereal selections from Mendelssohn's *Midsummer Night's Dream*.

While the orchestra was in New York, the Swiss embassy confirmed that Muck was a citizen of Switzerland and not Germany. In his ongoing effort to quell false news reports about the conductor, BSO manager Ellis sent a letter to concert subscribers in Washington, DC, that was also reprinted in the papers. In addition to reiterating Muck's high artistic standing and respect for the laws of America, he listed succinctly the facts about his citizenship:

- Dr. Muck is not a Prussian.
- He is not an enemy alien of the United States.
- He is not an official of the German Government.
- He is not a citizen of Germany.
- While he was born in Bavaria, he is a citizen of Switzerland, as was his father.

Most importantly, Ellis informed patrons that a careful investigation by federal authorities had revealed no evidence that Muck was a German agent or had done anything to undermine the United States.[9]

The second Carnegie Hall concert featured the Second *Indian* Suite, op. 48, by Edward MacDowell. The *Tribune* critic wrote extensively about the appeal of the piece and the composer's ability to capture the "genuine ring" of American music. Regarding Muck's performance of the work, the critic said it "took on a profound beauty that should warm the heart of the American musical patriot."[10] The *Sun*, in what was becoming a familiar refrain, complained about the orchestra's performance of the national anthem: "[The mood] was that of lugubrious depression in which Dr. Karl Muck conducted the national anthem of this country. The stars were dim and it was not easy to see that the flag was still there. The musicians from Boston really ought to buck up a bit and show more sanguine spirit when they come here."[11]

The rest of the month's performances were in the Boston area, where critics and audiences supported the orchestra with their accustomed loyalty. Muck continued to delight his audiences with insightful readings of familiar works like the Tchaikovsky Fourth Symphony and new works like Ravel's *Daphnis and Chloé* Suite no. 2, which was so much enjoyed on 14 and 15 December that it was brought back by popular demand on 4 and 5 January 1918. While his programs featured more French and Russian music than in previous years, he continued to play the German works that had always been central to his repertoire.

In Philadelphia, the issue of enemy aliens was resolved by the simple expedient of firing eight Germans and Austrians who had not completed the naturalization process. A statement to the press explained, "The Philadelphia Orchestra Association is a patriotic institution, and it is felt that the adoption of the course indicated is the only one which can be regarded as being compatible with the spirit and obligation of the times."[12] While Higginson stubbornly stood by his contractual obligation to the alien players in the BSO, the management of the Philadelphia Orchestra felt no such compunctions.

Stokowski's plans for "theme" concerts had to be modified as the season progressed and the political situation evolved. One concert that did not need to be modified, though, was the all-Tchaikovsky concert scheduled for 14 December, since Russia was one of America's allies. This concert opened with the ceremonial presentation of an American flag to the orchestra association by the women's committee. In her presentation, Frances A. Wister stated, "patriotism and art can not only walk hand in hand, but united they constitute a bulwark against enemies at home and abroad." Orchestra Association President Alexander Van Rensselaer responded by pledging the services of the orchestra "to be made use of in any way in which the government of the United States may deem wise."[13]

In this time of heightened patriotism, few could match Walter Damrosch. He and the players of his New York Symphony Orchestra were either native-born or naturalized US citizens, so they were not affected by the new restrictions on aliens. When he played his first concert of the season in Washington, DC, on 26 November, Mrs. Woodrow Wilson was joined in her box at the Belasco Theater by the duchess of Devonshire, wife of the governor-general of Canada, and the duchess's daughter, Lady Blanche Cavendish.[14] They had the opportunity to hear and see Percy Grainger performing with the orchestra in his US Army uniform.

Damrosch's first performance as conductor of the Oratorio Society of New York was scheduled for 5 December in Carnegie Hall. The program that Damrosch planned was a tribute to Belgium, which had suffered greatly during the battles between Germany and France (see Figure 12.2). The principal work was *The Children's Crusade*, an oratorio on a Flemish legend by the French composer Gabriel Pierné. The Oratorio Society chorus of 250 singers was supplemented by a 200-voice children's chorus and accompanied by the New York Symphony Orchestra, for a grand total of 540 musicians. The program also included a dramatic recitation by Frances Starr of a poem by the Belgian poet Émile Cammaerts, with orchestral accompaniment by the English composer Sir Edward Elgar. For months, it had also been announced that this occasion would include the first performance of the officially standardized version of "The Star-Spangled Banner."[15]

The concert was a qualified success, as critics agreed that the Pierné oratorio was more monotonous than interesting. The volume of sound produced by the combined forces of choruses and orchestra was impressive,

Figure 12.2 Announcement of the Oratorio Society concert (*Brooklyn Daily Eagle*, 1 December 1917).

but the melodic lines were not deemed to be inspired by reviewers of the *Tribune* and *Times*. The initial reviews of the concert were cautiously supportive of the new harmonization of the national anthem, but before long, complaints were heard about the overly ornate bass line. The *Brooklyn Daily Eagle* identified the challenge of creating an orchestral arrangement of a song for popular use:

> To the harmonization by Mr. Damrosch considerable objection might be made. He has introduced harmonies that are more musicianly than popular, and in the chorus has not hesitated to invest the bass part with no little counterpoint. The tendency is a natural one on the part of musicians these days, but is not

commendable, for simplicity is the foundation of popularity. There is not, nor has there ever been, a popular air which could not be learned by the general public after one or two hearings. . . . And in spite of the difficulty the general public has experienced in getting hold of the melody of "The Star-Spangled Banner," it can be a universal song provided its harmonic structure is restrained to the a, b, c's of music.[16]

Again and again throughout 1917, we have seen musicians struggling with issues of simplicity and complexity, artistic quality and popularity, highbrow and lowbrow. Here was the conductor of a symphony orchestra who was asked to create an accessible arrangement of the anthem for general use. Whereas in the spring Rector's orchestra had been criticized for and then forbidden from playing the anthem in a lowbrow manner, now Damrosch was criticized for making an arrangement that was too highbrow to be grasped in a single hearing. It seems that the national anthem was such an emotionally charged piece of music that there were many ways to do it wrong but no clear way to do it right.

Schumann-Heink's bout with bronchitis caused her to withdraw from the stage, but it did not stop her from being heard. On 1 December the Victor Talking Machine Company released her recording of "Nearer My God to Thee," a hymn of comfort that was associated with the sinking of the RMS *Titanic* in April 1912. This poignant recording became one of her most popular records. As she withdrew from the rigors of touring, she redoubled her efforts to support the military camps near her home in southern California. On the 17th, while presenting the regimental colors to the Twenty-First US Infantry in San Diego, she urged the men to "love the flag, stand by the flag, and die for the flag if need be."[17] On the 20th she sang for the troops at the naval training station, and as always, she had choice words for the reporters in attendance. The singer, who was still recovering from bronchitis, spoke in favor of smoking for the troops: "We ought to put our feet on the necks of the people who object to smoking tobacco for the soldiers and sailors. It is poor policy to begin reforming men who go forth to lay down their lives for you. Give the men all the comfort you can. We don't want booze in the army, but he's a pretty poor patriot who turns reformer in a world crisis."[18] On Christmas Eve she sang "The Star-Spangled Banner" for twenty thousand in the San Diego Plaza and then sang at a midnight mass at Camp Kearny, north of San Diego. On 15 December her twenty-eight-year-old son Walter enlisted in the US Army as a cook fourth class. With his enlistment, all her adult male relatives were serving in the military of the United States or Germany.

As Schumann-Heink continued to burnish her public reputation for patriotism, government investigators continued to build their file of evidence for her pro-German sympathies. Major Ralph Van Deman, chief of the Military Intelligence Section, assured Lieutenant Colonel Dennis Nolan in a 19 December letter that contrary to news reports, Schumann-Heink "will not go abroad in the capacity of a Red Cross nurse without our being better satisfied on some points than we are now." He added that she had been "a subject of observation for some months."[19] On 27 December, agents Weymouth and Watson spent the day in Grossmont, interviewing the singer and her gardener, Wilhelm Besthorn. They had received reports that he was "very rabidly pro-German," that he had attempted to visit Mexico in June 1917, and that his naval background had made him proficient in reading US semaphore signals. After a lengthy interrogation, the two agents left without making an arrest but no more confident than before of the loyalty of Schumann-Heink or her staff.[20]

The call to board the *Pocahontas* again came on 2 December, and the soldiers of the Fifteenth New York Infantry reassembled at Hoboken as the ship prepared to sail with another convoy (their third attempt, counting the convoy they missed in October). The ship was packed with two thousand enlisted men and fifty officers of the regiment, along with nearly four hundred "casual" officers and enlisted men who would serve in support capacities in France. Col. Hayward was especially annoyed by a volunteer company of automobile assembly mechanics under the command of Lieutenant J. Bradley Streit, whose drills and other metalworking equipment took up precious space in the hold and almost delayed their departure.

On 3 December, as the men completed last-minute preparations to sail, a fire broke out in one of the coal bunkers, forcing them to miss the convoy while the bunker was emptied, cleaned, repainted, and refilled. For the next ten days, unable to contact friends and family for security reasons, they waited impatiently on board the *Pocahontas* in Hoboken. During this time, they received several visits from Mrs. Amy G. Olney of the Red Cross, who brought sweaters, gloves, and other knitted things to warm them in the unseasonably frigid temperatures. Since the previous spring, women across the country had been knitting furiously to outfit the troops, and the click-clack of knitting needles was an added accompaniment to wartime concerts.[21] The soldiers of the Fifteenth Infantry benefited from that industriousness. On Mrs. Olney's last visit, she gathered a list of names and addresses of family members to let them know that the soldiers were safe but could not contact them yet. On 12 December, the ship pulled out of Hoboken and sailed out into the bay; it anchored off Sandy Hook to wait for the rest of its convoy.

The convoy began moving on the evening of 13 December. As the ships eased out, the winds increased and a storm moved in, leading the commander of the group to order all the ships to drop anchor for the night. As the men slept, the winds reached gale force of sixty to ninety miles an hour, driving a snowstorm that dumped six to fifteen inches on nearby towns.[22] The *Pocahontas*'s anchor held firm, but a nearby British tanker dragged anchor in the middle of the night and drifted into the transport ship, tearing a hole in the starboard side. At first light the two ships were disentangled, and the damage was assessed. Although the hole was well above the water line, the naval officers felt that they should return to port for repairs. Col. Hayward argued in favor of temporary repairs that would allow them to make the ocean crossing without another delay. The ship's captain pointed out that the ship could not be made seaworthy without sheet-metal drills and riveting equipment to repair the hull.

Hayward's luck finally turned, as he summoned Lieutenant Streit of the machinists' company. In civilian life, Streit had been an automobile salesman at the Studebaker dealership in Manhattan. A native of Birmingham, Alabama, he had joined the Alabama National Guard at eighteen and attended the officers' training camp. Now in charge of a unit of automotive repairmen, he was as eager as Hayward to see France. Streit assured the naval officers that his men had the necessary equipment and expertise to repair the hull themselves without returning to port, whereupon the naval men reluctantly gave them permission to proceed, on condition that the repairs be completed and the hull repainted by sundown if the ship were to sail with the convoy. Throughout the day, mechanics, working in shifts to keep their hands from freezing in the bitter cold, hung over the side of the ship in slings. At 6:20 p.m. the last painter was hauled on deck, the job complete.

The twelve days that the soldiers had already spent on board the *Pocahontas* made the thirteen-day crossing seem even longer. Knowing that they could encounter submarines at any time, the ships in the convoy used evasive maneuvers, changing course frequently. During the days the enlisted men exercised on deck, and the officers studied military subjects and took examinations. No lights were allowed after dark except for the tiny blue deck lights that Sissle compared to the floor lights lining the aisles of a movie theater. The December days were short, and supper was served at 3:30 p.m. so that all the cleaning was done before nightfall.

The long nights were boring but also anxious because of the threat of submarines.

As a noncommissioned officer, Noble Sissle had access to the quarters of the enlisted men below deck as well as the officers in the cabins, and his memoir contains vivid accounts of the way music comforted the men in both groups. The band played on deck during the afternoons, but after dark the sounds were more muted:

> On a tour of inspection way down in the lowest hold, below the water line, you would hear a chorus of voices singing with all the religious [sic] of a Georgia Camp Meeting—one voice, a natural lyric tenor, that with mellowness and celestial sweetness would start the old spiritual.
>
> Steal away, steal away
> Steal away to Jesus
> Steal away, steal away home
> Youn't got long to stay here
>
> Before he had gotten two bars with the song there would rise from that hatch a strain of heavenly harmony that would sweep from one section of the hold to another and in perfect harmony you could hear the resonant melody come floating up through hatchways.[23]

In the officers' quarters, there was an upright piano, and Europe played selections all evening with the help of Sissle and the Company K Quartet. Fellow officer John Wesley Castles Jr. recalled, "Jim's repertoire was practically without limit and he was as familiar with Wagner and Beethoven as he was with ragtime."[24] Sissle wrote that because of the circumstances, he had never sung for an audience that was more susceptible to emotional manipulation. He and Europe had to balance the officers' taste for sentimental songs with lively ragtime tunes to avoid sinking into a maudlin mood.[25]

The regiment was hit with measles and seasickness during the trip, especially in the cramped quarters below deck. According to Arthur Davis, the order "fall out!" was greeted with the response, "Can't make it, Sergeant, I'm dying." The quick-thinking sergeant replied, "Die and prove it. Fall out!"[26] Jim Europe suffered so much from seasickness that he threatened to stay in Europe forever when he reached the continent that was his namesake.

On Christmas Eve, the convoy entered the Danger Zone that had been mapped out by the Germans in February. They were accompanied by seven destroyers, "darting about, hither and yon, searching the seas, after the manner in which bird dogs search the fields."[27] For the rest of the trip, the men wore their clothes and life jackets around the clock, even while sleeping. They were treated to turkey and cranberries on Christmas, and on the morning of 27 December they sighted the French coast and dropped anchor in the harbor of Brest. The beautiful lawns and buildings were a welcome sight after so many weeks at sea. Owing to delays in the harbor management, though, they would not set foot on dry land until New Year's Day.

The Original Dixieland Jazz Band had settled into a comfortable routine by December. They had all the work they could handle, and the musical style they had introduced to New York at the beginning of the year showed no signs of going away. Many continued to hear a parallel between the frantic sound of jazz and the unsettled spirit of wartime. Their nightly performances at Reisenweber's were packed with dancers, and the "sugar jar" was filled with generous tips. In mid-December a rumor went around that the cabarets would be closed, but that rumor was quickly debunked.[28] The band played private parties, including a costume party called "The Silver Ball" in Greenwich Village on the Friday before Christmas. The advertising flyer read, "Music by the Best Orchestra in Brooklyn; augmented at one o'clock by the original Dixieland Jass Band who will come down all the way from the Rich Mr. Reisenweber's in a Fleet of Taxicabs, the same as they did for the Danse de la Lune."[29]

The draft had not affected the ODJB yet, as both LaRocca and Shields were granted medical deferments. LaRocca recalled taking off his shirt and waiting for a physical examination at the local draft board in New York, when a doctor strode across the room and pulled him out of line.

> "Do you *always* do that?" demanded the doctor.
> "Do what?" asked Nick.
> "This," said the doctor, jerking his shoulder.[30]

A group of doctors grilled him about a nervous twitch in his left shoulder that had been with him for months. After examining him and consulting about possible causes, they released him as unfit for military service. LaRocca noticed, though, that he was tailed by federal agents for a few weeks to verify that he was not faking it. Shields also received a deferment because of a nervous condition that caused him severe nightmares and insomnia. As none of the band members was among the five hundred thousand draftees of 1917, they were free to continue their performance routine.

If the band needed any more confirmation of popularity, they got it when Columbia Records began advertising its upcoming list of dance records in late December. Among them was a new record of "Livery Stable

Blues" by Handy's Orchestra of Memphis. The record had been cut on 25 September, before the Chicago trial, and the label credited Lopez and Nunez as composers. The record is clearly based on the ODJB's record, though, as virtually every element of the performance, including the animal sounds, is played precisely as on the Victor original but with a larger band. W. C. Handy was the well-known black composer of "Memphis Blues," "Beale Street Blues," "St. Louis Blues," and other standards. In his autobiography, *Father of the Blues*, he relates that Columbia sent him a contract in Memphis to bring a twelve-piece band to New York to record the ODJB cover and other numbers. His band members were so suspicious of the project that he needed to recruit additional players in Chicago to replace those who refused to travel to New York for the sessions.[31] Handy's recording of "Livery Stable Blues" is a strong indication of the popularity of LaRocca's creation, but it sounds underrehearsed.

Freddie Keppard and the Creole Band were also in a routine, albeit with the variety of changing theaters twice a week. Throughout December they continued to play smaller theaters in Indiana and Michigan, earning generally positive reviews and decent pay. Their position in the vaudeville hierarchy had fallen considerably because of the band's breakup in April, but the rising popularity of jazz meant that they were not lacking for work. The circuit of small-time vaudeville offered employment for the foreseeable future, much as it had a year earlier. Alone among the eight musicians in this book, Keppard ended the year exactly where he began it.

CHAPTER 13

☙

Epilogue

New Year's Day 1918

New Year's Day is a symbol of hope and optimism. The old year has been put away and the new year has just started, making anything possible. On New Year's Day 1918, the world was dramatically different from what it had been a year before. The US entry into World War I, the popularization of jazz, and the ostracizing of German musicians had made 1917 a year of momentous historical consequence; each of the musicians we have followed had been changed. Their activities on 1 January 1918 reflected what they had undergone and also where the years ahead would take them.

The sun rose on the coast of France six hours earlier than in New York, and New Year's Day allowed James Reese Europe and his band to touch dry land for the first time in a month. Col. Hayward had made special provisions for the band members to carry their instruments when they left the *Pocahontas* to avoid the possibility of damage if they were packed in a container but also to be prepared to provide music on request. As the tender pulled away from the ship that had been their home for the past month, the band played "Auld Lang Syne" while the crew of the *Pocahontas* saluted. In a short while the first black combat unit to reach France stepped onto the streets of Brest. Col. Hayward ordered Europe to play something for the crowd of curious French soldiers, sailors, and bystanders lining the streets, and he began with the French national anthem, "La Marseillaise," which the band had played often since the summer. Noble Sissle was puzzled that the listeners did not acknowledge the song as was customary in America, but suddenly after eight or ten measures a look of recognition came over their faces, and all the soldiers and sailors snapped to attention and saluted. The band later learned that their lively rendition of the anthem was so much faster than the hymn-like tempo of French bands as to be almost unrecognizable.[1] Their first musical performance on French soil was a foretaste of the impression they would make everywhere they went.

During the next year, the 369th US Infantry Regiment (as it was soon designated) earned a reputation for its tenacity and bravery as a military unit. They faced unimaginable hardships and devastating losses in battle, but one hardship they did not face was racial prejudice. The regiment was assigned to the French army, which had long incorporated North African soldiers and was pleased to welcome soldiers of the caliber of these New York troops. The band, meanwhile, played hundreds of performances in hospitals, training camps, and civilian gatherings (see Figure 13.1). Col.

Figure 13.1 James Reese Europe conducting the Harlem Hellfighters band in Paris (Library of Congress).

Hayward believed that Europe had indeed built the best military band in the United States, and he called on it repeatedly throughout the unit's tour of duty to foster good will. The band's ability to play in both a traditional military style and also in the emerging jazz style was profoundly influential in introducing jazz to the French public. Europe recalled the impact of their playing:

> Everywhere we gave a concert it was a riot, but the supreme moment came in the Tuileries Gardens when we gave a concert in conjunction with the greatest bands in the world—the British Grenadiers' Band, the band of Garde Republicaine, and the Royal Italian Band. My band of course, could not compare with any of these, yet the crowd, and it was such a crowd as I never saw anywhere else in the world, deserted them for us. We played to 50,000 people, at least, and, had we wished it, we might be playing yet.[2]

The leader of the Garde Republicaine was so impressed that he asked Europe to attend one of his rehearsals to demonstrate the playing techniques that made the 369th band sound so different from the European bands.

When the 369th Infantry returned to New York, they were given a hero's welcome, greeted by cheering crowds lining Fifth Avenue for their victory parade on 17 February 1919. The band made a series of records that spring and embarked on a ten-week tour of cities in the East and Midwest. By now the unit was nicknamed the Harlem Hellfighters, and this was the name the band used in its publicity. As they toured the country, they were welcomed by adoring crowds who admired their military precision and who could not get enough of their version of the jazz music that had swept the nation for the past two years. Near the end of the long and successful tour, James Reese Europe was attacked by a disgruntled band member in a dressing room at Mechanics Hall in Boston. What initially appeared to be a superficial knife wound to his neck led to internal bleeding that killed the famous bandleader at 11:45 p.m. on 9 May 1919. The man who told a friend that he would "startle the world with his music" after the war was cut down on the verge of a brilliant career.

The Original Dixieland Jazz Band rang in the New Year as the featured attraction at Reisenweber's exclusive 400 Club. The band that was playing a Chicago dive a year earlier was the toast of New York, and they could legitimately claim to have introduced the jazz genre to Broadway through their live performances and to the rest of the country through their hit Victor record. There was one small but significant change introduced to the

Reisenweber's Restaurant advertisements for New Year's Eve. Throughout the previous year, starting with the ODJB's first appearance in January 1917, the ads in New York papers had printed the name of the band in this way: "Original Dixieland 'Jazz' Band," with the word "jazz" in quotation marks. On 29 December, for the first time, the quotation marks were dropped from the band's name. The genre that had been strange and exotic a year earlier was now a part of mainstream American culture. Love it or hate it, jazz was here to stay, no longer set off by quotation marks.

Nick LaRocca had achieved more success in a year than most musicians earn in a lifetime, but his ambition was not satisfied. The band continued to play in Reisenweber's, temporarily replacing Edwards when he was drafted into the army and permanently replacing Ragas when he died of the Spanish flu. The band continued to make records for Victor and Columbia, though none matched the sales of the first Victor record, which sold over a million copies.[3] LaRocca's *Tiger Rag* went on to become one of the most frequently recorded jazz standards, as numerous bands covered it for decades. The ODJB enjoyed popular success during an extended run in England during 1920 and 1921, and then played in New York until LaRocca suffered a nervous breakdown in 1925.

As jazz developed in new stylistic directions in the 1920s and 1930s, LaRocca felt that the record collectors who were among the first critics and historians of the genre were not giving him the credit he deserved as a pioneer. This feeling of neglect evolved into an extreme resentment of African American musicians and their influence on the genre. By the time of his death on 22 February 1961, his legitimate role in bringing jazz to a national audience had been tarnished by his outlandish claims of having "invented" it. Thanks to the work of the Hogan Jazz Archive in New Orleans, his contributions are preserved and accorded the appreciation they deserve in the twenty-first century.

Freddie Keppard played in Flint, Michigan, on the first day of 1918. Unlike the other subjects of this book, he was right where he had started a year before. Owing to the breakup of the Creole Ragtime Band in April, the theater was smaller and less prestigious than the St. Louis venues he had played a year earlier, but the work was essentially the same. Vaudeville acts alternated with movies to give impatient patrons maximum variety in entertainment for an affordable price. Their formula of an antiquated plantation act that wrung cheap laughs out of racial stereotypes—supported by first-rate music—continued to earn them top billing. With the nationwide popularity of the ODJB records, audiences were now more informed about what they were hearing, and the promotional materials capitalized on their expectations: "The Original New Orleans Creole Ragtime Band. 8 Darkey Musicians in real syncopatin'—jazzcopatin'—harmonisin'—instrumental and vocal melodies. Laughs Galore."[4]

In March 1918 the Creole Ragtime Band ended its four-year vaudeville career. The popularity of jazz had created lucrative club opportunities in Chicago, and Keppard moved there when the band quit travelling. He spent most of the last fifteen years of his life in Chicago, where census records show that he lived with his wife, Sadie, and worked as a café musician. His childhood friend Sidney Bechet testified that he continued his hard-drinking ways as well as his inspired cornet playing as front man for a series of bands in cabarets and dance halls.[5] He died in 1933 after a five-year struggle with tuberculosis and chronic liver disease.

Assessing Keppard's role in the development of jazz is difficult because of the small number of recordings he made and because early jazz historians focused more on Joe Oliver and Louis Armstrong when the witnesses to Keppard's playing were still alive and could have been interviewed. His phrasing and rhythmic style seem to have been "excitable, even tense" in contrast to the relaxed swing popularized by Armstrong. His playing has been described as a bridge between the ragtime style of Buddy Bolden and the swing style of later players.[6] Though the recordings of the ODJB were the most potent influence on the national craze for jazz in 1917, the Creole Ragtime Band, Dunbar's Tennessee Ten, and a handful of other vaudeville acts must have been the first exposure to live jazz for many American listeners.

By New Year's Day, Fritz Kreisler and his wife Harriet settled into a reluctant retirement in the Wellington Hotel. He performed a few more modest charity engagements early in 1918 before withdrawing completely until fall 1919. During his forced absence from public life, he was most hurt by the callous attitude of former friends. Geraldine Farrar recalled in her memoirs that when she invited the Kreislers to a Christmas party in her home, she received a sheaf of anonymous complaints from other attendees. He later recalled the inconsistencies of this time period to his biographer: "British and French officers did not hesitate to come to my suite there, whereas some of my American friends were afraid even to greet me."[7]

When he had announced his retirement in November 1917, he stated his intention to "live quietly and devote myself to composing some serious works that I have long had in mind."[8] True to his word, he composed the score to an operetta entitled *Apple Blossoms*, which opened on Broadway on

7 October 1919. After two seasons dominated by jazz musicals and topical songs about the war, audiences were ready for something different. The Old World charm of the tuneful melodies that Kreisler had written during his "retirement," along with the Broadway debut of dancers Fred and Adele Astaire, made *Apple Blossoms* the surprise hit of the 1919/20 theatrical season.

A new Victor recording of Ernestine Schumann-Heink was released on 1 January 1918. The Irish folksong "Danny Boy" was a favorite with her audiences during wartime, and Victor's publicity called attention to her unique appeal:

> Those who like songs of tender sentiment, sweetly human, will find unusual pleasure in "Danny Boy," the latest record of Schumann-Heink. It is an old Irish folk-song—a woman's farewell to the lad who has heard the pipes calling across the glen. And who could better sing such a story? Schumann-Heink has lived through the whole gamut of human emotions. She is loved for her humanity as well as admired for a remarkable voice. She now has four sons in the service of the United States and is giving her art for the benefit of soldiers in camp as freely as she has always given herself for humanity's service.[9]

She was unable to follow through with her plan to sing for the troops in France, and her plan for an American Bayreuth never came to fruition, but she continued to sing frequent benefit performances at military bases in the United States. Her four sons in the American military survived the war; her oldest son August Heink died when the German submarine U-156 was sunk on 25 September 1918 between the Shetland Islands and the north coast of Scotland.

Schumann-Heink continued to perform for decades. Her remarkable vocal longevity resulted from both her strong constitution and careful management of her career. On 16 December 1926 the New York Symphony under Walter Damrosch honored her in a golden jubilee concert celebrating her first fifty years as a professional singer. She sang her last performance with the Metropolitan Opera as Erda in Wagner's *Siegfried* on 11 March 1932. That year she also sang four to five performances a day during a tour of vaudeville theaters. She never forgot her devotion to soldiers, singing often at military camps and bases, including an appearance at the American Legion convention two months before her death. She spoke out strongly against Hitler when he came to power in 1933 because of his persecution of Jews. She appeared in several motion pictures and had still not retired

when, at the age of seventy-five, she died on 17 November 1936.[10] Like
Kreisler, she thrived on the interaction between performer and audience,
and she was willing to choose repertoire that appealed to the American
public while remaining grounded in the European classics.

By the start of January, when Karl Muck shared a New Year's meal at the
home of Henry Higginson, the conductor was boxed in. His orchestra was
barred from entering Washington, DC, it was not wanted in Providence
and Baltimore, and a February tour to Chicago and the Midwest had
been cancelled. The orchestra had played for soldiers at Camp Devens in
Massachusetts on 30 December, but Muck was barred from conducting because of the restriction on enemy aliens in military facilities. The Swiss legation, which had verified his citizenship in early December, backed away
from that assertion and was no longer willing to vouch for the beleaguered
conductor. But Muck soldiered on with concerts in the Boston area,
Philadelphia, New York, and Brooklyn.

Protests were lodged in advance of the 7 January 1918 concert
in Philadelphia, the BSO's first appearance there since November. In
describing the protests, a reporter for the *Evening Ledger* reminded readers
of the complaints against Muck's playing of the national anthem at the
November concert. At that time, H. T. Craven's *Public Ledger* review had
criticized the arrangement of the anthem in this way:

> Void of soul and overweighted with astonishing instrumental embroidery was
> the national anthem as presented by the Prussian artist. Frivolous whirling
> figures on the strings curiously reminiscent of the Teutonic "Bacchanale" in
> "Tannhaeuser" twisted the composition almost out of all semblance to a pa-
> triotic song. Perhaps Doctor Muck, in his zeal for "art," sought to treat the
> "Star-Spangled Banner" "symphonically." In any event, the effect was eccentric,
> finickly [sic] and with a flavor of the perverse. The superfluous orchestral or-
> namentation very successfully excised all heroism from the song. Imagine the
> American flag converted into a silk lace "tidy" and some notion of last night's
> musical preface may be gleaned.[11]

Two months later, the *Public Ledger* reminded readers of that unsatisfac-
tory performance by stating, "Doctor Muck and his garbled version of 'The
Star-Spangled Banner,' as he played it in jazz style when he appeared here
November 5, will not be countenanced by Philadelphia's patriotic organizations."[12] The condensation of Craven's lengthy description of the performance into the phrase "in jazz style" is significant.

A year earlier, Philadelphia readers probably would not have known what jazz was. As shown by the graph in Figure 6.1, the word "jazz" had gone from obscurity to widespread currency in the course of 1917, its use increasing nearly fortyfold. The association of jazz with the Victor Herbert arrangement of the "Star-Spangled Banner" shows that the writer was familiar with the style as well as the word. Like the musical textures of the ODJB records, Herbert's arrangement features a principal melody surrounded by polyphonic embellishment. Herbert's score calls for an incessant triangle roll, cymbal crashes on the melody notes, and prominent snare drum parts, calling to mind the percussion "noise" that was so often decried in the jazz style. The closing measures of Herbert's setting feature polyrhythmic syncopation that would fit right into a jazz arrangement. In his response to the jazz slur, BSO manager Ellis stated of the November performance, "It would seem to be a sufficient commentary on this complaint to say that at the time one paper stated that the anthem was played at a 'funeral pace,' and another, that it was 'raced through.'"[13] Again, this describes perfectly the interplay of LaRocca's relaxed cornet melodies surrounded by Shields's dazzling clarinet embellishment.

Despite the best efforts of the Boston Symphony Orchestra management to protect Muck from criticism, they were ultimately unsuccessful. On the evening of 25 March 1918, Muck was arrested after a rehearsal at Symphony Hall and taken to Boston Police Station no. 16, where he spent the night in a cell and was delivered to federal authorities the following day.[14] It was a credit to the preparation of his orchestra that a scheduled performance of Bach's *St. Matthew Passion* the following day was led by assistant conductor Ernst Schmidt, who had never conducted the work before. An unauthorized search of Muck's home revealed no evidence of spying activity, but it turned up an extensive correspondence with twenty-two-year-old Boston heiress and aspiring singer Rosamond Young. When translated, Muck's letters to her were found to contain numerous unflattering comments about America, which damaged his public reputation further when published by the *Boston Post* starting in November 1918.

On 6 April 1918, a year after the declaration of war against Germany, Muck boarded a train for the internment camp at Fort Oglethorpe, Georgia, where he spent the remainder of the war along with Cincinnati Symphony conductor Ernst Kunwald and thousands of others. Considered a dangerous alien, Muck was detained until 21 August 1919, when he was deported from the country, never to return.[15] Violinist Carl Flesch, writing forty years later, encapsulated the paradox of this enigmatic musician: "He was a noble character endowed with all the gifts a good fairy can bestow, except benevolence and a love of humanity: he was a genuine misanthropist and had too few illusions about the world for his lack of imagination not to become noticeable in his art too. Nevertheless he must be counted among the great conductors of his time."[16]

On 1 January 1918, with great fanfare, Victor Records placed the first recordings of the Philadelphia Orchestra on sale. Unlike their promotion of the BSO recordings a month earlier, the company highlighted the role of the conductor: "New Victor Records for January: Under the guiding genius of Leopold Stokowski the whole orchestra brings the utmost art to these two brilliant and famous Brahms numbers, Hungarian Dance no. 5 and Hungarian Dance no. 6."[17] A month later Victor released Stokowski's recording of the Scherzo from Mendelssohn's *Midsummer Night's Dream*. Over the next sixty years, Stokowski became one of the most versatile and prolific conductors ever to make recordings. He created a body of work that has seldom been equaled.[18] By contrast, only one more of the records that Muck made for Victor in October 1917—the Tchaikovsky "Marche Miniature" from the First Orchestral Suite—was released in 1918; the others had to wait until the BSO issued a CD of the complete recording session in 1995.[19]

On 3 January 1918, Olga Samaroff joined Clara and Ossip Gabrilowitsch, cellist Hans Kindler, and violinist Thaddeus Rich in a benefit concert for the Settlement Music School of Philadelphia. Her playing was highly acclaimed as always, and her husband Stokowski gave an impassioned speech on behalf of the charity. The Gabrilowitsches had recently moved to the Philadelphia area, bringing them close to their Seal Harbor friends. This friendship proved crucial later in 1918 when Clara Clemens Gabrilowitsch and Olga Samaroff, disturbed by the growing American animosity toward German music, met with Woodrow Wilson and his advisor Colonel Edward House to secure a statement from the president decrying this form of extremism.[20]

Samaroff continued her distinguished career as one of America's leading piano virtuosos. She was divorced from Stokowski in 1923, two years after the birth of their daughter, Sonya. An injury to her left arm forced her to curtail her performing in 1926. Her subsequent activities as a critic, author, and lecturer were much admired, but it was as a teacher that she had the most profound influence. Among the illustrious pianists she taught at the Philadelphia Conservatory and the Juilliard School were Richard Farrell, Natalie Hinderas, William Kapell, Eugene List, Jerome Lowenthal, Vincent

Persichetti, and Rosalyn Tureck. Students recalled that even decades after her divorce from Stokowski, her teaching was profoundly influenced by his musical insights.[21]

None of Walter Damrosch's ensembles performed on New Year's Day 1918. He had led the Oratorio Society in its annual performance of Handel's *Messiah* on 27 December, and he was preparing to lead the New York Symphony Orchestra in an all-Brahms program on 3 January that featured the composer's Third Symphony as well as the Second Piano Concerto with soloist Ossip Gabrilowitsch. Both concerts opened with "The Star-Spangled Banner." Damrosch had been constantly in the public eye during 1917, both because of his many performances and also because of his participation in the debates over the national anthem, German repertoire, Austro-German musicians, and the leadership of the Oratorio Society.

But even Damrosch was not immune to the war hysteria that swept the country. In the summer of 1918, the conductor was invited to lead an orchestra of elderly French musicians at American army camps in France under the auspices of the YMCA. At the last minute, the French leaders of the sponsoring organization attempted to block his participation in this charity effort because of his German birth. The incident was publicly aired, causing Damrosch great embarrassment before clearance was finally granted. In November 1918, Damrosch was taken to task in the pages of *The Chronicle* by Mrs. William Jay, who after disposing first of German-language opera at the Met and then of Karl Muck, had expanded her crusade to all German repertoire of any era. He wrote bitterly of this campaign in his memoir: "There was in New York a small but noisy group led by a few women who sought to demonstrate their 'patriotism' by hysterical outbursts and newspaper protests against the performance of all music composed by Germans, no matter how many years ago. Some of these women, through the curious psychosis of war, really thought that they were serving their country by their protests."[22]

Damrosch found the ideal medium for his combination of musical knowledge and verbal skill in 1923, the same year his memoir was published. He began broadcasting lecture recitals on the radio, and with them he reached a larger audience than ever before. After several years of broadcasting programs for adults, he created the *NBC Music Appreciation Hour* as an educational program for children. Broadcasts of this show, heard by millions of children between 1928 and 1942, enabled him to introduce young people to the music he admired in a format that allowed for conversational immediacy and the widest possible exposure. These radio broadcasts reached a vastly greater audience than even the most active conductor of live concerts could ever hope to reach.

The experiences of these eight individuals illustrate the sweeping changes that occurred in 1917, a year like no other in American musical history. They were among the most influential musicians of their era, but their stories did not unfold in isolation. Each of them actively changed the musical hierarchy of the time, and all were also swept along by forces beyond their control. The old order of January 1917 had given way to a new hierarchy in January 1918. This transformation of the American musical landscape went on to shape the twentieth century.

Afterword

The year 1917 brought significant changes, not only to the lives of the eight musicians we have followed through the year, but to American musical culture as a whole. World War I served as a political, social, and musical watershed whose effects resonated throughout the twentieth century. The circumstances of these eight musicians differed so markedly that it would be presumptuous to draw too many parallels between them. Nonetheless, their unfolding stories reflect the changes occurring in American music and culture during this crucial year. They discovered that in a time of national crisis, no one is immune from the influence of politics. Walter Damrosch embraced the challenge of responding to the national political climate, while Karl Muck tried unsuccessfully to remain aloof from current events. Ernestine Schumann-Heink and Fritz Kreisler discovered that nationality and perceptions of nationality can be fluid and that loyalties of public figures will be reassessed continually. Nick LaRocca and Freddie Keppard benefited from the widespread popularity of their new musical style, but they also found that old stereotypes of race and class were difficult to surmount. Olga Samaroff found that even the most talented woman can be limited by her marriage to a famous and charismatic husband. James Reese Europe redefined the possibilities open to black musicians through his discipline, determination, and the support of a sympathetic commanding officer. The ripple effects of this year continued for generations, as both classical musicians and popular musicians adapted to the fallout of 1917.

Among the biggest stories of the year was the power of new technologies to shape listening. The unprecedented success of "Livery Stable Blues" illustrated the sales potential of popular music, which proved more successful than classical music records for the first time. Jazz benefited enormously from records in the 1920s, as did blues and country music. The development of the electronic microphone in 1925 ushered in a golden age of recording, both for regional artists who could be recorded with portable equipment in the field and for classical musicians, whose performances could be recorded with greater fidelity. By the 1930s the explosion of recordings had spawned a cadre of avid record collectors, among whom were the first historiographers of jazz music. Their perspectives on the genre, along with their propensity for creating indexes of recordings, shaped historical writing on jazz for generations.[1]

The growing popularity of movies also helped to reshape American entertainment culture. In 1917, vaudeville shows were already being supplemented by movies shown in the same theaters, but vaudeville proved remarkably tenacious. Through the late 1920s, the genre that had made the Creole Band famous remained an important form of American entertainment until the introduction of talking pictures in 1927 made it possible for theater owners to offer big-name stars on the screen for lower admission prices than small-time vaudeville acts. By 1932, when the Palace Theatre in New York was converted to a movie house, vaudeville was essentially dead. A generation later, television undermined the dominance of cinema in similar fashion, and by the twenty-first century, the Internet continued the cycle by undermining broadcast television.

The American tendency to allow technology to alter musical entertainment also affected the world of classical music. Orchestral performance is the most expensive form of music because of the large numbers of highly trained musicians required for its presentation. The growth of radio broadcasts and high fidelity records after the 1920s reduced employment opportunities for orchestral musicians and forced orchestras to consolidate. Most famous was the 1928 consolidation of the New York Philharmonic and New York Symphony Orchestra, a merger in which many of Damrosch's musicians lost their jobs. The orchestral musicians' perspective on the demise of the orchestra is detailed by violinist Winthrop Sargeant, who picturesquely noted, "The sound movies and other varieties of 'canned' music were already cutting down the possibilities of outside work. . . . The symphonic musician's mind is geared to a small specialty whose entire function and meaning is dependent on the organization of which he forms a part. A symphony orchestra is incomplete without a contra bassoonist. But there is in the world no more lonely, futile and helpless spectacle than that of a contra bassoonist without a symphony orchestra."[2]

The rise of popular music was a second major outcome of 1917. There had been other fads in popular music dating to the nineteenth century, but none had demonstrated the sheer money-making capacity of jazz. As the recording industry exploded, supplemented after the mid-1920s by commercial radio, jazz only grew in popularity and cultural influence. The decade of the 1920s has been called the Jazz Age not only because of that musical style's popularity but because of what it represented culturally.

The publicity surrounding the Original Dixieland Jazz Band portrayed it as a challenge to traditional authority. The musicians claimed to be completely spontaneous and untrained, as for instance when Eddie Edwards (who could read music as well as improvise) told an interviewer, "I don't know how many pianists we tried before we found one who couldn't read music."[3] Contemporary descriptions of the music presented it as musical anarchy, with wild young men making unmusical sounds to the delight of rebellious audiences. Gunther Schuller has argued that the consistency and discipline of their recordings belie this claim of anarchy, but the message overpowered the music.[4] At this historical moment, the challenge to traditional musical authority may be seen as a symbol of the American military challenge to traditional European authority.

America's first intervention in a European war was not only a gesture of support for the Allied community of nations but also an assertion of nationalism. It was no coincidence that the strongest reactions against Muck, Kreisler, and their world of cosmopolitan music occurred at precisely the moment when American soldiers began dying in the trenches. When the war ended, the suspicion of immigrants aroused in the early months of the conflict intensified. Across the country, the campaign for "100-percent Americanism" fomented nativist sentiments and led to laws restricting the number of immigrants from certain countries. As American society became more insular after the war, jazz was recognized as a musical genre that was national rather than international.

The small-combo format of the ODJB served as a metaphor for individualism. A ninety-five-man symphony orchestra needed a conductor, but a jazz group did not need a leader; it was small and nimble enough for each member to do his own thing while still ending together in a Dixieland tag. Small combos remained at the core of jazz style throughout the 1920s, even as Fletcher Henderson and others expanded the size of the jazz orchestra. After the era of big-band swing music in the 1930s, small combos made a comeback in the bebop style of the 1940s. Rock and roll in the 1950s, like jazz in 1917, established itself as a small-combo genre that encouraged individualism.

The anti-authoritarian message of jazz in 1917 was perhaps its greatest contribution to American musical aesthetics. The notion that popular music can and should challenge the musical establishment shows no sign of abating a century later. The bebop jazz pioneered by Dizzy Gillespie and Charlie Parker in the 1940s explicitly challenged the hegemony of big-band swing. The 1950s rock and roll revolution of Elvis Presley, Little Richard, and others was a rebellious antidote to bland popular song styles. Punk rock of the 1970s protested the industrialization of pop music culture, while hip-hop won an enormous following in the 1980s by protesting the dominant culture's injustices.

The power of technology and the rise of popular music were important musical developments, but on a broader level the musical events of 1917 reflected social and political changes in the United States that would continue for generations. The decade of the 1920s saw the first of the twentieth century's "culture wars," epitomized by a popular song published in early 1919, just a few months after the armistice:

How ya gonna keep 'em, down on the farm,
After they've seen Paree?
How ya gonna keep 'em away from Broadway;
Jazzin' aroun', and paintin' the town?[5]

The chorus of the song effectively captures the tensions that ignited the culture war: rural versus urban, traditional versus modern, national versus foreign, and conservative versus liberal. (Tellingly, James Reese Europe's 369th Regiment band performed the song frequently on its national tour after returning from France.)[6] The 1920 US census was the first in which the urban population exceeded the rural population, a trend that continued for the rest of the century.[7] Conservatives felt that their way of life was threatened by a growing non-Anglo-Saxon Protestant population that was primarily urban and liberal. Jazz symbolized this growing threat, especially as African American performers became more prominent.

Ann Hagedorn, in *Savage Peace: Hope and Fear in America, 1919*, observed that winning the war did not give Americans a sense of security. If anything, the mood at home grew more restive. The returning doughboys brought with them new attitudes and mores that conflicted with traditional rural values. The fear of terrorism and the threat of Bolshevism in the wake of the Russian Revolution led to enhanced restrictions on civil liberties in the United States. Many of the wartime security measures were extended in the face of real and imagined threats to the country. The freedoms and gratitude the soldiers had experienced in France were not part of their postwar experience after the victory parades were over.

For African Americans, the homecoming was especially bitter. They had been treated as equals in the French army, but they quickly discovered that the United States was not ready to accord them the same courtesy at home. Lynchings increased sharply in 1919, and Ku Klux Klan membership surged in the early 1920s. James Reese Europe's hopes for a national Negro orchestra were not realized, and his untimely death deprived the Harlem Renaissance of one of its most aspirational voices. He was succeeded, though, by an exceptionally influential cohort of black jazz musicians from around the country. New Orleans players like Joe Oliver, Louis Armstrong, and Jelly Roll Morton shaped small-ensemble jazz in the 1920s, and black bandleaders like Duke Ellington and Count Basie were influential in establishing big-band swing in the 1930s. For Nick LaRocca, the ascendancy of black jazz musicians was a bitter pill to swallow, as he grew increasingly strident in his claims to have been the sole originator of jazz.[8]

For German Americans, the anti-immigrant furor immediately after World War I created a powerful incentive for assimilation. Before the war, when German immigrants were perceived as valuable contributors to American society, they had been largely shielded from the discrimination leveled at Irish and southern European immigrants. As a consequence, many of the millions of German Americans before the war succeeded in reaping the social and economic benefits of American citizenship while maintaining strong ties to their cultural heritage. German-language schools and newspapers, German social clubs, and German music all helped to foster cohesiveness in this immigrant group. The war brought this biculturalism to an abrupt end in much of the country, as the descendants of nineteenth-century German immigrants hastened to distance themselves from more recent immigrants by abandoning their ties to German culture.[9]

Fritz Kreisler experienced this animosity firsthand when he returned to the concert stage in the fall of 1919. He waited nearly a year after the armistice to resume performing, but he found uncanny parallels to his experiences in 1917. At his first public concert on 27 October 1919, a relief concert in New York's Carnegie Hall, his entrance was greeted by a five-minute standing ovation, and the applause at the end went on so long that the house manager dimmed the lights as in his prewar concerts. But in the weeks following Kreisler faced stiff opposition in smaller cities: protests by the American Legion (a veteran's organization founded after the war) led to cancelled concerts in Louisville, Kentucky, and Rochester, New York. In Lynn, Massachusetts, the mayor gave a permit for a "sacred concert" only and then announced that he had arranged for a jury of twelve musicians to alert the police if Kreisler played any secular music.[10] The mayor of Scranton, Pennsylvania, urged the citizens of that town to boycott the concert there, but three thousand attended anyway. The controversy came to a head in Ithaca, New York, where a 10 December 1919 concert was supported by the Cornell University president but opposed by the city's mayor. Protestors nearly succeeded in thwarting the concert, but Kreisler persisted, even when he was forced to play in the dark because someone cut the power to the building. When asked in late December why he persisted in touring in the face of such opposition, Kreisler gave his artistic credo, affirming his belief in the universality of art even in a time of nationalism:

> I am staying here upon the unbiased basis of art for the sake of art. I feel that I can give America something. And my message is a purely artistic one and always will be in every country under every circumstance. I will never stand for any inclusion of the national element in art. I would as quickly oppose any attempt in Vienna to agitate against French music. The higher art goes the less it has to do with terrestrial things. It is like religion and philosophy. Music has no vehicle in which it is held down and confined to nationalities any more than religion is for one favored people alone.[11]

In January 1920, Kreisler returned to Pittsburgh, the scene of his blocked concerts in 1917. In advance of the concert, the women of the Service Star Legion of Allegheny County issued a letter of protest, and the American Legion threatened a disturbance. One reporter noted that at the concert "there were almost as many policemen as there were auditors" but that as soon as Kreisler began to play, "everything was as happy as a wedding bell."[12]

The events of 1917 challenged the belief in the universal nature of art. Kreisler and Damrosch argued that the universal language of music knew no national boundaries and therefore the music of Beethoven and Bach was not restricted by time and place. Their detractors, on the other hand, argued that any music written by a German composer, no matter how long ago or how noble in its aims, was inseparable from the heinous crimes that were being committed by German soldiers and spies in the name of the Kaiser. This fundamental disagreement over whether art music was universal or national resonated strongly in an era when politics and economics were undergoing similar debates. World War I abruptly ended a period of globalism, when banking systems, trade networks, and diplomatic ties had grown increasingly interdependent. The war forced nations to break those international bonds and rely instead on their internal resources or those of their allies. This sudden rise of "statism" influenced the political climate for most of the twentieth century, until globalism again saw a resurgence starting in the 1990s.[13]

The musical lessons of World War I were inconsistently applied during World War II, which the United States entered after the Japanese attack on Pearl Harbor on 7 December 1941. The government employed even more draconian methods against Americans of Japanese ancestry than it had against German Americans in the First World War. Japanese Americans were excluded by executive order from the West Coast, including the entire state of California, and over a hundred thousand were placed in internment camps between February 1942 and March 1946. This mass internment was possible because of the much smaller number of Japanese Americans in 1942 compared to the millions of German Americans in 1917. In Hawaii, then still a territory, where over one-third of the population was of Japanese ancestry, fewer than two thousand were interned. After decades of denial, the US government finally agreed to pay reparations to survivors of the internment camps in the Civil Liberties Act of 1988.[14]

In the concert hall, American music played a much more prominent role during World War II than it had during World War I. The major symphony orchestras were still conducted almost exclusively by Europeans, but the old prejudices against American composers had begun to break down. Days after the attack on Pearl Harbor, conductor Andre Kostelanetz commissioned a series of musical portraits from composers Aaron Copland, Virgil Thomson, and Jerome Kern. Conductor Eugene Goossens of the Cincinnati Symphony Orchestra commissioned a series of patriotic fanfares by American composers, inspiring among others the enduringly popular *Fanfare for the Common Man* by Aaron Copland, premiered in March 1943. Many conductors, including Arturo Toscanini, featured American music prominently on their programs. In her study of music during the war, Annegret Fauser points out that conductors took a much more inclusive approach to repertoire than their counterparts in the previous war. They continued to perform music from both allied and enemy nations, "demonstrating an ability to rise above national enmities in matters of culture."[15]

Finally, the musical events of 1917 reinforced the emotional power of "The Star-Spangled Banner." The question of whether a performer should be obligated to perform the national anthem was at the heart of the controversy over the Boston Symphony Orchestra's failure to play it in Providence. (It should be noted that though President Wilson recognized "The Star-Spangled Banner" for performance at official government functions in 1916, the song was not legally adopted as the country's national anthem until Congress passed a resolution to that effect on 3 March 1931.) But that controversy was only a symbol of American resentment and mistrust of foreign musicians. Equally important was the debate over the correct stylistic rendering of the anthem. Complaints about cabaret performances of the anthem in popular styles showed how politically charged the anthem could be, and reactions to Damrosch's "official" harmonization of the anthem and Muck's lethargic performance in Philadelphia illustrated how easy it was to get the anthem wrong.

Damrosch's harmonization was never given official status. There are no laws forbidding interpretive license in performing the song, which allows popular singers to embellish it to suit their own personal tastes. When Jose Feliciano sang a Latin-styled interpretation of the anthem before a World Series game on 7 October 1968, the reaction was so strong that some radio stations blacklisted his records temporarily. Another personal interpretation, the ornate electric guitar embellishment performed by Jimi Hendrix at the Woodstock Festival in 1969, has been heard by some as an iconoclastic assault on the anthem and by others as a uniquely personal homage to the anthem. Whitney Houston's performance of the anthem at the Super Bowl on 27 January 1991, ten days after the start of the Gulf War, was rapturously praised, while her modification of the triple meter to quadruple earned barely a mention.[16]

In the twenty-first century, the anthem remains a flashpoint, ready to ignite passions and stimulate debate at moments of national conflict. Athletes have used the performance of the anthem as a vehicle for protest against social injustice, notably at the Mexico City Olympics in 1968 and at National Football League games in 2016 and 2017. The vigorous reactions for and against these protests raise fundamental questions about the nature of American democracy. Is the anthem a symbol of American freedom or a symbol of national unity? If it is a symbol of freedom, why is it so divisive when protestors use the anthem to call attention to injustice and inequity? If it is a symbol of unity, how can audiences be urged to participate in its symbolism without evoking forced compliance? Clearly, "The Star-Spangled Banner" is much more than just a song, and its ability to inspire controversy two centuries after its composition is an ongoing testimony to its symbolic power.

Each of the eight performers in this study shows in a different way how strongly our musical history is tied to our social and political history. Kreisler, Muck, and Schumann-Heink discovered that the security and freedom they had taken for granted as aliens could become tenuous in wartime. Europe and Keppard found that the war and the emergence of jazz brought new opportunities for African American musicians but did not erase the legacy of discrimination. Damrosch and Samaroff saw their commitment to the international traditions of classical music questioned during an era of intense patriotism. LaRocca was in the right place at the right time to capitalize on the surge of nationalism and nervous energy in the United States with his version of jazz style. Each of the eight performers learned that in wartime, artistic expression cannot remain aloof from patriotic sentiment. And each of them learned that reputations can be made and broken through the power of public opinion. Their experiences in 1917 form a microcosm of the musical culture of their time as well as a harbinger of the century to come.

NOTES

CHAPTER 1

1. Their correspondence is preserved in the Spaulding Library, New England Conservatory of Music.
2. This descriptive phrase was used by the Military Intelligence agent who searched the home (without a search warrant or a member of the family present) after Muck's arrest in March 1918. Report by Agent Weiss, 30 March 1918, Military Intelligence Division, Correspondence 1917–1941, Record Group 165, File 9140–4175, 2, National Archives and Records Administration.
3. "Mme. Samaroff's Concert: An American Pianist with a Russian Name Makes Her First Appearance," *New York Times*, 19 January 1905, 9.
4. Onah L. Spencer, "Trumpeter Freddie Keppard Walked Out on Al Capone!," *Music and Rhythm* 2/6 (June 1941), 14–15.
5. "Chicago Has 'Sanest' New Year's Eve: Churches, Movies and Theaters Claim Crowds That Watch 1916 Vanish; Loop Undemonstrative," *Chicago Examiner*, 1 January 1917, 1.
6. For a wide-ranging discussion of the "trans-ethnic cultural exchange" that characterized New Orleans musicians in LaRocca's youth, see Bruce Boyd Raeburn, "Stars of David and Sons of Sicily: Constellations beyond the Canon in Early New Orleans Jazz," *Jazz Perspectives* 3/2 (August 2009), 123–52.
7. Lowell Mellett, "Speculators Roll in Wealth—New York a Modern Babylon," *Day Book*, 12 December 1916, 30.
8. Quoted in Al Rose, *Eubie Blake* (New York: Schirmer, 1979), 60.

CHAPTER 2

1. B. D. "Russian Pianist not Wearied by Labors: Gabrilowitsch Plays with Undying Art on Boston's Fine Romantic Program," *Philadelphia Evening Public Ledger*, 2 January 1917, 9.
2. "Symphony Delights: Dr. Muck Reveals Much Temperament in Third Concert," *Washington Times*, 3 January 1917, 6.
3. M.E.H. "Boston Symphony," *Baltimore Sun*, 4 January 1917, 6.
4. "The Boston Orchestra: Franck's Symphony and Three Wagner Overtures Played," *New York Times*, 5 January 1917, 3.
5. A. H., "Muck Translates Franck and Wagner," *Musical America* 25/11 (13 January 1917), 18.
6. H.F.P., "The Saturday Concert," *Musical America* 25/11 (13 January 1917), 18.

7. "Boston Symphony Concerts," *Musical Courier* 74/2 (11 January 1917), 14. The first line is misquoted from Longfellow's original, "When she was good, she was very very good."

8. "Walter Damrosch Delights Music Lovers with his Wagner Concert," *Washington Post*, 10 January 1917, 7.

9. Sylvester Rawling, "'Marta' Given First of Seven Winning Operas," *New York Evening World*, 27 January 1917, 7.

10. "Damrosch Greeted on 55th Birthday," *New York Times*, 31 January 1917, 9.

11. "Mr. Higginson Explains Boston Symphony's Non-Unionism," *Musical America* 25/11 (13 January 1917), 27.

12. Quoted in Arthur W. Little, *From Harlem to the Rhine: The Story of New York's Colored Volunteers* (New York: Covici, Friede, 1936), 120.

13. Noble Sissle, "Memoirs of Lieutenant 'Jim' Europe," Typescript, Library of Congress Manuscript Division, NAACP Papers, Box II, Folder J56, 44.

14. Donna Staley Kline, *Olga Samaroff Stokowski: An American Virtuoso on the World Stage* (College Station: Texas A&M University Press, 1996), 95.

15. "Madame Olga Samaroff, Famous Piano Soloist: She will be the Star of Two Concerts by the Philadelphia Orchestra," *Daily Republican*, 16 January 1917, 2.

16. "Mosque Concert Attracts Crowd: New Temple Opened to Orchestra by Stokowski and Mme. Samaroff," *Pittsburgh Daily Post*, 30 January 1917, 7.

17. "Fair's Spirit Will Live On: Exhibits and Music to Keep Exposition Site Gay," *Los Angeles Times*, 14 January 1917, 12. A detailed description of her plans for the initial festival may be found in "For an American Bayreuth," *Wellington (Kansas) Daily News*, 29 January 1917, 1.

18. "Diva Sings for Ohio Soldiers: Mme. Schumann-Heink in Splendid Concert at Camp Pershing Sunday," *El Paso Herald*, 15 January 1917, 11.

19. G. A. M., "Schumann-Heink Sings to an Appreciative Audience," *El Paso Herald*, 15 January 1917, 11.

20. "A 'Gala Concert': Boston Orchestra, Kreisler, and Paderewski in One Program," *New York Times*, 17 January 1917, 7.

21. Victor Records, May 1917 (Victor Talking Machine Company), n.p.

22. For a detailed discussion of their perambulations, see Lawrence Gushee, *Pioneers of Jazz: The Story of the Creole Band* (Oxford and New York: Oxford, 2005), 179–98.

23. "At the Majestic," *Cedar Rapids Evening Gazette*, 22 December 1916, 9.

24. Copyright Office of the United States of America, Record of the Filing of Copyright Deposits under the Act of March 4, 1909, Class E.—Musical Compositions, Entry 396303.

25. Gushee, *Pioneers of Jazz*, 169–77.

26. Gushee, *Pioneers of Jazz*, 173–74.

27. "Reisenweber's Celebrates: 60 Years Old—Once a Roadhouse, but now seats 3,500 at One Time," *New York Evening World*, 18 January 1917, 6.

28. The entire correspondence is preserved in Edwards's scrapbook, Hogan Jazz Archive.

29. For a photo of this interior design, see J. H. Phillips, "Interiors for Dining and Dancing," *Architectural Review* 10/1 (January 1920), 22.

30. H. O. Brunn, *The Story of the Dixieland Jazz Band* (Baton Rouge: Louisiana State University Press, 1960), 51–57.

CHAPTER 3

1. "Text of the Annex to German Note, Outlining Barred Zones and Prescribing Conditions for American Vessels," *New York Times*, 1 February 1917, 1.

2. For a compelling account of the Lusitania tragedy, see Erik Larson, *Dead Wake: The Last Crossing of the Lusitania* (New York: Crown, 2015).

3. Quoted in "Fervid Patriotism Inspired by Music," *Washington Times*, 23 February 1917, 8.

4. "Mme Samaroff Ill Here: Wife of Conductor Stokowski Suffers from Amnesia After Tour," *New York Times*, 4 February 1917, 13.

5. "Mephisto's Musings," *Musical America* 25/16 (17 February 1917), 7–8. For a discussion of similar episodes in Samaroff and other female musicians, see Beth Abelson MacLeod, *Women Performing Music: The Emergence of American Women as Instrumentalists and Conductors* (Jefferson, NC: McFarland, 2001), 66–70.

6. "Comes in Special Train," *Sandusky Star-Journal*, 9 February 1917, 4.

7. "All Bows Moved Up at the Same Time—Also the Violinists, Well Drilled, Drew Them Down in Perfect Unison—No Long Hair, Some Bald—Musicians Didn't Beat Time with Their Feet, Either; Some Folks Talked," *Sandusky Star-Journal*, 12 February 1917, 12.

8. Winthrop Sargeant, *Geniuses, Goddesses, and People* (New York: Dutton, 1949), 42.

9. Letter, Walter Damrosch to Margaret Blaine Damrosch, "Friday 4 p.m." (9 February 1917), Damrosch-Blaine Collection, Box 3, Folder 2, Library of Congress Music Division.

10. Leonard Liebling, "Variations," *Musical Courier* 74/6 (8 February 1917), 21.

11. Leonard Liebling, "Variations," *Musical Courier* 74/8 (22 February 1917), 21.

12. "Status of German Opera Stars at Metropolitan Remains Unchanged," *Musical America* 25/15 (10 February 1917), 1.

13. "Mephisto's Musings," *Musical America* 25/18 (3 March 1917), 7–8.

14. "Cabarets," *Variety* 45/11 (9 February 1917), 13.

15. Brunn, *The Story of the Dixieland Jazz Band*, 58.

16. Feist hit the jackpot with this song. An unpublished melody entitled "Everybody Loves a Jass Band" had been copyrighted on 16 December 1916, and publication under the same title was registered on 10 January 1917. The sheet music hit the stores at precisely the right moment to capitalize on the arrival of the ODJB in New York, and the change of spelling to "Jazz" on the title page came shortly thereafter.

17. Milton Bronner, "Pity, Like Art, Has No Nationality, Says the World's Greatest Violinist," *Evansville (Indiana) Press*, 1 February 1917, 2.

18. "Schumann-Heink in Concert: In Prospect Hall to Aid German Sufferers from the War," *Brooklyn Daily Eagle*, 4 February 1917, 30; "German Concert Off," *Brooklyn Daily Eagle*, 20 February 1917, 10.

19. "Kreisler Plays Again: Violinist Appears at the Philharmonic Concert," *New York Sun*, 26 February 1917, 7.

20. T.C.L., "Worcester Audience, 2,000 Strong, Arises to Cheer Kreisler," *Musical America* 25/15 (10 February 1917), 30.

21. Quoted in "War and the Universality of Art," *Musical America* 25/17 (24 February 1917), 39.

22. "'Siegfried' in 'The Ring': Mr. Sembach and Mme. Gadski in the Leading Parts," *New York Times*, 17 February 1917, 9.

23. Shirley Victor Brooks, "Largest Audience of Season Hears Schumann-Heink: Orchestra and Contralto at Their Best in Wagnerian Festival," *St. Louis Star and Times*, 24 February 1917, 4.

24. "Schumann-Heink Loses $100,000 by Cancellations: Singer Resting Well Although Still in Pain after Friday's Auto Accident," *St. Louis Star and Times*, 26 February 1917, 10.

25. Brooks, "Largest Audience of Season"; see also Richard C. Stokes, "Schumann-Heink at Height of Her Genius: Grandmother of Nine Packs Odeon for Symphony Orchestra's Wagner Program," *St. Louis Post Dispatch*, 24 February 1917, 8.

26. Joseph L. Howard, *Madame Ernestine Schumann-Heink: Her Life and Times* (Sebastopol, CA: Grizzly Bear, 1990), 237.

27. Marc Myers, "Start Spreadin' the Blues," *Wall Street Journal*, 21 February 2012, D7.

28. Quoted in Brunn, *The Story of the Dixieland Jazz Band*, 67.

29. Brunn, *The Story of the Dixieland Jazz Band*, 65–68; Samuel Charters, *A Trumpet around the Corner: The Story of New Orleans Jazz* (Jackson: University Press of Mississippi, 2008), 141–43.

30. For a discussion of the origins and significance of these techniques, see Thomas Brothers, *Louis Armstrong's New Orleans* (New York: Norton, 2006), 121–24, 130–31, 264–65.

31. *Indianapolis Star*, 26 January 1917, 7; quoted in Gushee, *Pioneers of Jazz*, 199.

32. *Chicago Herald*, 7 February 1917, 4; quoted in Gushee, *Pioneers of Jazz*, 201.

33. *Detroit Free Press*, 27 February 1917; quoted in Gushee, *Pioneers of Jazz*, 202.

CHAPTER 4

1. "Woodrow Wilson Takes Oath of Office for Another Term; Armed Neutrality Bill Defeated by Filibuster in Senate," *Charlotte Observer*, 5 March 1917, 1.

2. "Farrar a True American, She Declares at Banquet: Soprano Indignant at Reports Which Credited Her with Being Ardently a Germanophile," *Musical America* 25/22 (31 March 1917), 2; "Mme. Farrar Proves Her Americanism: Soprano Sings National Anthem in Boston—Denies That She Is Germanophile," *Musical America* 25/22 (31 March 1917), 32.

3. Geraldine Farrar, *Such Sweet Compulsion: The Autobiography of Geraldine Farrar* (New York: Greystone, 1938), 141.

4. Lenore McDougall, "Rag-Time Patriotism," *New York Tribune*, 8 March 1917, 10. A "busby" is a large Hungarian military hat.

5. George S. Kaufman, "Broadway and Elsewhere," *New York Tribune*, 11 March 1917, 29.

6. S. Jay Kaufman, "Jass," *(New York) Globe and Commercial Advertiser*, 14 March 1917, 14. This definition was widely reprinted without the author's name under the title "The Latest in Music."

7. O. O. McIntyre, "New York Day-by-Day," *Arkansas Democrat*, 22 March 1917, 6.

8. "Cabarets," *Variety* 46/3 (16 March 1917), 15.

9. Two Reisenweber's display ads indicate the schedule: *New York Times*, 9 March 1917, 8.

10. Gill, "What is a Jass Band?" *Ragtime Review* 3/3 (March 1917), 10.

11. Quoted in "Origin of Jazz Music Traced to Negro Player," *Pittsburgh Post-Gazette*, 12 March 1917, 7.

12. Quoted in Gushee, *Pioneers of Jazz*, 208.

13. Gushee, *Pioneers of Jazz*, 206–10.

14. *New York Clipper*, 4 April 1917, 21; quoted in Gushee, *Pioneers of Jazz*, 209.

15. Brunn *The Story of the Original Dixieland Jazz Band*, 59–60. For recordings by several of Durante's bands, see *Pioneer Recording Bands, 1917–1920* (Retrieval RTR 79043).

16. "Kreisler-Konzert," *Tägliches Cincinnatier Volksblatt*, 9 March 1917, 3. Translation mine.

17. "Roosevelt Bars the Hyphenated: No Room in this Country for Dual Nationality, He Tells Knights of Columbus," *New York Times*, 13 October 1915, 1.
18. For an in-depth study of German and British propaganda aimed at German Americans before the US entry into World War I, see Chad R. Fulwider, *German Propaganda and U.S. Neutrality in World War I* (Columbia: University of Missouri Press, 2016).
19. "Woodward & Lothrop," *Washington Post*, 27 February 1917, 7.
20. "Mme. Ernestine Schumann-Heink," *Musical Courier* 74/10 (8 March 1917), 33.
21. B. D., "Dr. Muck's Adieu Mozartianly Said: Boston Orchestra Heard in a Fine Farewell Program at the Academy," *Evening Public Ledger*, 13 March 1917, 9.
22. "Boston Symphony Orchestra," *Baltimore Sun*, 15 March 1917, 10.
23. *Musical Courier* 34/12 (22 March 1917), 20.
24. "Boston Symphony at Last Matinee," *New York Herald*, 18 March 1917, 8.
25. Quoted in Joseph Horowitz, *Moral Fire: Musical Portraits from America's Fin de Siècle* (Berkeley: University of California Press, 2012), 42.
26. Quoted in Bliss Perry, *Life and Letters of Henry Lee Higginson* (Boston: Atlantic Monthly, 1921), 480.
27. Quoted in Perry, *Life and Letters*, 480–81.
28. "Symphony Plays Farewell: 'The Star-Spangled Banner' Brings a Patriotic Outburst," *New York Times*, 18 March 1917, 22.
29. "N.Y. Symphony Orchestra Will Play in Winnipeg," *Winnipeg Tribune*, 14 March 1917, 5.
30. Winthrop Sargeant, *Geniuses, Goddesses, and People* (New York: Dutton, 1949), 42–43. Sargeant played with the orchestra from 1926 to 1928, but his characterization of Damrosch's touring presumably applies to the 1917 tour as well.

CHAPTER 5

1. Frederick J. Spencer, *Jazz and Death* (Jackson: University of Mississippi Press, 2002), 170–80.
2. "President Calls for War Declaration, Stronger Navy, New Army of 500,000 Men, Full Co-operation with Germany's Foes," *New York Times*, 3 April 1917, 1–2.
3. "Patriotism at the Metropolitan Opera," *Musical Courier* 74/14 (5 April 1917), 5; "Demonstration at Opera When War Message Arrives," *Musical America* 25/23 (7 April 1917), 1.
4. Quoted in Glenn Watkins, *Proof through the Night: Music and the Great War* (Berkeley: University of California Press, 2003), 259.
5. "Sits during U.S. Anthem; Mobbed: Socialist Plastered with Salad at Rector's and Then Arrested," *Chicago Daily Tribune*, 7 April 1917, 1.
6. "Failed to Stand When the Orchestra Played National Air," *Santa Cruz Evening News*, 18 April 1917, 2.
7. "Musical Notes," *Los Angeles Times*, 3 May 1917, 18.
8. "Fritz Kreisler Is Always Welcomed," *San Francisco Chronicle*, 18 March 1917, 23.
9. Fritz Kreisler, *Four Weeks in the Trenches: The War Story of a Violinist* (Boston: Houghton Mifflin, 1915).
10. "Kreisler Tells of Horrors of War in Europe," *Oakland Tribune*, 8 April 1917, 32.
11. W.R.M., "Kneisel Quartet Ends Distinguished Career: Final Program and Performance of Rare Proportions, Graces and Perfections," *Evening Public Ledger*, 6 April 1917, 12.
12. "Schumann-Heink Talks of Sons Fighting Son," *St. Louis Star and Times*, 7 April 1917, 2.

13. "Her Sons at War, Schumann-Heink Is Prostrated," *Chicago Daily Tribune*, 7 April 1917, 1.

14. "Fifteenth Regiment Is Now Under U.S. Government Supervision; Hayward Makes Statement," *New York Age*, 19 April 1917, 1.

15. Noble Sissle, "Memoirs of Jim Europe," NAACP Collection, Library of Congress Manuscript Division, 49–50.

16. "Symphony Renders Last Concert Here," *Providence Journal*, 11 April 1917, 12.

17. Olin Downes, "Symphony Performs New Work: Noren's 'Life' Heard for First Time in Boston," *Boston Post*, 21 April 1917, 7.

18. "Higginson Withdraws Support from Boston Symphony Orchestra?" *Musical America* 25/26 (28 April 1917), 1.

19. Sylvester Rawling, "Gabrilowitsch as Conductor; Bauer, Soloist," *New York Evening World*, 28 April 1917, 5.

20. "Boston Symphony Orchestra to Continue: Contrary Report Declared False," *Musical Courier* 74/18 (3 May 1917), 5.

21. Walter Anthony, "Symphony Orchestra Draws Huge Crowd to Auditorium: San Franciscans Prove at Sunday Afternoon Concert That They Are True Music Lovers," *San Francisco Chronicle*, 30 April 1917, 7.

22. "'Kaiser Has No Place in New World'—Says Damrosch: Famous Conductor of New York Symphony Is Wonderful Hyphenate," *Seattle Star*, 14 April 1917, 1.

23. "Damrosch, Here, Says Patriotism Loves Music," *San Francisco Chronicle*, 22 April 1917, 36. See also "Artists Only Can Bring Peace: Walter Damrosch Says World Must Look to Its Poets, Painters and Musicians, *Reno (Nevada) Gazette-Journal*, 24 April 1917, 7.

24. Jeanne Redman, "Damrosch: An Intimate View of the Great Musician Who Admires Waiters," *Los Angeles Times*, 26 April 1917, 19.

25. "All-Night Revelry Ended by the War: Mayor Prohibits Sale of Liquor after 1 O'Clock A.M., Beginning on May 1," *New York Times*, 18 April 1917, 3.

26. "Cabarets," *Variety* 46/11 (11 May 1917), 15.

27. "Variety Actors Partners Now," *New York Sun*, 8 April 1917, sec. 3, 5.

28. Eddie Edwards interview, 1 July 1959, 2, Hogan Jazz Archive.

29. Telegram, 14 March 1917, and letter, 29 March 1917, Edwards Scrapbook, Hogan Jazz Archive.

30. "Special List: New Victor Records Jass Band and Other Dance Selections." Copies of this are preserved in both the LaRocca and Edwards Scrapbooks in the Hogan Jazz Archive. A tiny notation on the back page (3552—UQA—3-7-17) led LaRocca and Brunn to assume that it was published on 7 March, but the letter from Victor in the Edwards Scrapbook clearly indicates that it still was not available on 29 March.

31. B. L. Aldridge, *The Victor Talking Machine Company*, 73–74; reprinted in *The Encyclopedic Discography of Victor Recordings: Pre-Matrix Series*, comp. Ted Fagan and William R. Moran (Westport, CT: Greenwood, 1983).

32. Spear & Company of Pittsburgh included a description of Record no. 18255 and a brief description of a Jass Band in display ads in both the *Pittsburgh Daily Post* and the *Pittsburgh Press* on 8 April.

33. "Attention! Dancing Folks Only!" *New Orleans Times Picayune*, 15 April 1917. A copy of this advertisement is pasted in LaRocca's Scrapbook, Hogan Jazz Archive, which is also reproduced on the archive's website. See also Bruce Boyd Raeburn, "Jazz and the Italian Connection," *Jazz Archivist* 6/1 (May 1991), 1–4.

34. Manuel Manetta Interview, 21 March 1957, Reel VI, Hogan Jazz Archive.

35. Letter, Kenner B. George, 30 April 1917, Edwards Scrapbook, Hogan Jazz Archive.
36. Brunn, *The Story of the Original Dixieland Jazz Band*, 74.
37. The saga of the Creole Band's activities in April 1917 is told in detail in Gushee, *Pioneers of Jazz*, 210–17.

CHAPTER 6

1. "About Jazz Music," *Daily Missourian*, 1 May 1917, 2.
2. "'His Little Widows' an Amusing Show: All the Humors of Mormonism in the Latest Musical Comedy at the Astor," *New York Times*, 1 May 1917, 1.
3. These two papers were inserted unattached in the Edwards scrapbook, Hogan Jazz Archive.
4. Samuel Charters, *A Trumpet around the Corner: The Story of New Orleans Jazz* (Jackson: University Press of Mississippi, 2008), 132.
5. Quoted in Brunn, *The Story of the Original Dixieland Jazz Band*, 72.
6. "Spartanburg Music Festival," *Greenville News*, 9 May 1917, 7.
7. "A Music Man Talks Alfalfa: Walter Damrosch Is Concerned about Nation's Supply of Food," *Wichita Beacon*, 10 May 1917, 9.
8. [William Allen White], "Don't Coddle Us," *Emporia Gazette*, 10 May 1917, 1.
9. "A Blessing in Disguise?," *Wichita Beacon*, 23 May 1917, 1.
10. All three anecdotes reported in Leonard Liebling, "Variations," *Musical Courier* 74/20 (17 May 1917), 21.
11. "Bars Enemy Aliens from Hotel Zone: Rule May Also Close Many Theatres and Cabarets to Them after June 1," *New York Times*, 18 May 1917, 4.
12. "Teutons Battle in Permit Rush: Reserves Called to Federal Building as 17,000 File Applications," *New York Sun*, 30 May 1917, 2.
13. "A Distinction to Keep in Memory," *New York Times*, 24 May 1917, 12.
14. "Review of Musical Season," *Boston Globe*, 6 May 1917, 36.
15. Quoted in Perry, *Life and Letters*, 482.
16. "Mme. Schumann-Heink Cries 'United States Forever!'" *Musical Courier* 74/21 (24 May 1917), 8. See also "Demonstrate Love, Esteem: San Diego Gives Remarkable Luncheon to Diva," *Los Angeles Times*, 10 May 1917, 17.
17. "Schumann-Heink Sues U.R.: Asks for $95,000 Damages for Injuries Sustained in Accident," *St. Louis Post Dispatch*, 12 May 1917, 9; "Schumann-Heink Effects Compromise," *San Diego Union*, 8 April 1926, 5.
18. "Son of Schumann-Heink Registers and May Fight against Brothers," *San Francisco Chronicle*, 27 May 1917, 34.
19. Sissle's "Memoirs" states that Europe brought fifteen Puerto Rican musicians, while Badger's *A Life in Ragtime* lists thirteen musicians. The ship's manifest clearly lists twelve Puerto Rican musicians aged eighteen to thirty-two, plus Europe.
20. Sissle, "Memoirs," 54.
21. "Hampton Musicians Join 15th," *New York Age*, 17 May 1917, 6.
22. "Raw Recruits of the Fifteenth Learn Quickly at Peekskill; Complimented on Deportment," *New York Age*, 24 May 1917, 1.
23. Little, *From Harlem to the Rhine*, 22.

CHAPTER 7

1. Carl Wittke, *German-Americans and the World War (With Special Emphasis on Ohio's German-Language Press)* (Columbus: Ohio State Archaeological and Historical Society, 1936), 185–86.

2. "Nora Bayes at Palace," *Brooklyn Daily Eagle*, 12 June 1917, 9.
3. "Negro Registration Exceeds That of the Whites in Many Regions throughout South," *New York Age*, 14 June 1917, 1.
4. Noble Sissle, "Memoir," 72. The importance of the band in recruiting is confirmed in "Secure Colored Recruits," *Brooklyn Daily Eagle*, 9 November 1917, 20.
5. "Fifteenth Reaches Full War Strength; Candidates for Commissions Off for Iowa," *New York Age*, 14 June 1917, 1; "Negro Regiment First on War Basis: Col. Hayward's Command Leads New York Infantry in Readiness for Service," *New York Times*, 20 June 1917, 6.
6. Charles T. Magill, "15th Regiment Pageant Draws a Record Crowd," *Chicago Defender*, 30 June 1917, 3; Lester A. Walton, "15th Regiment Band," *New York Age*, 28 June 1917, 6.
7. Sissle, "Memoirs," 64–65.
8. "Clever Colored Artists Support Nora Bayes," *New York Age*, 10 May 1917, 6.
9. Lester A. Walton, "Nora Bayes in Song," *New York Age*, 17 May 1917, 6.
10. Telegram, Max Hart to Edwards, 23 June 1917, Edwards scrapbook, Hogan Jazz Archive.
11. United States Copyright Office, Library of Congress.
12. Quoted in "Directors Choose Damrosch to Lead Oratorio Society: But Members Express Strong Preference for Koemmenich—Court Action Threatened," *Musical Courier* 75/1 (5 July 1917), 5.
13. "Oratorio Society So Keyed Up It Squeaks: Damrosch-Koemmenich Row Turns Harmony into Savage Discord," *New York Sun*, 30 June 1917, 7.
14. "Oratorien-Mißklänge," *Tägliches Cincinnatier Volksblatt*, 4 July 1917, 7.
15. Quoted in "Artists Only Can Bring Peace: Walter Damrosch Says World Must Look to Its Poets, Painters and Musicians," *Reno Gazette-Journal*, 24 April 1917, 7.

CHAPTER 8

1. "A Virtuoso's Summer," *Musical Courier* 75/5 (2 August 1917), 21.
2. Olga Samaroff Stokowski, *An American Musician's Story* (New York: Norton, 1939), 141–42.
3. Kline, *Olga Samaroff Stokowski*, 93. "List or Manifest of Alien Passengers," SS *Noordam*, 24 August 1914, ancestry.com, accessed 25 August 2016.
4. Like her father, Clara Clemens was an engaging writer. Her recollections of the harrowing experience of Ossip's arrest and their eventual escape to America are recounted in Chapter 6 of *My Husband Gabrilowitsch*, 61–83.
5. The dramatic story of her escape in the summer of 1914 is vividly chronicled in Mary Lawton, *Schumann-Heink: The Last of the Titans* (New York: Macmillan, 1928), 268. The speed and urgency of these events may have been embellished, as the SS *Rotterdam*, whose passenger list included her, three of her eight children, and two companions, sailed on 29 August (a month after the declaration of war) and arrived in New York on 13 September.
6. Muck's failed attempt to enlist in the German army is described in a letter from Muck to Wilhelm Schuler, 11 September 1914, quoted in Peter Muck, *Karl Muck: Ein Dirigentenleben in Briefen und Dokumenten* (Tutzing: Hans Schneider, 2003), 96. Ellis's use of Anita Muck to convince her husband to return to the United States is described in a letter from Ellis to Henry Lee Higginson, 20 August 1914, cited in Gayle K. Turk, "The Case of Dr. Karl Muck: Anti-German Hysteria and Enemy Alien Internment during World War I" (BA thesis, Harvard University, 1994), 24.

7. "Kreisler, Wounded, Tells of War," *New York Times*, 29 November 1914, V, 4.

8. Fritz Kreisler, *Four Weeks in the Trenches: The War Story of a Violinist* (Boston: Houghton Mifflin, 1915). The publishing contract for this book is preserved in the Music Division, Library of Congress, Fritz Kreisler Collection, Box 16, Folder 15.

9. Clemens, *My Husband Gabrilowitsch*, 88.

10. Greg A. Hartford, "Acadia National Park History," http://www.acadiamagic.com/acadia_national_park.html, accessed 25 August 2016.

11. "Mount Desert Island: Many Fine Drives and Walks Connecting Bar Harbor with Nearby Resorts," *Bar Harbor Times*, 7 July 1917, 3.

12. Samaroff Stokowski, *An American Musician's Story*, 151.

13. "Mount Desert Island—the World's Playground," *Bar Harbor Times*, 28 April 1917, 3.

14. [L. H. Behymer], "Musicians Gather on Maine Coast: Distinguished Group Is Enjoying Vacation There and Having Good Time," *San Francisco Chronicle*, 17 September 1916, 24; Clara Clemens, "Famous Musicians Off Guard at Seal Harbor: Mark Twain's Daughter Writes of Impression Kreisler, Bauer, Gabrilowitsch, Godowsky, and Others of Colony Made on Natives," *New York Times Magazine*, 24 September 1916, 15.

15. Clemens, *My Husband Gabrilowitsch*, 90.

16. Samaroff Stokowski, *An American Musician's Story*, 147.

17. The documents detailing this process are housed at the National Archives and Records Administration (NARA), Record Group 12, Entry 6, Historical Files, File Class 900, Box 68. I am grateful to Patrick Warfield for his help in finding them.

18. Samaroff Stokowski, *An American Musician's Story*, 149. Although she states in the memoir that these rehearsals took place during the summer of 1918, they were more likely during the summer of 1917, since the performances in Philadelphia and on tour were during the winter of 1917/18.

19. "Music and Musicians," *Boston Sunday Globe*, 14 October 1917, 40. The process of planning the Philadelphia Orchestra's season in the face of potential opposition to German music and musicians is discussed in James M. Doering, "World War I and Programming Issues," in *The Great Orchestrator: Arthur Judson and American Arts Management* (Urbana: University of Illinois Press, 2013), 48–55.

20. "Boston Symphony," *Boston Sunday Post*, 23 September 1917, 39.

21. "Further Plans of the Boston Symphony Orchestra," *Musical Courier* 75/11 (13 September 1917), 13.

22. Schelling's report and the other documents relating to suspicious activities on Mount Desert Island are preserved in NARA, Military Intelligence Section, files 10080-361 and 10468.

23. George Martin, *The Damrosch Dynasty: America's First Family of Music* (Boston: Houghton Mifflin, 1983), 242–43.

24. Walter Damrosch, *My Musical Life* (New York: Scribner, 1923), 1.

25. The initial announcement was made in "Kreisler with Kneisel Quartet," *New York Times*, 18 June 1917, 9; for more details, see "Work of Kneisels Will Be Resumed: Fritz Kreisler to Be a Member of Famous Quartet in Three Concerts Next Year," *Williamsport Sun-Gazette*, 23 June 1917, 5.

26. A photo of the two playing together—McCormack in a white tennis outfit and Kreisler in a tie and dress shoes—was published in *Musical Courier* 75/4 (26 July 1917), 13, and their enthusiasm is discussed in "Tennis Favorite Sport," *El Paso Herald*, 17 August 1917, 9.

27. "Two Great Stars," *Asbury Park Press*, 13 August 1917, 5.
28. "Ocean Grove Hears Two Famous Artists: Kreisler and McCormack Perform Before 10,000 People," *Washington Herald*, 19 August 1917, 22.
29. "10,000 Hear McCormack—Kreisler," *New York Times*, 19 August 1917, 10.
30. D. H. W., "Schumann-Heink Draws $5,000 in 'Frisco," *Musical Courier* 75/11 (13 September 1917), 7.
31. Quoted in "Ragtime Scorned by Soldiers; Want Opera," *Indiana Gazette*, 26 June 1917, 3.
32. Howard Mann, "Mme. Schumann-Heink Sends Younger Sons to Battle Their Eldest Brother, Who Is Fighting for Kaiser," *Medford (Oregon) Mail Tribune*, 22 August 1917, 3.
33. Zoe Beckley, "Sons in Opposing Armies: Mme. Schumann-Heink's Problem Is One Only Mothers Understand," *Kansas City Times*, 2 July 1917, 5.
34. The voluminous files on Schumann-Heink at NARA are found in Military Intelligence files 9140–2266 and Department of Justice "Old German" files 31262, 36954, and 300302.
35. Editorial cartoon signed "Russell," *New York Age*, 5 July 1917, 1.
36. John Love, quoted in Badger, *A Life in Ragtime*, 154.
37. Badger, 153, describes the recruitment and early contributions of these two drummers who in 1919 played a decisive role in Europe's death.
38. "Names Are Given 32 Army Cantonments: War Department Designates New Camps in Honor of American Heroes," *New York Sun*, 16 July 1917, 3. The woeful state of US military preparedness at the start of the war is described in Bill Harris, *The Hellfighters of Harlem: African-American Soldiers Who Fought for the Right to Fight for their Country* (New York: Carroll & Graf, 2002), 29–31.
39. "State Guard Ready to Mobilize Monday: New York Troops Ordered to Form Sixth Division of National Army. To Go to Spartanburg," *New York Sun*, 14 July 1917, 4; "Three N.Y. Regiments to Be Brigaded with a Southern Division: Extra Units—10th, 14th and 47th—to Mobilize at Alexandria, La.," *New York Tribune*, 22 July 1917, 2; "One Great Division for Old N.Y. Guard: All Organized Units of State Troops Expected to Form Body as Large as Army Corps," *New York Times*, 29 July 1917, 6.
40. "Rousing 'Send Off' Assured as Governor Orders Parade of New York Guardsmen: *Evening World*'s Plan to Bid Boys Farewell Meets Hearty Approval," *New York Evening World*, 12 July 1917, 1.
41. "Fifteenth at Camp Whitman: Col. Hayward's 'Billy Boys' Given a Big Send Off as They Entrain Monday," *New York Age*, 19 July 1917, 1.
42. "Governor Visits Camp Whitman; Reviews 15th Regt.," *Poughkeepsie Eagle News*, 13 August 1917, 5.
43. Jerome B. Courtney, "Billy Boy," *New York Sun*, 18 August 1917, 12. The deposit copy of the published song in the Library of Congress is dated 25 August 1917.
44. "Construction Records Smashed at Camp Dix: Barracks to Accommodate 200 Men Completely Erected within Space of Ten Hours," *Philadelphia Evening Public Ledger*, 20 August 1917, 13; "Fifteenth Regiment Doing Guard Duty," *New York Age*, 23 August 1917, 1.
45. Robert V. Haynes, *A Night of Violence: The Houston Riot of 1917* (Baton Rouge: Louisiana State University Press, 1976).

46. Quoted in "Fear Negro Troops in Spartanburg: Citizens Make Protest When It Is Reported That Fifteenth Infantry Will Be Trained There," *New York Times*, 31 August 1917, 4.
47. "Columbia's Mid-Month Specials—August 10th," *Indianapolis News*, 9 August 1917, 5.
48. *Pioneer Recording Bands: 1917–1920*, Retrieval RTR 79043.
49. The authorship of this tune was vigorously disputed in the early years of its popularity, when LaRocca collected royalties on the publication and later recordings. Recent scholarship has supported his claim to authorship in the New Orleans tradition of combining fragments of previously existing tunes. For a summary, see Bruce Boyd Raeburn, preface to Vincenzo Caporaletti, *Jelly Roll Morton, the Old Quadrille and Tiger Rag: A Historiographic Revision* (Lucca: Libreria Musicale Italiana, 2011), 47–49.
50. See Chapter 5.
51. Walter Kingsley, "Whence Comes Jass? Facts from the Great Authority on the Subject," *New York Sun*, 5 August 1917, 3.
52. For discussions of the inaccuracies and discrepancies in Kingsley's article, see Alan P. Merriam and Fradley H. Garner, "Jazz—the Word," *Ethnomusicology* 12/3 (September 1968), 373–96; and Dick Holbrook, "Our Word Jazz," *Storyville* no. 50 (December 1973–January 1974), 46–58.
53. "The Appeal of Primitive Jazz," *Literary Digest* 55 (25 August 1917), 26–29. For a discussion of the importance of band photos in corny poses, see Alan John Ainsworth, "Early New Orleans Band Photography," *Jazz Research Journal* 11, no. 1 (2017), 28–61.
54. "The Cry for Jazz," *Musical Courier* 75/3 (19 July 1917), 9.
55. Hiram Kelly Moderwell, "A Modest Proposal," *Seven Arts* 2/2 (July 1917), 368–69.

CHAPTER 9

1. The photo is reproduced in Geraldine Farrar, *Such Sweet Compulsion: The Autobiography of Geraldine Farrar* (New York: Greystone, 1938).
2. "Making the World Safe for Music," *Musical Courier* 75/12 (20 September 1917), 23.
3. Rose L. Sutro, "The Sleeping Giant," *Musical Courier* 75/9 (30 August 1917), 15–16.
4. "Seizing the Moment," *Musical Courier* 75/10 (6 September 1917), 15–16.
5. Doering, *The Great Orchestrator*, 49–51.
6. "Phila. Orchestra's Brilliant Plans: Veritable Host of Soloists Engaged for Ensuing Season of Symphony Music," *Wilmington News Journal*, 7 September 1917, 5.
7. "Orchestra Outlines New Season's Plans: Mr. Stokowski Will Direct Symphonic Band of 94 Players; Begins October 12," *Philadelphia Evening Public Ledger*, 5 September 1917, 6.
8. "Academy's Seating Capacity Enlarged: New Chairs Replace Rear Balcony Boxes to Accommodate Orchestra Patrons," *Philadelphia Evening Public Ledger*, 22 September 1917, 14.
9. Quoted in "News and Notes," *New York Sun*, 23 September 1917, 29. Roentgen served over a year in the American Expeditionary Forces in Europe and rejoined the New York Symphony upon his return to the United States in 1919.
10. "Symphony Orchestra: Dr. Karl Muck, Conductor," *Boston Sunday Post*, 2 September 1917, 31.

11. "American premieres at the BSO," http://www.bso.org/brands/bso/about-us/historyarchives/archival-collection/american-premieres-at-the-bso.aspx, accessed 14 September 2016.
12. National Archives and Records Administration, Military Intelligence Section files, 9140–4175, doc. 5.
13. Clemens, *My Husband Gabrilowitsch*, 94.
14. Letter, Anita Muck to Ida Chadwick, 29 September 1917, Spaulding Library, New England Conservatory of Music.
15. These details were shared in a revealing interview by Rochester, New York, manager James E. Furlong: "Recitalists Come High," *Rochester Democrat and Chronicle*, 26 August 1917, 23.
16. Oliver Daniel, *Stokowski: A Counterpoint of View* (New York: Dodd, Mead, 1983), 180.
17. Quoted in Oliver, *Stokowski*, 180.
18. "Schumann-Heink Sucks Snake Poison from Boy's Arm: Youth Bitten by Rattler Will Recover as Result of Singer's Prompt Action," *St. Louis Post-Dispatch*, 12 September 1917, 6.
19. "Pianist Grainger now Oboeist, U.S.A.: Celebrated Artist Plays for 15th Coast Artillery for $36 a Month," *New York Sun*, 28 June 1917, 7.
20. "The Humanitarian Cult Concert Starts New York Musical Season: Galaxy of Prominent Stars Appears Before Huge and Appreciative Audience," *Musical Courier* 75/14 (4 October 1917), 26. See also the display ad entitled "The Greatest Concert of the Age!" *New York Times*, 13 September 1917, 6.
21. *New Victor Records* 3/9 (September 1917), 18.
22. Tim Gracyk with Frank Hoffmann, *Popular American Recording Pioneers 1895–1925* (New York: Haworth, 2000), 73–85.
23. Gunther Schuller, *Early Jazz: Its Roots and Development* (New York: Oxford University Press, 1968), 184.
24. "Cabarets," *Variety* 48/3 (21 September 1917), 23.
25. "Afternoon Teas at Reisenweber's," *New York Sun*, 23 September 1917, 29.
26. "Construction Records Smashed at Camp Dix," *Philadelphia Evening Public Ledger*, 20 August 1917, 13.
27. "Negro Soldiers Police Camp Dix: Officials Deny That Troops Have Clashed with White Workmen," *Asbury Park Press*, 8 September 1917, 2.
28. "General Hershey, Guest at Camp Dix, Praises Soldiers," *New York Tribune*, 8 September 1917, 6.
29. "Wrightstown Camp Will Accommodate 60,000 Soldiers," *Wilkes-Barre Times Leader*, 13 September 1917, 3.
30. "15th Regiment Band at Bordentown School," *New York Age*, 13 September 1917, 1.
31. "Organized Sports for Soldiers in Wrightstown Camp: Regiments Will Have Football Teams Featured by Varsity Stars," *Wilkes-Barre Times Leader*, 14 September 1917, 2.
32. "Second Contingent of Rookies Now Pouring into Camp Dix," *Philadelphia Evening Public Ledger*, 19 September 1917, 5.
33. "Two Weeks Change Men to Soldiers," *Asbury Park Press*, 6 October 1917, 2. For a contradictory report of this incident, which credits southern members of the engineering company with deliberately provoking the black guards, see "Men of 15th N.Y. Resent Insult: Tear Down Obnoxious Signs at Camp Dix," *Philadelphia Tribune*, 6 October 1917, 1.

34. Jeffrey T. Sammons and John H. Morrow Jr., *Harlem's Rattlers and the Great War* (Lawrence: University Press of Kansas, 2014), 153–55.
35. Arthur W. Little to Col. Edward M. House, 25 September 1917, quoted in Sammons and Morrow, *Harlem's Rattlers*, 155.

CHAPTER 10
1. Hamilton Fish to Franklin Roosevelt, 4 October 1917, quoted in Sammons and Morrow, *Harlem's Rattlers*, 160.
2. "Fifteen Leaves for Spartanburg, S. C.," *New York Age*, 11 October 1917, 1.
3. "Many Novelties Offered by Director Mees at Worcester's Sixtieth Annual Music Festival," *Musical Courier* 75/15 (11 October 1917): 16.
4. Lynne Johnson, "Liszt and Saint-Saëns" (PhD diss., University of Hawaii, 2009).
5. "Many Novelties," *Musical Courier*, 16.
6. "Full Orchestra Records under Way: Victor Machines Will 'Can' Art of Philadelphia and Boston Symphonies," *Evening Public Ledger*, 29 September 1917, 14.
7. Raymond Sooy, "Memoirs of My Recording and Traveling Experiences for the Victor Talking Machine Company," MS transcribed and edited by Janet Swartz, http://www.davidsarnoff.org/soo-maintext.html, accessed 21 September 2016.
8. David Milsom, "Conditional Gifts: Acoustic Orchestral Recordings of Edouard Colonne and Karl Muck and Their Testament to Late Nineteenth-Century Performing Practices," *Early Music Performer* 16 (November 2005): 4–5.
9. *The Phonograph Monthly* (November 1926); quoted in Martin Bookspan, "The BSO and the Talking Machine," *High Fidelity* 8/1 (January 1958): 124.
10. Christopher Dyment, "Karl Muck's Boston Recordings," *International Classical Record Collector* 6 (Autumn 1996): 39.
11. Quoted in Brian Bell, liner notes to *The First Recordings of the Boston Symphony Orchestra* (1995), BSO Classics 171002.
12. Quoted in "Schumann-Heink Draws Capacity House: Artist at Her Best in Fargo, N.D. Program," *Musical Courier* 75/18 (1 November 1917): 39.
13. "Extraordinary Demonstration for Schumann-Heink at Orchestra Hall," *Musical Leader* 34/17 (25 October 1917): 407.
14. "Discoverer of Jazz Elucidates in Court: 'Kid' Tells How He Wrote 'The Livery Stable Blues' in Burst of Genius Animals Inspired 'Tune,'" clipping in Hogan Jazz Archive, Dominic LaRocca Collection, Series 8, Folder 17.
15. "Nobody Wrote Those Livery Stable Blues: At Least, So Says Man Who Combats the Jazz Kid's Claim to Musical Fame," *Chicago Daily News*, 12 October 1917, 3.
16. "Blues and More Blues Go Blooey in Music Suit: Jazz Band in Lobby and Jazz Testimony Get Nowhere," *Chicago Tribune*, 12 October 1917, 11.
17. "Nobody Wrote Those Livery Stable Blues."
18. The full text of the judgment is found in Hogan Jazz Archive, Dominic LaRocca Collection, Series 8, Box 12, Folder 2, Item 4.
19. "Blues Are Blues, Court Decrees, and No One Wins: Solomonesque Decision on Jazz Issue Ends Suit" and Frederick Donaghey, "The Orchestra Starts Its Season," *Chicago Daily Tribune*, 13 October 1917, 13. For a dispassionate view of the legal issues at stake minus the sensationalism, see "'Blues Are Blues, They Are' Says Expert in 'Blues' Case," *Variety* 48/8 (19 October 1917): 16.
20. The story of the case as related by LaRocca's recollections and the court documents is detailed in Brunn, *The Story of the Original Dixieland Jazz Band*, 74–87.
21. Glendinning Keeble, "Music," *Pittsburgh Post-Gazette* , 14 October 1917, 37.
22. "Kreisler Concert," *Pittsburgh Press*, 28 October 1917, 20.

23. H.T.C., "American Music Well Presented: Philadelphia Orchestra Opens Season with Interesting Works by Native Composers," *Philadelphia Evening Public Ledger*, 13 October 1917, 9.

24. "Opening Event of Musical Season: Philadelphia Orchestra Resumes Performances at the Academy of Music Heard in Programme Exclusively Derived from Writings of American Composers," *Philadelphia Inquirer*, 13 October 1917, 13.

25. G.M.W., "Kelley's New England Symphony, Feature of the Opening Philadelphia Symphony Concert: Stokowski and His Men in Splendidly Played, All-American Program," *Musical Courier* 75/16 (18 October 1917): 7.

26. See E. Douglas Bomberger, *"A Tidal Wave of Encouragement": American Composers' Concerts in the Gilded Age* (Westport, CT: Praeger, 2002); and Douglas W. Shadle, *Orchestrating the Nation: The Nineteenth-Century American Symphonic Enterprise* (New York: Oxford University Press, 2015).

27. Larry Huffman, "Leopold Stokowski and the Philadelphia Orchestra 1917—First Acoustic Recordings," www.stokowski.org, accessed 23 September 2016.

28. "Camp Wadsworth," *Brooklyn Daily Eagle*, 12 October 1917, 3.

29. Sammons and Morrow, *Harlem's Rattlers*, 163.

30. "Fifteenth Regiment May Soon See Service in France," *New York Age*, 18 October 1917, 1. Little, *From Harlem to the Rhine*, 54–55, gives an extended version of the speech that is considerably more flowery but agrees in its main points.

31. Little, *From Harlem to the Rhine*, 56.

32. "Colored Troops May Sail Soon," *Middletown Times-Press*, 16 October 1917, 1; and "Colonel Hayward's Regiment Expects to Embark Soon: Fifteenth (Negro) Infantry Gets Latest Equipment in Shoes and Underwear," *New York Tribune*, 16 October 1917, 6.

33. "15th Completes Hike in Storm at Camp Wadsworth: Negro Regiment Shows Mettle by Marching in Mud," *New York Tribune*, 20 October 1917, 7.

34. "Allied Officers Will Train Troops: First of Ten Assigned to Camp Wadsworth Arrive after Delay from U-Boats," *New York Times*, 16 October 1917, 10.

35. Sissle, "Memoirs," 78.

36. Little, *From Harlem to the Rhine*, 57.

37. Little, *From Harlem to the Rhine*, 59–62. For a southern perspective on this incident, see Lee Kennett, "The Camp Wadsworth Affair," *South Atlantic Quarterly* 74/2 (Spring 1975): 197–211.

38. This confrontation was described by two participants, Noble Sissle and Arthur W. Little, in the memoirs cited above. For additional perspectives on this pivotal incident, see Reid Badger, *A Life in Ragtime*, 159–60, and Sammons and Morrow, *Harlem's Rattlers*, 165–69.

39. Quoted in Little, *From Harlem to the Rhine*, 65–66.

40. Quoted in "Damrosch Insists on German Music: Would Rather Lay Down Baton Than Ignore Masters, He Tells Audience," *New York Tribune*, 26 October 1917, 13.

41. "Music of Friend and Foe Played: American and German Art Displayed at Opening of Concert Season," *New York Sun*, 26 October 1917, 9.

42. "Are Stransky and Damrosch Making German Propaganda?" *Musical Leader* 34/18 (1 November 1917): 439.

43. [Editorial page], *Musical Courier* 75/18 (1 November 1917): 20.

44. "Sunday's Concerts: Kreisler, the Symphony, Friedheim, and Dostal Appear," *New York Times*, 29 October 1917, 11.

45. "Dr. Muck's Program," *New York Times*, 28 October 1917, E2.

46. Farrar, *Such Sweet Compulsion*, 142.

47. "Incident of National Anthem Overshadows Other Boston Happenings," *Musical Courier* 75/19 (8 November 1917), 12.
48. "Pension Fund Concert," *Boston Post*, 29 October 1917, 2.
49. "Pension Concert: Capacity Audience Enjoys a Feast of Music, Geraldine Farrar Casts Her Spell as of Old—Dr. Muck Conducts," *Boston Daily Globe*, 29 October 1917, 9.

CHAPTER 11

1. "Patriotic Fury Directed at Boston Symphony," *Musical Courier* 75/19 (8 November 1917): 19.
2. "Symphony does not Play U. S. Anthem: This Despite Request of Providence Women," *Boston Daily Globe*, 31 October 1917, 8.
3. "Ask that Orchestra Play 'Star Spangled Banner': Ten Local Organizations Telegraph Symphony Manager," *Providence Evening Bulletin*, 30 October 1917, 1.
4. "American Anthem Entirely Ignored. Symphony Orchestra Does Not Play 'Star Spangled Banner'—Tickets Refused to Many," *Providence Daily Journal*, 31 October 1917, 1.
5. Quoted in "American Anthem Entirely Ignored," 1.
6. Turk, "The Case of Dr. Karl Muck," 6–8.
7. "The Boston Symphony in Providence," *Providence Daily Journal*, 2 November 1917, 8.
8. "Maj. H. L. Higginson Defends Symphony: Says National Anthem Has No Place in Art," *Boston Globe*, 1 November 1917, 4.
9. "Request to Play Nation's Hymn Hurts Dr. Muck: Embarrasses Artistic Sensibilities, Says Boston Orchestra Leader," *New York Tribune*, 1 November 1917, 1.
10. "Let Muck Play Anthem or Go to Jail, Says T. R.," *New York Evening World*, 2 November 1917, 1.
11. H. Earle Johnson, *Symphony Hall, Boston* (Boston: Little, Brown, 1950), 76. Johnson states that this coaching took place on the 3rd, but press reports confirm that the anthem was first played on the 2nd.
12. "Dr. Muck Conducts National Anthem," *Boston Post*, 3 November 1917, 10.
13. "Dr. Muck Conducts," 10.
14. "Our First Trench Losses," *Brooklyn Daily Eagle*, 6 November 1917, 6.
15. Quoted in "Aroused over Dr. Muck: Ex-Gov. Warfield Seeks to Prevent Boston Symphony Orchestra," *Baltimore Sun*, 2 November 1917, 14.
16. "German Opera under Ban by Metropolitan," *New York Sun*, 2 November 1917, 1.
17. Quoted in "Dr. Muck Resigns, Then Plays Anthem," *New York Times*, 3 November 1917, 22.
18. Richard Aldrich, "The Case of Doctor Muck, Major Higginson, and 'The Star-Spangled Banner,'" *New York Times*, 4 November 1917, X5.
19. H. T. C[raven], "National Anthem Directed by Muck: But 'Star-Spangled Banner' Boston Symphony Style Lacks Heroic Quality," *Evening Public Ledger*, 6 November 1917, 11.
20. "Dr. Muck Plays Anthem to Open Local Concert," *Washington Herald*, 7 November 1917, 1.
21. "Ex-Gov. Warfield Would Mob Muck: Volunteers to Lead Baltimore Citizens to Prevent Concert Conducted by German," *New York Times*, 5 November 1917, 13.
22. "It's Too Exclusive Even for Perusal by the Hoi Polloi," *Pittsburgh Press*, 8 August 1917, 8. The United Press journalist who wrote the article visited the editorial office in New York but was not allowed to see a copy because "They're for our

subscribers only, and, you know, our subscribers are invited to subscribe." Since the journal was not available for general sale, there are few extant copies. The Library of Congress owns a complete run from March 1917 to November 1918. Census and selective service records confirm that "Fletcher" was actually Richard Fechheimer, born in Ohio in 1880. The UP article hints that the British accent was an affectation in support of the exclusive mystique he was cultivating.

23. Mrs. William (Lucie) Jay, "German Music and German Opera," *The Chronicle* 2/3 (November 1917), n.p.

24. Quoted in "War-time Antagonism Halts Wagner Operas," *Musical Courier* 75/19 (8 November 1917): 5.

25. F. T. Vreeland, "Jazz, Ragtime By-Product, Revives a Lost Art of Rhythm," *New York Sun*, 4 November 1917, sec. 5, 2.

26. All of the preceding quotations are from Vreeland, "Jazz, Ragtime By-Product."

27. Quoted in "Dr. Muck Coming to Brooklyn; Will Play National Air," *Brooklyn Daily Eagle*, 3 November 1917, 1.

28. "Boston Symphony Orchestra Plays National Anthem at B'klyn Academy," *Brooklyn Daily Eagle*, 10 November 1917, 6.

29. Quoted in Louis P. Lochner, *Fritz Kreisler* (New York: Macmillan, 1950), 163.

30. Quoted in "Police Refuse Permit for Kreisler," *Pittsburgh Post-Gazette*, 8 November 1917, 7.

31. "Kreisler Quits Concert Stage: Austrian Violinist Cancels All Engagements Owing to Hostile Criticism," *New York Sun*, 26 November 1917, 1. See also "An Inevitable Loss," *New York Tribune*, 27 November 1917, 8.

32. "Trials of Dr. Muck and His Men Have Not Affected Their Work," *Musical Courier* 75/21 (22 November 1917): 32.

33. H. T. C[raven], "Three Pianists Triumph: Bauer, Gabrilowitsch and Samaroff Heard in Unique Philadelphia Orchestra Concert," *Evening Public Ledger*, 1 December 1917, 8.

34. Bruce Boyd Raeburn, "The Storyville Exodus Revisited, or Why Louis Armstrong Didn't Leave in November 1917, Like the Movie Said He Did," *Southern Quarterly* 52/2 (Winter 2015): 10–33.

35. Quoted in Brunn, *Original Dixieland Jazz Band*, 111.

36. A cast list for the film may be found on the Internet Movie Database, http://www.imdb.com/title/tt0008025/ (accessed 1 November 2017), but no copy of the film is known to have survived. For Nick LaRocca's recollections of the film, see Jean-Christophe Averty, "Contribution à l'Histoire de l'Original Dixieland Jass Band (II)," *Cahiers du Jazz* 4 (1960): 94–95.

37. Quoted in Gushee, *Pioneers of Jazz*, 227.

38. "Schumann-Heink Sings: A Very Large Audience Hears Her in Carnegie Hall," *New York Times*, 4 November 1917, 23.

39. *Washington Post*, 2 December 1917, 2.

40. "Mme. Schumann-Heink Is Heard in Recital," *Washington Herald*, 28 November 1917, 10.

41. "Schumann-Heink Is Ill: Contralto Suffers Collapse after Concert Given Here Tuesday—Bronchitis Attack Serious," *Washington Post*, 29 November 1917, 5. See also "Sängerin Schumann-Heink völlig erschöpft," *Der Tägliche Demokrat* (Davenport, IA), 28 December 1917, 1.

42. Martin, *The Damrosch Dynasty*, 249.

43. "Walter Damrosch Discusses the Effect of Prussianism on Music," *New York Sun*, 25 November 1917, 32. See also "German Music," *Des Moines Register*, 16 November 1917, 6.

44. "Damrosch's Men Play Nation's Air: Their Performance of 'Star-Spangled Banner' Thrills Big Audience at Academy," *Brooklyn Daily Eagle*, 4 November 1917, 66.

45. The Pianola Institute, "The Reproducing Piano—Duo-Art," www.pianola.org/reproducing/reproducing_duo-art.cfm, accessed 12 December 2016.

46. "Symphony Players in Novel Concert," *New York Sun*, 18 November 1917, 9.

47. For a discussion of the convoy system and its importance to wartime crossings of the Atlantic, see John U. Bacon, *The Great Halifax Explosion: A World War I Story of Treachery, Tragedy, and Extraordinary Heroism* (New York: William Morrow, 2017), 9–12.

48. "15th New York and Southerners in Fight: Alabamans Get Worst of Mixup," *Chicago Defender*, 2 November 1917, 1. See also "Camp No Place for Race Riots," *Brooklyn Daily Eagle*, 28 October 1917, 20; and "Alabama Troops and Negro Soldiers Clash: Excitement at Camp Mills When Southerners Threaten to Drive Out Negroes," *Greensboro (North Carolina) Daily News*, 29 October 1917, 2.

49. "City Sees Its New Negro Regiment: 15th Infantry Presents Fine Appearance at Review in Central Park," *New York Tribune*, 3 November 1917, 8. Little, *From Harlem to the Rhine*, 75 gives the incorrect date of 8 November, which has been copied in subsequent books.

50. For a detailed discussion of the murder and the problems with desertion, see Sammons and Morrow, *Harlem's Rattlers*, 171–84.

CHAPTER 12

1. W. J. Henderson, "Rising Tide of Sentiment against German Music," *New York Sun*, 2 December 1917, 8.

2. Henderson, "Rising Tide," 8.

3. "Kreisler Retires, His Bow Stilled by Attacks," *New York Tribune*, 2 December 1917, 42.

4. "Kreisler Fails to Appear: Too Ill to Play at Hippodrome Benefit for Children," *New York Times*, 3 December 1917, 13.

5. For a thorough discussion of this incident and its aftermath, see Bacon, *The Great Halifax Explosion*.

6. Olin Downes, "Great Trio in Concert for Halifax: Kreisler, Melba and the Symphony at One Hearing," *Boston Post*, 17 December 1917, 9.

7. The full text of the proclamation was printed in "By the President of the United States of America: A Proclamation," *Washington Post*, 20 November 1917, 4.

8. "Boston Symphony Orchestra NOTICE!" *Washington Times*, 4 December 1917, 22.

9. "Dr. Muck, Citizen of Switzerland: Boston Symphony Director Is Not a German Subject, Swiss Legation Declares," *New York Times*, 8 December 1917, 13; "Swiss Subject, Says Legation: Boston Symphony Director, Born in Bavaria, Naturalized in Republic," *Washington Herald*, 10 December 1917, 4.

10. "Boston Symphony Orchestra Gives Two Recitals in Carnegie Hall," *New York Tribune*, 9 December 1917, 17.

11. "Boston Symphony 'Lame' in Anthem: Dr. Muck and His Orchestra Apparently in Full Keeping with the Weather," *New York Sun*, 9 December 1917, 9.

12. "Orchestra Drops Teutons," *Pittsburgh Post-Gazette*, 2 December 1917, 1.

13. H. T. C[raven], "Old Glory at Academy: Flag Presentation Interpolated in the Philadelphia Orchestra's Tschaikowsky Concert," *Evening Public Ledger*, 15 December 1917, 6.

14. "Washington Women Wear Costly Furs Both for Day and Evening Functions," *Brooklyn Daily Eagle*, 9 December 1917, 4.

15. An interview with Damrosch explained the procedure for preparing the standardized edition: "Damrosch Was One of Five to Revise the National Anthem," *Harrisburg Evening News*, 24 November 1917, 9.

16. "Opera and Musical News of the Week," *Brooklyn Daily Eagle*, 9 December, 1917, 8.

17. "Mme. Schumann-Heink Presents U.S. Flag," *Santa Ana Register*, 18 December 1917, 1.

18. "Let 'em Smoke, She Says," *Los Angeles Times*, 21 December 1917, 22.

19. National Archives and Records Administration, Military Intelligence file 9140–2266 (4).

20. National Archives and Records Administration, "Old German Files" 31263.

21. For a colorful description of the impact of knitting on concerts, see Frederick Donaghey, "The Orchestra Starts Its Season," *Chicago Daily Tribune*, 13 October 1917, 13. Further parsing of the types of concerts that attracted knitters is found in "Notes on Knitting," *Musical Courier* 75/26 (27 December 1917), 21, and Mary H. Radcliffe, "Knitting at Concerts," *Philadelphia Record*, 2 January 1918, 8.

22. "General Weather Indications," *Brooklyn Daily Eagle*, 14 December 1917, 10.

23. Sissle, "Memoirs," 95.

24. Quoted in Sammons and Morrow, *Harlem's Rattlers and the Great War*, 185.

25. Sissle, "Memoirs," 96–99.

26. Quoted in Sammons and Morrow, *Harlem's Rattlers and the Great War*, 185.

27. Little, *From Harlem to the Rhine*, 96.

28. "Broadway Cabarets to Keep Jazz Bands," *New York Tribune*, 13 December 1917, 11.

29. "Biggest, Gayest Spectacle of the Year: The Silver Ball, Greenwich Village's Christmas Costume Party," advertising flyer in Greenwich Village Clubs Ephemera, Committee of Fourteen Papers, Box 31, New York Public Library. For information on the "Danse de la Lune" in November, see "Danse de la Lune Shocks Village by Its Tameness: Tendency to Camouflage with Real Clothes Robs Greenwich of 'Thrills,'" *New York Evening World*, 17 November 1917, 5. I am grateful to Dale Cockrell for calling my attention to the advertising flyer.

30. Quoted in Brunn, 114.

31. W. C. Handy, *Father of the Blues: An Autobiography* (New York, 1941; reprint London: Sidgwick and Jackson, 1957), 171–75. Brian Rust, *Jazz Records A—Z, 1897–1931*, 2nd ed. (Middlesex, England, self-published, 1961), 268–69.

CHAPTER 13

1. Noble Sissle, "Memoirs," 106–7.

2. Quoted in Badger, *A Life in Ragtime*, 193.

3. Letter from E. E. Oberstein of RCA Victor to H. O. Brunn, 22 September 1937, cited in Brunn, *Original Dixieland Jazz Band*, 70.

4. Colonial Theater advertisement, *Logansport (IN) Pharos-Reporter*, 12 January 1918, 3.

5. Sidney Bechet, *Treat It Gentle: An Autobiography* (New York: Hill and Wang, 1960), 118–19.

6. Lawrence Gushee, *Pioneers of Jazz*, 255–60.

7. Quoted in Louis Lochner, *Fritz Kreisler* (New York: Macmillan, 1950), 170.
8. "Kreisler Quits Concert Tour: Violinist Finds That He Can't with Self-Respect Accept America's Money," *New York Times*, 26 November 1917, 1.
9. "Schumann-Heink Sings Irish Folk-Song," *Pittsburgh Daily Post*, 30 December 1917, sec. 4, 5.
10. Richard W. Amero, "Madame Schumann-Heink: A Legend in Her Time," www. balboaparkhistory.net, accessed 19 December 2016.
11. H. T. C[raven], "National Anthem Directed by Muck: But 'Star-Spangled Banner' Boston Symphony Style Lacks Heroic Quality," *Philadelphia Public Ledger*, 6 November 1917, 11.
12. "Patriotism of City Rises against Muck: Thousands Join to Oppose Appearance of German as Orchestra Leader," *Philadelphia Public Ledger*, 4 January 1918, 3.
13. C. A. Ellis, "Hounding Dr. Muck," *Philadelphia Record*, 7 January 1918, 8.
14. "U.S. Agents Arrest Muck: Symphony Orchestra Leader Seized under Alien Enemy Act—Placed in Cell for the Night," *Boston Daily Globe*, 26 March 1918, 1.
15. For further information on this incident, see Edmund A. Bowles, "Karl Muck and His Compatriots: German Conductors in America during World War I (And How They Coped)," *American Music* 25/4 (Winter 2007): 405–40; and Matthew Mugmon, "Patriotism, Art, and 'The Star-Spangled Banner' in World War I: A New Look at the Karl Muck Episode," *Journal of Musicological Research* 33/1–3 (2014): 4–26.
16. Carl Flesch, *The Memoirs of Carl Flesch*, trans. by Hans Keller (London: Rockliff, 1957), 286.
17. "New Victor Records for January," *Poughkeepsie Eagle News*, 11 January 1918; see also "Victor Company Opens New Field of Musical Delight: Full Symphony Orchestra Has Been Successfully Recorded in Brahm's [*sic*] Dances," *Leavenworth (KS) Times*, 1 January 1918, 7.
18. Extensive information on Stokowski's recorded legacy may be found at Larry Huffman, *The Stokowski Legacy*, www.stokowski.org, accessed 18 December 2016.
19. *The First Recordings of the Boston Symphony Orchestra* (BSO Classics 171002, 1995).
20. Samaroff Stokowski, *An American Musician's Story*, 155–56.
21. Nancy Bachus, "Teacher Profile: Madame Olga Samaroff," *Clavier Companion* 5/6 (November/December 2013): 28–33.
22. Walter Damrosch, *My Musical Life* (New York: Scribner, 1923), 261.

AFTERWORD

1. For a discussion of the influence of record collectors on the emerging field of jazz historiography in the 1930s, see Bruce Boyd Raeburn, *New Orleans Style and the Writing of American Jazz History* (Ann Arbor: University of Michigan Press, 2009).
2. Sargeant, *Geniuses, Goddesses, and People*, 75.
3. Quoted in *Jazzmen*, ed. Frederic Ramsey Jr. and Charles Edward Smith (New York: Harcourt Brace, 1939), 51.
4. Schuller, *Early Jazz*, 176–82.
5. Walter Donaldson (composer), Joe Young, and Sam M. Lewis (lyricists), "How Ya Gonna Keep 'Em Down on the Farm (After They've Seen Paree?)" (New York: Waterson, Berlin & Snyder, 1919).
6. Ann Hagedorn, *Savage Peace: Hope and Fear in America, 1919* (New York: Simon & Schuster, 2007), 99–101.

7. United States Census Bureau, *Census Urban/Rural Populations 1900–1990*, https://www.census.gov/population/censusdata/urpop0090.txt, accessed 7 October 2017.

8. For a discussion of LaRocca's feud with writer Marshall Stearns over the issue of race in jazz, see Raeburn, *New Orleans Style*, 52–53.

9. Though this characterization is generally true, there were enclaves where German Americans managed to perpetuate their bicultural traditions in the 1920s, as documented in Don Heinrich Tolzmann, *The Cincinnati Germans after the Great War* (New York: Peter Lang, 1987).

10. "Cancel Kreisler Concert," *New York Times*, 30 November 1919, sec. I, 19.

11. "Fritz Kreisler Discusses America's Attitude toward Him," *Literary Digest* (3 January 1920), 50.

12. "Kreisler, McCormack and Cortot Make Pittsburgh's Week Thrice Notable," *Musical America* 31/13 (24 January 1920), 43.

13. Carl Strikwerda, "World War I in the History of Globalization," *Historical Reflections* 42/3 (Winter 2016), 112–32.

14. Marta Robertson, "Ballad for Incarcerated Americans: Second Generation Japanese American Musicking in World War II Camps," *Journal of the Society for American Music* 11/3 (August 2017), 284–312.

15. Annegret Fauser, *Sounds of War: Music in the United States during World War II* (New York: Oxford, 2013), 51.

16. Jordan Runtagh, "Remembering Whitney Houston with Her Super Bowl National Anthem Performance That United the Country, *People Music* (posted 11 February 2017), http://people.com/music/whitney-houston-super-bowl-national-anthem-death-anniversary/, accessed 28 October 2017.

BIBLIOGRAPHY

ARCHIVAL SOURCES

Boston Symphony Orchestra Archives
Hogan Jazz Archive, Tulane University, New Orleans
    Edwin ("Eddie") Edwards Collection
    Dominic ("Nick") LaRocca Collection
International Piano Archives at Maryland, College Park, MD
Library of Congress Copyright Deposits
Library of Congress Manuscript Division
    NAACP papers
Library of Congress Music Division
    Damrosch-Blaine Collection
    Damrosch-Tee Van Collection
    Geraldine Farrar Collection
    Fritz Kreisler Collection
    Mannes-Damrosch Collection
Library of Congress Prints and Photographs Division
National Archives and Records Administration, College Park, MD
    Military Intelligence Files
    Bureau of Investigation "Old German" Files
    Star-Spangled Banner Files
Spaulding Library, New England Conservatory, Boston
    George Whitefield Chadwick Collection
University of Pennsylvania, Kislak Special Collections Library
    Diary from a Maine island vacation home
    Leopold Stokowski Collection

NEWSPAPERS

Asbury Park Press
Baltimore Sun
Bar Harbor Times
Boston Globe
Boston Post
Brooklyn Daily Eagle
Chicago American
Chicago Daily News

Chicago Daily Tribune
Chicago Defender
Daily Republican
Der Tägliche Demokrat (Davenport, Iowa)
Des Moines Register
El Paso Herald
Emporia Gazette
Evansville (Indiana) Press
Harrisburg Evening News
Indiana Gazette
Los Angeles Times
Medford (Oregon) Mail Tribune
Musical America
Musical Courier
Musical Leader
New York Age
New York Globe and Commercial Advertiser
New York Herald
New York Sun
New York Times
New York Tribune
New York World
Oakland Tribune
Philadelphia Evening Public Ledger
Philadelphia Inquirer
Philadelphia Tribune
Pittsburgh Daily Post
Pittsburgh Post-Gazette
Pittsburgh Press
Poughkeepsie Eagle News
Providence Bulletin
Providence Journal
Rochester Democrat and Chronicle
San Diego Union
San Francisco Chronicle
Santa Ana Register
Santa Cruz Evening News
St. Louis Post-Dispatch
St. Louis Star and Times
Tägliches Cincinnatier Volksblatt
Washington Herald
Washington Post
Washington Times
Wellington (Kansas) Daily News
Wilkes-Barre Times Leader
Williamsport Sun-Gazette
Wilmington News Journal
Winnipeg Tribune

ARTICLES AND BOOKS

"About Jazz Music," *Daily Missourian*, 1 May 1917, 2.

Ainsworth, Alan John. "Early New Orleans Band Photography." *Jazz Research Journal* 11, no. 1 (2017): 28–61.

Aldrich, Richard. "The Case of Doctor Muck, Major Higginson, and 'The Star-Spangled Banner.'" *New York Times*, 4 November 1917, X5.

Amero, Richard W. "Madame Schumann-Heink: A Legend in Her Time." www. balboaparkhistory.net. Accessed 19 December 2016.

Anderson, Maureen. "The White Reception of Jazz in America." *African American Review* 38/1 (Spring 2004): 135–45.

"The Appeal of Primitive Jazz." *Literary Digest* 55/8 (25 August 1917), 26–29.

Ardoin, John. *The Philadelphia Orchestra: A Century of Music*. Philadelphia: Temple University Press, 1999.

"The Argot of Vaudeville," *New York Times*, 23 December 1917, 38.

Averty, Jean-Christophe. "Contribution à l'Histoire de l'Original Dixieland Jazz Band." *Les Cahiers du Jazz* 3 (1959): 60–107; 4 (1960): 74–117.

Bachus, Nancy. "Teacher Profile: Madame Olga Samaroff." *Clavier Companion* 5/6 (November/December 2013): 28–33.

Bacon, John U. *The Great Halifax Explosion: A World War I Story of Treachery, Tragedy, and Extraordinary Heroism*. New York: William Morrow, 1917.

Badger, Reid. *A Life in Ragtime: A Biography of James Reese Europe*. New York: Oxford University Press, 1995.

Barker, Danny. *Buddy Bolden and the Last Days of Storyville*. Alyn Shipton, ed. London: Cassell, 1998.

Bechet, Sidney. *Treat It Gentle: An Autobiography*. New York: Twayne, 1960. Reprint, New York: Da Capo, 1978.

Beckley, Zoe. "Sons in Opposing Armies: Mme. Schumann-Heink's Problem Is One Only Mothers Understand." *Kansas City Times*, 7 July 1917, 5.

[Behymer, L. H.] "Musicians Gather on Maine Coast: Distinguished Group Is Enjoying Vacation There and Having Good Time." *San Francisco Chronicle*, 17 September 1916, 24.

Berlin, Edward A. *King of Ragtime: Scott Joplin and His Era*. 2nd ed. New York: Oxford University Press, 2016.

Berresford, Mark. *That's Got 'Em! The Life and Music of Wilbur C. Sweatman*. Jackson: University Press of Mississippi, 2010.

Biancolli, Amy. *Fritz Kreisler: Love's Sorrow, Love's Joy*. Portland, OR: Amadeus Press, 1998.

"A Blessing in Disguise?" *Wichita Beacon*, 23 May 1917, 1.

Bomberger, E. Douglas. *"A Tidal Wave of Encouragement": American Composers' Concerts in the Gilded Age*. Westport, CT: Praeger, 2002.

Bookspan, Martin. "The BSO and the Talking Machine." *High Fidelity* 8/1 (January 1958), 50–51, 124–26.

Bowen, Louise de Koven. *The Public Dance Halls of Chicago*. Rev. ed. Chicago: Juvenile Protective Association of Chicago, 1917.

Bowles, Edmund A. "Karl Muck and His Compatriots: German Conductors in America during World War I (and How They Coped)." *American Music* 25/4 (Winter 2007): 405–40.

Brasington, Bruce C. "The Doughboy Comes to Chartres: *Stars and Stripes* and the Middle Ages." *Studies in Medievalism* XVI (2008): 83–97.

Bronner, Milton. "Pity, like Art, Has No Nationality, Says the World's Greatest Violinist." *Evansville (Indiana) Press*, 1 February 1917, 2.

Brooks, Shirley Victor. "Largest Audience of Season Hears Schumann-Heink: Orchestra and Contralto at Their Best in Wagnerian Festival." *St. Louis Star and Times*, 24 February 1917, 4.

Brooks, Tim. *Lost Sounds: Blacks and the Birth of the Recording Industry, 1890–1919*. Urbana: University of Illinois Press, 2004.

Brothers, Thomas. *Louis Armstrong's New Orleans*. New York: Norton, 2006.

Brown, Jonathan. *Great Wagner Conductors: A Listener's Companion*. Canberra: Parrot Press, 2012.

Brunn, Harry O. *The Story of the Original Dixieland Jazz Band*. Baton Rouge: Louisiana State University Press, 1960.

"By the President of the United States of America: A Proclamation." *Washington Post*, 20 November 1917, 4.

Caporaletti, Vincenzo. *Jelly Roll Morton, the* Old Quadrille *and* Tiger Rag: *A Historiographic Revision*. Lucca: Libreria Musicale Italiana, 2011.

Carney, Court. *Cuttin' Up: How Early Jazz Got America's Ear*. Lawrence: University Press of Kansas, 2009.

Carney, Court. "New Orleans and the Creation of Early Jazz." *Popular Music and Society* 29/3 (July 2006): 299–315.

Cassidy, Daniel. "How the Irish Invented Jazz." *Counterpunch*, 14 July 2006. http://www.counterpunch.org/2006/07/14/how-the-irish-invented-jazz/. Accessed 28 October 2017.

Charters, Samuel. *A Trumpet around the Corner: The Story of New Orleans Jazz*. Jackson: University Press of Mississippi, 2008.

Chilton, John. *Sidney Bechet: The Wizard of Jazz*. New York: Oxford University Press, 1987.

Church, Lucy Claire. "Music, Morality, and the Great War: How World War I Molded American Musical Ethics." PhD diss., Florida State University, 2015.

Clemens, Clara. "Famous Musicians off Guard at Seal Harbor: Mark Twain's Daughter Writes of Impression Kreisler, Bauer, Gabrilowitsch, Godowsky, and Others of Colony Made on Natives." *New York Times Magazine*, 24 September 1916, 15.

Clemens, Clara. *My Husband Gabrilowitsch*. New York: Harper, 1938.

"The Cry for Jazz." *Musical Courier* 75/3 (19 July 1917), 9.

Cullen, Frank, with Florence Hackman and Donald McNeilly. *Vaudeville Old and New: An Encyclopedia of Variety Performers in America*. 2 vols. New York: Routledge, 2006.

Damrosch, Walter. *My Musical Life*. New York: Scribner, 1923.

Daniel, Oliver. *Stokowski: A Counterpoint of View*. New York: Dodd, Mead, 1983.

Daughtry, J. Martin. *Listening to War: Sound, Music, Trauma, and Survival in Wartime Iraq*. Oxford: Oxford University Press, 2015.

"Delving into the Genealogy of Jazz." *Current Opinion* 67/2 (August 1919): 97–99.

Doering, James M. *The Great Orchestrator: Arthur Judson and American Arts Management*. Urbana: University of Illinois Press, 2013.

Dyment, Christopher. *Conducting the Brahms Symphonies: From Brahms to Boult*. Woodbridge, UK: Boydell, 2016.

Dyment, Christopher. "Karl Muck's Boston Recordings," *International Classical Record Collector* 6 (Autumn 1996), 38–41.

Dyment, Christopher. "The Recordings of Karl Muck: Some Unresolved Problems." *Association for Recorded Sound Collections Journal* 9/1 (1977): 67–69.

Ellis, C. A. "Hounding Dr. Muck." *Philadelphia Record*, 7 January 1918, 8.

Fagan, Ted, and William R. Moran, comps. *The Encyclopedic Discography of Victor Recordings: Pre-Matrix Series.* Westport, CT: Greenwood Press, 1983.

Farrar, Geraldine. *Such Sweet Compulsion: The Autobiography of Geraldine Farrar.* New York: Greystone, 1938.

Fauser, Annegret. *Sounds of War: Music in the United States during World War II.* New York: Oxford University Press, 2013.

Ferris, Marc. *Star-Spangled Banner: The Unlikely Story of America's National Anthem.* Baltimore: Johns Hopkins University Press, 2014.

Finnegan, John Patrick. *Military Intelligence.* Washington, DC: Center of Military History, US Army, 1998.

First Recordings of the Boston Symphony Orchestra, The. BSO Classics 171002, 1995.

Flesch, Carl. *Memoirs of Carl Flesch.* Hans Keller, trans. London: Rockliff, 1957.

Fulwider, Chad R. *German Propaganda and U.S. Neutrality in World War I.* Columbia: University of Missouri Press, 2016.

Gates, Henry Louis, and Gene Andrew Jarrett, eds. *The New Negro: Readings on Race, Representation and African American Culture, 1892–1938.* Princeton, NJ: Princeton University Press, 2007.

Giddens, Gary. *Visions of Jazz: The First Century.* New York: Oxford University Press, 1998.

Gienow-Hecht, Jessica C. E. *Sound Diplomacy: Music and Emotions in Transatlantic Relations, 1850–1920.* Chicago: University of Chicago Press, 2009.

Gilbert, David. *The Product of Our Souls: Ragtime, Race, and the Birth of the Manhattan Musical Marketplace.* Chapel Hill: University of North Carolina Press, 2015.

Gilbert, James L. *World War I and the Origins of U.S. Military Intelligence.* Lanham, MD: Scarecrow, 2012.

Gill, "What Is a Jass Band?" *Ragtime Review* 3/3 (March 1917), 10.

Gracyk, Tim, with Frank Hoffmann. *Popular American Recording Pioneers: 1895–1925.* New York: Haworth, 2000.

Grant, Mark N. *Maestros of the Pen: A History of Classical Music Criticism in America.* Boston: Northeastern University Press, 1998.

Grossman, James R. *Land of Hope: Chicago, Black Southerners, and the Great Migration.* Chicago: University of Chicago Press, 1989.

Gushee, Lawrence. "The Nineteenth-Century Origins of Jazz." *Black Music Research Journal* 14/1 (Spring 1994): 1–24.

Gushee, Lawrence. *Pioneers of Jazz: The Story of the Creole Band.* Oxford: Oxford University Press, 2005.

Hagedorn, Ann. *Savage Peace: Hope and Fear in America, 1919.* New York: Simon & Schuster, 2007.

Handy, W. C. *Father of the Blues.* Arna Bontemps, ed. New York: Macmillan, 1941.

Harding, Henry J. "Musical Echoes from the Hub." *Jacobs' Orchestra Monthly* 8/12 (December 1917): 18–19, 53.

Harris, Bill. *The Hellfighters of Harlem: African-American Soldiers Who Fought for the Right to Fight for Their Country.* New York: Carroll & Graf, 2002.

Harris, Stephen L. *Harlem's Hell Fighters: The African-American 369th Infantry in World War I.* Washington, DC: Brassey's, 2003.

Hart, Philip. *Orpheus in the New World: The Symphony Orchestra as an American Cultural Institution.* New York: Norton, 1973.

Hartford, Greg A. "Acadia National Park History." http://www.acadiamagic.com/acadia_national_park.html. Accessed 25 August 2016.

Haynes, Robert V. *A Night of Violence: The Houston Riot of 1917.* Baton Rouge: Louisiana State University Press, 1976.

Henderson, W. J. "Rising Tide of Sentiment against German Music." *New York Sun*, 2 December 1917, sec. 3, 3.

Hersch, Charles. *Subversive Sounds: Race and the Birth of Jazz in New Orleans*. Chicago: University of Chicago Press, 2007.

Hobson, Vic. "How Did the ODJB Learn to Play 'Livery Stable Blues?'" *Jazz Archivist* 30 (2017): 15–24.

Holbrook, Dick. "Our Word Jazz." *Storyville*, no. 50 (December 1973–January 1974): 46–58.

Holsinger, M. Paul, ed. *War and American Popular Culture: A Historical Encyclopedia*. Westport, CT: Greenwood Press, 1999.

Horowitz, Joseph. *Artists in Exile: How Refugees from Twentieth-Century War and Revolution Transformed the American Performing Arts*. New York: Harper, 2008.

Horowitz, Joseph. *Moral Fire: Musical Portraits from America's Fin de Siècle*. Berkeley: University of California Press, 2012.

Howard, Joseph L. *Madame Ernestine Schumann-Heink: Her Life and Times*. Sebastopol, CA: Grizzly Bear, 1990.

Howe, M., A. DeWolfe, and John N. Burk. *The Boston Symphony Orchestra, 1881–1931*. Boston: Houghton Mifflin, 1931.

H. T. C[raven]. "National Anthem Directed by Muck: But 'Star Spangled Banner' Boston Symphony Style Lacks Heroic Quality," *Philadelphia Evening Ledger*, 6 November 1917, 11.

Huffman, Larry. *The Stokowski Legacy*. www.stokowski.org. Accessed 18 December 2016.

Jasen, David A., and Gene Jones. *Black Bottom Stomp: Eight Masters of Ragtime and Early Jazz*. New York: Routledge, 2002.

Jay, Mrs. William [Lucie]. "German Music and German Opera." *The Chronicle* 2/3 (November 1917), n.p.

Johnson, H. Earle. *Symphony Hall, Boston*. Boston: Little, Brown, 1950.

Johnson, Lynne. "Liszt and Saint-Saëns." PhD diss., University of Hawai'i, 2009.

Joyce, John J., Jr., Bruce Boyd Raeburn, and Anthony M. Cummings, eds. *Sam Morgan's Jazz Band: Complete Recorded Works in Transcription*. Music of the United States of America (MUSA), vol. 24. Middleton, WI: A-R Editions, 2012.

Kagan, Sheldon S. "Trial by Newspaper: The Strange Case of Dr. Karl Muck." *New Jersey Journal of Communication* 1/1 (1993): 50–62.

Kaufman, George S. "Broadway and Elsewhere." *New York Tribune*, 11 March 1917, 29.

Kaufman, S. Jay. "Round the Town: Jass." *New York Globe and Commercial Advertiser*, 14 March 1917, 12.

Keen, John. "Joplin in New York: A Post-mortem Walking Tour." *Rag-Time Ephemeralist* 3 (2002): 216–25.

Kennett, Lee. "The Camp Wadsworth Affair." *South Atlantic Quarterly* 74/2 (Spring 1975): 197–211.

Kenney, William Howland. *Chicago Jazz: A Cultural History, 1904–1930*. New York: Oxford University Press, 1993.

Kimball, Robert, and William Bolcom. *Reminiscing with Sissle and Blake*. New York: Viking Press, 1973.

Kingsley, Walter. "Whence Comes Jass? Facts from the Great Authority on the Subject." *New York Sun*, 5 August 1917, 3.

Kirchner, Bill. *The Oxford Companion to Jazz*. New York: Oxford University Press, 2000.

Kline, Donna Staley. *Olga Samaroff Stokowski: An American Virtuoso on the World Stage*. College Station: Texas A&M University Press, 1996.

Kreisler, Fritz. *Four Weeks in the Trenches: The War Story of a Violinist.* Boston: Houghton Mifflin, 1915.

Larson, Erik. *Dead Wake: The Last Crossing of the* Lusitania. New York: Crown, 2015.

Lawton, Mary. *Schumann-Heink: The Last of the Titans.* New York: Macmillan, 1928.

Levin, Michael David. "Louise de Koven Bowen: A Case History of the American Response to Jazz." PhD thesis, University of Illinois at Urbana-Champaign, 1985.

Levy, Alan H. "The American Symphony Orchestra at War: German-American Musicians and Federal Authorities during World War I." *Mid-America* 71 (1989): 5–13.

Little, Arthur W. *From Harlem to the Rhine: The Story of New York's Colored Volunteers.* New York: Covici Friede, 1936.

Lochner, Louis P. *Fritz Kreisler.* New York: Macmillan, 1950.

Lomax, Alan. *Mister Jelly Roll: The Fortunes of Jelly Roll Morton, New Orleans Creole and Inventor of Jazz.* New York: Pantheon, 1950. Reprint, Berkeley: University of California Press, 1973.

Lowens, Irving. "L'affaire Muck: A Study in War Hysteria (1917–1918)." *Musicology* 1 (1947): 265–74.

Luebke, Frederick C. *Bonds of Loyalty: German-Americans and World War I.* DeKalb: Northern Illinois University Press, 1974.

MacLeod, Beth Abelson. *Women Performing Music: The Emergence of American Women as Instrumentalists and Conductors.* Jefferson, NC: McFarland, 2001.

"Making the World Safe for Music." *Musical Courier* 75/12 (20 September 1917), 23.

Mann, Howard. "Mme. Schumann-Heink Sends Younger Sons to Battle Their Eldest Brother, Who Is Fighting for Kaiser." *Medford (Oregon) Mail Tribune,* 22 August 1917, 3.

Martin, George Whitney. *The Damrosch Dynasty: America's First Family of Music.* Boston: Houghton Mifflin, 1983.

McCusker, John. *Creole Trombone: Kid Ory and the Early Years of Jazz.* Jackson: University Press of Mississippi, 2012.

McDonough, John. "Jass Record #1." *Downbeat* 59/2 (February 1992), 26–77.

McIntyre, O. O. "New York Day-by-Day." *Arkansas Democrat,* 22 March 1917, 6.

Mellett, Lowell. "Speculators Roll in Wealth—New York a Modern Babylon." *Day Book,* 12 December 1916, 30.

Merriam, Alan P., and Fradley H. Garner. "Jazz—the Word." *Ethnomusicology* 12/3 (September 1968): 373–96.

Miller, James. "Walter Damrosch Conducts." *Fanfare* 37/4 (March/April 2014), 510–12.

Milsom, David. "Conditional Gifts: Acoustic Orchestral Recordings of Edouard Colonne and Karl Muck and Their Testament to Late Nineteenth-Century Performing Practices." *Early Music Performer* 16 (November 2005): 4–13.

Moderwell, Hiram. "Two Views of Ragtime: A Modest Proposal." *Seven Arts* 2/3 (July 1917), 368–76.

Morris, Ronald L. *Wait until Dark: Jazz and the Underworld, 1880–1940.* Bowling Green, OH: Bowling Green University Popular Press, 1980.

Muck, Peter. *Karl Muck: Ein Dirigentenleben in Briefen und Dokumenten.* Tutzing: Hans Schneider, 2003.

Mueller, John H. *The American Symphony Orchestra: A Social History of Musical Taste.* Bloomington: Indiana University Press, 1951.

Mugmon, Matthew. "Patriotism, Art, and 'The Star-Spangled Banner' in World War I: A New Look at the Karl Muck Episode." *Journal of Musicological Research* 33/1–3 (2014): 4–26.

Myers, Marc. "Start Spreadin' the Blues." *Wall Street Journal,* 21 February 2012, D7.

"A Negro Explains 'Jazz.'" *Literary Digest* 61/4 (April 1919), 28–29.

Nelson, Peter. *A More Unbending Battle: The Harlem Hellfighters' Struggle for Freedom in WWI and Equality at Home*. New York: Basic Civitas, 2009.

Osgood, Henry O. *So This Is Jazz*. Boston: Little, Brown, 1926.

Ostransky, Leroy. *Jazz City: The Impact of Our Cities on the Development of Jazz*. Englewood Cliffs, NJ: Prentice Hall, 1978.

Peretti, Burton. *The Creation of Jazz: Music, Race, and Culture in Urban America*. Urbana: University of Illinois Press, 1992.

Perry, Bliss. *Life and Letters of Henry Lee Higginson*. Boston: Atlantic Monthly, 1921.

Phillips, J. H. "Interiors for Dining and Dancing." *Architectural Review* 10/1 (January 1920), 19–23.

Pietrusza, David. *1920: The Year of the Six Presidents*. New York: Carroll & Graf, 2007.

Raeburn, Bruce Boyd. "Jazz and the Italian Connection." *Jazz Archivist* 6/1 (May 1991): 1–4.

Raeburn, Bruce Boyd. *New Orleans Style and the Writing of American Jazz History*. Ann Arbor: University of Michigan Press 2009.

Raeburn, Bruce Boyd. "Stars of David and Sons of Sicily: Constellations beyond the Canon in Early New Orleans Jazz." *Jazz Perspectives* 3/2 (August 2009): 123–52.

Raeburn, Bruce Boyd. "The Storyville Exodus Revisited, or Why Louis Armstrong Didn't Leave in November 1917, Like the Movie Said He Did." *Southern Quarterly* 52/2 (Winter 2015): 10–33.

Redman, Jeanne. "Damrosch: An Intimate View of the Great Musician Who Admires Waiters." *Los Angeles Times*, 26 April 1917, 19.

Reich, Howard, and William Gaines. *Jelly's Blues: The Life, Music, and Redemption of Jelly Roll Morton*. New York: Da Capo Press, 2003.

Robertson, Marta. "Ballad for Incarcerated Americans: Second Generation Japanese American Musicking in World War II Camps." *Journal of the Society for American Music* 11/3 (August 2017): 284–312.

Rose, Al. *Eubie Blake*. New York: Schirmer, 1979.

"Rounding Up Reviews: '1917–1921.'" *IAJRC Journal* 26/4 (1993): 86.

Rust, Brian. *The American Dance Band Discography, 1917–1942*. 2 vols. New Rochelle, NY: Arlington House, 1975.

Rust, Brian, comp. *Jazz Records, A–Z, 1897–1931*. 2nd ed. Middlesex, England: Brian Rust, 1962.

Sager, David. "Unraveling the Dawn of Recorded Jazz." *Jazz Archivist* 30 (2017): 3–14.

Samaroff Stokowski, Olga. *An American Musician's Story*. New York: Norton, 1939.

Sammons, Jeffrey T., and John H. Morrow Jr. *Harlem's Rattlers and the Great War*. Lawrence: University Press of Kansas, 2014.

Sargeant, Winthrop. *Geniuses, Goddesses, and People*. New York: Dutton, 1949.

Schafer, William J. "Jas, Jass, Jasz, Jazz!" *Mississippi Rag* 34/4 (April 2007): 8–9.

Schuller, Gunther. *Early Jazz: Its Roots and Musical Development*. New York: Oxford University Press, 1968.

Schumann-Heink, Ernestine. "Hints for the Singer's Daily Practice." *The Etude* 35/1 (January 1917), 17.

Schumann-Heink, Ernestine. "Keeping the Voice in Prime Condition." *The Etude* 34/12 (December 1916), 843–44.

Seagrove, Gordon. "Blues Is Jazz and Jazz Is Blues." *Chicago Daily Tribune*, 11 July 1915, sec. VIII, 8.

Sengstock, Charles A. *Jazz Music in Chicago's Early South-Side Theaters*. Northbrook, IL: Canterbury Press of Northbrook: 2000.

Sengstock, Charles A., Jr. *That Toddlin' Town: Chicago's White Dance Bands and Orchestras, 1900–1950*. Urbana: University of Illinois Press, 2004.

Shadle, Douglas W. *Orchestrating the Nation: The Nineteenth-Century American Symphonic Enterprise*. New York: Oxford University Press, 2015.

Sissle, Noble. "Memoirs of Lieutenant 'Jim' Europe." Typescript, Library of Congress Manuscript Division, NAACP Papers, Box II, Folder J56.

Sonneck, Oscar George Theodore. *"The Star Spangled Banner."* Washington, DC, 1914. Reprint, New York: Da Capo, 1969.

Sooy, Raymond. "Memoirs of My Recording and Traveling Experiences for the Victor Talking Machine Company." MS. Janet Swartz, transcriber and ed. http://www.davidsarnoff.org/soo-maintext.html. Accessed 21 September 2016.

Spencer, Frederick J. *Jazz and Death*. Jackson: University of Mississippi Press, 2002.

Spencer, Onah L. "Trumpeter Freddie Keppard Walked Out on Al Capone!" *Music and Rhythm* 2/6 (June 1941), 14–15.

Strikwerda, Carl. "World War I in the History of Globalization." *Historical Reflections* 42/3 (Winter 2016): 112–32.

Sudhalter, Richard M. *Lost Chords: White Musicians and Their Contributions to Jazz, 1915–1945*. New York: Oxford University Press, 1999.

Sutro, Rose L. "The Sleeping Giant." *Musical Courier* 75/9 (30 August 1917), 15–16.

Tischler, Barbara, "One-Hundred Percent Americanism and Music in Boston during World War I." *American Music* 4/2 (Summer 1986): 164–76.

Tolzmann, Don Heinrich. *The Cincinnati Germans after the Great War*. New York: Peter Lang, 1987.

Tolzmann, Don Heinrich, ed. *German-Americans in the World Wars* Munich: K. G. Saur, 1995–98.

Turk, Gayle K. "The Case of Dr. Karl Muck: Anti-German Hysteria and Enemy Alien Internment during World War I." BA thesis, Harvard University, 1994.

Tyler, Don. *Music of the First World War*. Santa Barbara, CA: Greenwood Press, 2016.

Vaillant, Derek. *Sounds of Reform: Progressivism and Music in Chicago, 1873–1935*. Chapel Hill: University of North Carolina Press, 2003.

Vandenbergh, Lydia, and Earle G. Shettleworth Jr. *Revisiting Seal Harbor and Acadia National Park*. Charleston, SC: Arcadia, 1997.

Vermazen, Bruce. *That Moaning Saxophone: The Six Brown Brothers and the Dawning of a Musical Craze*. New York: Oxford University Press, 2004

"A Virtuoso's Summer." *Musical Courier* 75/5 (2 August 1917), 21.

Vreeland, F. T. "Jazz, Ragtime By-Product, Revives a Lost Art of Rhythm." *New York Sun*, 4 November 1917, sec. 5, 2.

Wang, Richard. "Researching the New Orleans–Chicago Jazz Connection: Tools and Methods." *Black Music Research Journal* 8/1 (1988): 101–12.

"War and the Universality of Art." *Musical America* 25/17 (24 February 1917), 39.

Waters, Ethel. *His Eye Is on the Sparrow*. New York: Doubleday, 1951.

Watkins, Glenn. *Proof through the Night: Music and the Great War*. Berkeley: University of California Press, 2003.

"What Is a Jazz Band?" *Ragtime Review* (June 1917), 7–8. Reprint of a *New York Globe* article.

White, William Allen]. "Don't Coddle Us." *Emporia Gazette*, 10 May 1917, 1.

"Why 'Jazz' Sends Us Back to the Jungle." *Current Opinion* 65/3 (September 1918): 165.

Williams, Lisa R. "A Furious Battleground: World War I and the Development of Jazz in American Popular Culture." *Jazz Perspectives* 8/2 (August 2014): 153–84.

Wittke, Carl. *German-Americans and the World War (with Special Emphasis on Ohio's German-Language Press)*. Columbus: Ohio State Archaeological and Historical Society, 1936.

Wright, Ben. "Victory and Defeat: World War I, the Harlem Hellfighters, and a Lost Battle for Civil Rights." *Afro-Americans in New York Life and History* 38/1 (January 2014): 35–70.

Zimmer, Ben. "How Baseball Gave Us 'Jazz': The Surprising Origins of a 100-Year-Old Word." *Boston Globe*, 25 March 2012.

INDEX